W9-DJH-014

Advance praise for De Colores Means All of Us

"Elizabeth Martínez's work comprises one of the most important living histories of progressive activism in the contemporary era.... [Martínez is] inimitable...irrepressible...indefatigable."

—From the foreword by Angela Y. Davis

"Please do yourself a favor and read this essay collection by Elizabeth Martínez! Share it with your friends, students, neighbors. Free yourself from the onslaught of misinformation and ignorance regarding racism in the United States and Latino politics. It is an up-to-date news flash on what is going on regarding Mexicans on both sides of the border. 'Betita' (to those of us who know her, love her, and continue to learn from her) is a veteran activist and Chicana pundit of the highest order."

—Ana Castillo, author, Massacre of the Dreamers

"Elizabeth Martínez has played a unique and extraordinary role as chronicler of Chicana-Chicano history, and De Colores beautifully captures her passion, her intelligence, her powerful commitment to universal human values. I am very happy this volume exists, and hope it will be widely read."

—Howard Zinn, author, A People's History of the United States

"This is one of the most important books to be published as we prepare to continue our struggle for a multiracial democracy in the twenty-first century.... Elizabeth (Betita) Martínez embodies the courage and tenacity exemplified by Latina activists, and women of color generally, who have been the backbone of our movements for social justice."

—Prof. Carlos Muñoz, Jr., Ethnic Studies, UC Berkeley; author, Youth, Identity, Power: The Chicano Movement

"Elizabeth Martínez speaks eloquently about class, race, identity, and the problems of achieving real 'democracy' today. Her essays in this book are thought-provoking, fierce, and often humorous. De Colores is powerful testament, a loving work that encourages us never to lose the idealism that can move worlds and achieve human rights and equality against all odds."

—John Nichols, author, The Milagro Beanfield War

DE COLORES MEANS ALL OF US

ALL OF US

Latina Views for a Multi-Colored Century

Elizabeth Martínez

South End Press

Cambridge, MA

Copyright © 1998 by Elizabeth Martínez
Cover design by Beth Fortune
Author photo by Margaret Randall
Text design and production by the South End Press collective
Printed in the U.S.A. on acid-free paper
First edition

Library of Congress Cataloging-in-Publication Data

Martínez, Elizabeth Sutherland, 1925-
De colores means all of us: Latina views for a multi-colored century/ by Elizabeth Martínez.
    p.   cm.
Includes index.
ISBN 0-89608-583-x (alk. paper). — ISBN 0-89608-584-8 (alk. paper)
    1. Pluralism (Social sciences)—United States. 2. United States—Ethnic relations. 3. United States—Race relations.
    4. Minorities—United States—Social conditions. 5. Mexican Americans—Ethnic identity. 6. Mexican Americans—Social conditions. 7. Mexican-American women—Political activity.
    I. Title.
E184.A1M313   1998
305.8'00973—dc21   98-6841
                                                        CIP

South End Press, 7 Brookline Street, #1, Cambridge, MA 02139

For la juventud,

the youth, and their

revolutionary vision

out by 2,000 high school students for better schools. April 22, 1998. Concord, California

Contents

PART IV:
RACISM AND THE ATTACK ON MULTICULTURALISM

PART V:
WOMAN TALK: No Taco Belles Here

PART VI:
LA LUCHA CONTINUA: Youth In The Lead

FOREWORD

by Angela Y. Davis

From her involvement with the Student Nonviolent Coordinating Committee during the 1960s to her current leadership of the Institute for Multi-Racial Justice, Elizabeth (Betita) Martínez' work comprises one of the most important living histories of progressive activism in the contemporary era. Furthermore, her writings recording countless struggles for social justice—some won, some lost, some still raging with varying degrees of intensity, and many having international implications—offer us an invaluable reader in the rich history of radical activism in the Americas.

That this collection of Martínez' writings is being published on the eve of the twenty-first century is a propitious event indeed, for it simultaneously chronicles the at-times glorious, at-times tedious work of progressive activists everywhere to keep "los movimientos" alive during the latter half of the twentieth century, *and* it reminds us as we move forward, youth and elders alike, that we have much work to do as the century and the millennium turn. The reader will find in these pages a tone that is by turns celebratory, angry, challenging and delightfully witty; Martínez' words are always powerful, never mournful as she addresses the role of U.S. people of color in forging the past, present and future of leftist activism.

The articles and essays that make up *De Colores Means All of Us* recount and critically analyze pivotal struggles of Latino/a peoples against the scourges of White Supremacy, patriarchy and class domination. Martínez' perspective is one that has developed through her involvement in Black, Native American and Asian-American movements as well. Her voice, one of wisdom gained through a wide range of experiences across a broad spectrum of social movements, speaks to all marginalized people, whether she is citing alarming statistics about hate crimes or imagining the future possibilities of an energized multiracial youth movement. "The oppressed," she writes in "Seeing More Than Black and White," have always survived by becoming experts on the oppressor's ways. But that can become a prison of sorts, a trap of compulsive vigilance. Let us liberate ourselves, then, from the tunnel vision of whiteness and behold the many colors around us! Let us summon the courage to reject outdated ideas and stretch our imaginations into the next century.

In this same piece, which urges a more comprehensive view of racial issues than the established tendency toward an exclusive Black-white binary analysis, she acknowledges the centrality of the historical, collective experience of Black Americans to any analysis of U.S. racism.

Simultaneously, her overall message is one of coalition building among groups subject to social domination—be they Black, Asian-American, Latino/a, Native American, gay, lesbian or white working-class—in what must become a more collaborative fight for social justice at every level. Evoking a term that will be recognized by many who have heard her speak, she urges us not to engage in "Oppression Olympics," not to create a futile hierarchy of suffering, but, rather, to harness our rage at persisting injustices in order to strengthen our opposition to an increasingly complex system of domination, which weaves together racism, patriarchy, homophobia and global capitalist exploitation.

In "Reinventing America," Martínez critiques the problematics of our national identity, which is based on an "origin myth" that demonizes and completely discredits populations of color—Native Americans, Africans, Mexicans and Chinese—of whose blood and sweat this country was founded. "Urging a more truthful origin myth," she writes, "and with it a different national identity, does not mean Euro-Americans should wallow individually in guilt. It does mean accepting collective responsibility to deal with the implications of a different narrative."

Examining issues such as anti-immigrant violence, which is fueled by politicians and governmental policy, and the gross human rights violations by major corporations that simultaneously exploit immigrant labor in the U.S. and themselves migrate to the Third World in order to find even more profitable labor arrangements, Martínez contextualizes what are commonly perceived as U.S. domestic matters within the global arena. Here, she salutes the work of United Farm Workers leader César Chávez and that of Fuerza Unida, the dynamic organization of women garment workers that arose in

1992 from a crucial battle with the Levi Strauss company. She shares with us her experience of the 1994 reunion marking the 30-year anniversary of the Mississippi Summer Project and the voter-registration drive in Mississippi. She also spells out the realities of environmental racism, making the important distinction between environmentalism as conservationism and environmentalism as a matter of short-term survival, which it has become for so many communities of color. And she demystifies the contests over affirmative action and multiculturalism in university curricula and corporate settings, urging their proponents to understand these strategies within a more productive context of anti-racist activism, as opposed to simply treating them as ends in themselves.

De Colores Means All of Us is not the work of a journalistic observer of social movements, but rather that of a passionately engaged participant. Throughout all these pieces runs the understated thread of Betita Martínez' personal involvement in many of the movements and struggles about which she writes. In this sense, *De Colores Means All of Us* may be read as a political autobiography. Martínez manages to assert her voice powerfully—lending impenetrable credibility to her arguments and analyses on the basis of her lived experiences as an activist—while simultaneously refraining from placing her formidable personality between her readers and her ideas. She handles every one of her topics with a fierce seriousness, demanding nothing less from her readers. Her approach is no-nonsense, yet it reflects the sharp sense of humor that so effectively keeps the weightiness of her subjects from overwhelming. An example: a reference to the 1846–48 war over Mexican land as a "territorial drive-by" by white settlers. The result is an engaging and highly accessible assessment of where we have been, where we are now and where we should go from here.

As we who have come to be known as movement veterans—or inveterate radicals—strive to inject our experiences and wisdom into the fires of young rebels, our work increasingly demands that we draw connections, that we forge radical political relationships across boundaries of gender, race, class, sexuality and national borders. Betita Martínez' life and work stand as a living monument to the possibilities for success that reside in our collective knowledge, commitment, persistence and plain old hard work.

As such, these writings are a fitting tribute to and assessment of the work we have done so far. Even more important, however, they are an indispensable guidebook of principles with which we are well armed for the coming millennium and for all of the battles it already has begun to present.

Here, then—for all our benefit—in all her glory, is the inimitable, the irrepressible, the indefatigable Betita Martínez.

ACKNOWLEDGMENTS

From the laid-off Mexican garment workers for Levi Strauss in San Antonio, to the aging Hispanos of northern New Mexico fighting for land the gringos seized, to the teenage Latinas discovering they can organize and lead big walkouts protesting school conditions, the people who made this book possible are innumerable. They gave me their experiences and thoughts so their struggles might become useful to others through my writing.

Many friends and colleagues helped steer my course as a writer in different ways: providing source material and analysis, reading and editing, keeping up my spirits when they wilted. Among old friends, some of the names that stand out are: José Calderón, Roxanne Dunbar, Phil Hutchings, Sharon Martinas, Richard Moore, Carlos Muñoz, Jr., Tony Platt, María Elena Ramírez, and Nancy Stein. Young comrades in my efforts include Kim Furumoto, Gabriel Hernández, Raquel Jiménez, Van Jones, Raquel Laviña, Adriana Montes, José Palafox, and others from Voices of Struggle (VOS) and the Xicano Moratorium Coalition. Professor Julia Curry has been a valued advisor on women's issues and Arnoldo García is the poet friend who taught me, among other things, why Chicanos in Texas call Anglos *los godames* (because they so often say "Goddam Mexicans!").

Two organizations that have been especially helpful in research and analysis are the National Network for Immigrant and Refugee Rights and the Northern California Coalition for Immigrant Rights, especially Renée Saucedo. Warm thanks also to Max Elbaum, former editor of *CrossRoads* magazine, and the editors of *Z* as the original publishers of many articles you will find here, which have now been updated and expanded. Other such journals are *Social Justice, Signs, The Progressive, Razateca,* and *Rethinking Schools.*

Most recently Anthony Arnove at South End Press has not only offered many helpful comments and suggestions but also patience with my editorial and design compulsions. Above all, he has been a pleasure to work with—and all writers know how much that means.

In a class by herself is Tessa Martínez, my daughter, who reads my stuff with great sensitivity, makes really cool suggestions, and lets me get away with nothing. I mean, *nada. Gracias, amor.*

INTRODUCTION
A Call for Rainbow Warriors

Visiting Cuba a few years after the 1959 revolution that overthrew the Batista dictatorship, I went to several teacher-training centers to see how new educators were being developed. The program took them through several stages, each in different parts of the island. The first center was located in a remote, mountainous area, so the students—who often came from the city—would understand *campesino* life.

When I asked them about their goals, they said: "to help make life better for all Cubans." Then one of them added proudly, "after that, we'll help teachers in Africa, Asia, all over the world!" I was thinking over this ambitious statement when another young student caught my eye. "After that," he said with a big, happy smile as the whole group nodded, "We'll just go help on another planet!" They were absolutely sincere.

Such was the spirit of revolutionary Cuba. Such was the spirit of many people engaged in struggle around the world, including these United States, in those years. A little optimistic? You could say so. Is this book too optimistic? You may come to think so. I hope, instead, that you will see my attempt to avoid both empty nostalgia and paralyzing cynicism. To learn from both past and present. And above all to listen to young activists, whose fiery demands for social justice light up a new path today. They weave for all of us a garment of brightness.

We surely need that light. For we live in an era of counter-revolution, when the gains made against racism during the 1960s—which I fought for alongside millions of other people—face constant assault. A century ago, the Reconstruction that followed the Civil War and offered real hope to Black people was brutally undone. Today, the Reconstruction that was launched by the Civil Rights Movement and offered hope to all people of color faces a similar reversal.

Latinos and Latinas are often victims of that reversal, with California the scene of the greatest abuse. The last few years have seen that state's denial of human rights to immigrants and its elimination of bilingual education. Also, California's abolition of affirmative action has excluded Latinos along with African Americans and other people of color, as well as many women, from higher education and better jobs.

The reversal of our twentieth-century Reconstruction doesn't stop there. Every day we see drastic cutbacks in programs that once helped the poor, at a time when the poor of all colors are getting steadily poorer. The poverty rate among Latinos—who are the focus of this book—has surpassed that of all other ethnic/racial groups in the United States. Census Bureau data published in 1996 showed that Latinos formed nearly 24 percent of the nation's poor. Among Latinos, 30 percent were officially poor (earning less than $15,569 for a family of four), with Puerto Ricans being the most impoverished subgroup. Child poverty ran equally high among Latinos and Blacks, at an outrageous 40 percent. Latinos had the lowest proportion of high school graduates: 53 percent of adults aged 25 and older, compared to 83 percent of whites and 74 percent of African Americans in the same age group, according to *Black Issues in Higher Education* (September 19, 1996). Recent immigration explains some of those figures but far from all, as other studies have shown.

In this era of counter-revolution and its deadly effects, we can be discouraged into silence or reduced to caring only about our immediate, personal world. Or we can, as I heard poet June Jordan say at a conference in Arizona, fight back against "those pistol-packing gatekeepers of a house that never belonged to them in the first place."

That sounds better! And let's remember: there would be no counter-attack today if we hadn't made some significant changes yesterday.

<<< >>>

This book is a collection of writings about Latinos—mostly Chicanas and Chicanos—that appeared in various publications during recent years and have been updated. It is rooted in a basic demand for respect, beginning with recognition that our presence in the United States goes back more than 400 years. Elsewhere in América, our history goes back thousands of years. We have a long record of building vast wealth for others, and a proud tradition of militant resistance by women and men. All that, yet in racist eyes we remain trapped under that big sombrero, taking an endless siesta.

Sometimes we have resisted oppression with humor, like the cartoon by Lalo Alcaraz featuring Cuco Rocha (a pissed-off Chicano cockroach) saying: *"Esos pinches gringos* ... they stole our land ... but left us the yardwork!" We also hear seriously angry cries of "Ya basta"—that's enough—from many Raza (Latinas and Latinos), like those you will find here.

Repression and resistance are the historical twins that dominate my own four decades of thinking, acting, struggling, and rethinking how to transform not only Latino life but the entire human condition in these United States. We are all inseparable from our times, whether we realize it or not. It took me a while to understand that there is quite a straight line from my injustice-hating mother and my Mexican immigrant father who had watched the 1910 revolution as a young Zapatista enthusiast, to five years as a United Nations researcher on colonialism at a time when independence movements raged around the world, to working in the Black civil rights/human rights movement, to years in the Southwest with the Chicano movimiento, to a decade of trying to serve the socialist vision, and now to today's struggles.

Strengthened by that sense of continuous linkage to human history, I am making two commitments with this book: to remember something ancient and to imagine something new (as Peter Bratt, director of the movie *Follow Me Home*, said). Something ancient includes the pre-Columbian roots of Raza and the best of our indigenous traditions, which honor balance and respect for all living creatures. Something new—now, there's the trick. It needs to include the promise of transformation.

Transformation will elude us until we envision our society in very new ways. This requires ending the inequality-based system called capitalism, a monstrous task when we recall that our nation was *born* capitalist—without passing through primitive communalism, feudalism, and so forth—so most people here identify as such. It was also born racist, thanks to unbridled genocide. We need a vision, then, in which we abolish the prevailing definition of the United States as a nation with a single, Euro-American culture and identity. Then we must re-imagine it as a community of communities that recognize their inter-dependence and relate on the basis of mutual respect. The nation's very boundaries may have to change; after all, they're only two centuries old and they were drawn through conquest and genocide. Think *sin fronteras*—without borders. Think what may seem unthinkable, and envision revolution.

This book will speak to you, I hope, of a transformative, feminist worldview that can help move us toward a rainbow century. The rainbow as a symbol of unity-in-diversity can be found among many indigenous peoples of Turtle Island—today called North America. It takes different forms, but all versions resonate with respect for the Earth, for ourselves and each other, for the plants and animals that make human existence possible.

In many versions the legend tells how Turtle Island was healthy until the light-skinned ones arrived and enslaved or killed the native people. Vinson Brown recalls in his book *Voices of Earth and Sky* that the great chief of the Oglala Sioux, Crazy Horse, had a vision around 1871:

> He saw his people being driven into spiritual darkness and poverty while the white people prospered in a material way all around them.... He saw the coming of automobiles and airplanes and twice he saw great darkness and heard screams and explosions when millions died in two great world wars. But then he saw a time come when his people began to awaken, not all at once but a few here and there....

The legend continues with all the races and religions banding together against the disaster. Under the symbol of the rainbow they spread the great wisdom of living in harmony with each other and with all the creations of the world. "Those who teach this way will be the Warriors of the Rainbow," says another version of this legend. Armed only with the truth, after a great struggle they will bring an end to the destruction. Eventually they will save life itself.[*]

Here is a call, a most urgent call, for Rainbow Warriors: something ancient, something new.

---

[*] With thanks to Steven McFadden for his book *Ancient Voices, Current Affairs: The Legend of the Rainbow Warriors.*

part one

SEEING MORE THAN
BLACK AND WHITE

Queremos ser libres
y la nueva forma
de ser libres
es serlo juntos.

We want to be free
and the new way
of being free
is to be free together.

—*palabras zapatistas/EZLN*
—from the Zapatista movement

chapter one

A WORD ABOUT
THE GREAT TERMINOLOGY QUESTION

When you have a name like Martínez, sooner or later someone will ask the Great Terminology Question. Say that you prefer to be called a Chicana, not Mexican American, and you'll have to explain it at some length. Say that you prefer to be called Latina rather than Hispanic, and prepare for an even longer discussion. Say you are indigenous, and you'd better make another pot of coffee for a long night's debate. So it goes in this land of many identities, with new ones emerging all the time.

On one hand, there are real grounds for confusion. The term "Chicano" or "Chicana" eludes simple definition because it stands for a mix that is both racial and cultural. It refers to a people who are neither strictly Mexican nor strictly Yankee—as well as both. Go to Mexico and you will quickly realize that most people there do not see Chicanos as Mexican. You may even hear the term "brown gringo." Live in the United States, and you will quickly discover that the dominant population doesn't see Chicanos as real Americans.

Confusion, ignorance and impassioned controversy about terminology make it necessary, then, to begin this book with such basic questions as: what is a Chicana or Chicano? (And remember, Spanish is a gendered language, hence Chicana/Chicano.)

For starters, we combine at least three roots: indigenous (from pre-Columbian times), European (from the Spanish and Portuguese invasions) and African (from the many slaves brought to the Americas, including some 200,000 to Mexico alone). A smattering of Chinese should be added, which goes back to the sixteenth century; Mexico City had a Chinatown by the mid-1500s, some historians say. Another *mestizaje,* or mixing, took place—this time with Native Americans of various nations, pueblos and tribes living in what is now the Southwest—when Spanish and Mexican colonizers moved north. Later our Chicano ancestors acquired yet another dimension through intermarriage with Anglos.

The question arises: is the term "Chicano" the same as "Mexican American" or "Mexican-American"? Yes, except in the sense of political self-definition. "Chicano/a" once implied lower-class status and was at times derogatory. During the 1960s and 1970s, in an era of strong pressure for progressive change, the term became an outcry of pride in one's peoplehood and rejection of assimilation as one's goal. Today the term "Chicano/a" refuses to go away, especially among youth, and you will still hear jokes like "A Chicano is a Mexican American who doesn't want to have blue eyes" or "who doesn't eat white bread" or whatever. (Some believe the word itself, by the way, comes from "Mexica"—pronounced "Meshica"—which was the early name for the Aztecs.)

People ask: are Chicanos different from Latinos?

At the risk of impassioned debate, let me say: we are one type of Latino. In the United States today, Latinos and Latinas include men and women whose background links them to some 20 countries, including Mexico. Many of us prefer "Latino" to "Hispanic," which obliterates our indigenous and African heritage, and recognizes only the European, the colonizer. (Brazilians, of course, reject "Hispanic" strongly because *their* European heritage is Portuguese, not Spanish.) "Hispanic" also carries the disadvantage of being a term that did not emerge from the community itself but was imposed by the dominant society through its census bureau and other bureaucracies, during the Nixon administration of the 1970s.

Today most of the people who say "Hispanic" do so without realizing its racist implications, simply because they see and hear it everywhere. Some who insist on using the term point out that "Latino" is no better than "Hispanic" because it also implies Eurocentricity. Many of us ultimately prefer to call ourselves "La Raza" or simply "Raza," meaning "The People," which dates back many years in the community. (Again we find complications in actual usage: some feel that Raza refers to people of Mexican and perhaps also Central American origin, and doesn't include Latinos from other areas.)

We are thus left with no all-embracing term acceptable to everyone. In the end, the most common, popular identification is by specific nationality: Puerto Rican, Mexican, Guatemalan, Colombian and so forth. But those of us who seek to build continental unity stubbornly cling to some broadly inclusive way of defining ourselves. In my own case, that means embracing both "Chicana" and "Latina."

<<< >>>

At the heart of the terminology debate is the historical experience of Raza. Invasion, military occupation and racist control mechanisms all influence the evolution of words describing people who have lived through such trauma. The collective memory of every Latino people includes direct or indirect (neo-)colonialism, primarily by Spain or Portugal and later by the United States.

Among Latinos, Mexicans in what we now call the Southwest have experienced U.S. colonialism the longest and most directly, with Puerto Ricans not far behind. Almost one-third of today's United States was the home of Mexicans as early as the 1500s, until Anglos seized it militarily in 1848 and treated its population as conquered subjects. (The Mexicans, of course, themselves occupied lands that had been seized from Native Americans.) Such oppression totally violated the Treaty of Guadalupe Hidalgo, which ended the 1846–48 war and promised respect for the civil and property rights of Mexicans remaining in the Southwest. The imposition of U.S. rule involved taking over millions of acres of Mexican-held land by trickery and violence. Colonization also brought the imposition of Anglo values and institutions at the expense of Mexican culture, including language. Hundreds of Mexicans were lynched as a form of control.

In the early 1900s, while colonization continued, the original Mexican population of the Southwest was greatly increased by an immigration that continues today. This combination of centuries-old roots with relatively recent ones gives the Mexican-American people a rich and varied cultural heritage. It means that Chicanos are not by origin an immigrant people in the United States (except compared with the Native Americans); their roots go back four centuries. Yet they also include immigrants. Too many Americans see only the recent arrivals, remaining blind to those earlier roots and what they signify.

We cannot understand all that history simply in terms of victimization: popular resistance is its other face. Raza resistance, which took the form of organized armed struggle in the Southwest during the last century, continues today in many forms. These include rejecting the colonized mentality, that pernicious, destructive process of internalizing a belief in the master's superiority and our inferiority.

The intensity of the terminology debate comes as no surprise, then, for it echoes people's struggles for non-racist—indeed, anti-racist—ways of defining themselves. Identity continues to be a major concern of youth in particular, with reason. But an obsession with self-definition can become a trap if that is all we think about, all we debate. If liberatory terminology becomes an end in itself and our only end, it ceases to be a tool of liberation. Terms can be useful, even vital tools, but the house of La Raza that is waiting to be built needs many kinds.

chapter two

SEEING MORE THAN BLACK AND WHITE

Introduction

When today's activists try to learn from the movements of the 1960s, one simple lesson should be remembered: liberation has similar meanings for all people of color engaged in struggle. It means an end to racist oppression, the birth of collective self-respect and genuine hope of the social justice that we sometimes call equality. That common dream requires us to build alliances among progressive people of color.

Such alliances require a knowledge and wisdom that we have yet to acquire. Today it remains painful to see how divide-and-conquer strategies succeed among people of color. It is painful to see how prejudice, resentment, petty competitiveness and sheer ignorance fester. It is positively pitiful to see how we echo Anglo stereotypes about each other.

These divisions indicate that we urgently need some fresh and fearless thinking about racism, which might begin with analyzing the strong tendency to frame U.S. racial issues in strictly Black-white terms. Such terms make little sense when a 1996 U.S. Census report says that 33 percent of our population will be Asian/Pacific Island-American, Latino, Native American/Indigenous (which includes Hawaiian) and Arab-American by the year 2050—in other words, neither white nor Black. (Steven A. Holmes, "Census Sees a Profound Ethnic Shift in U.S.," *New York Times,* March 14, 1996.) Also, we find an increasing number of mixed people who incorporate two, three or more "races."

The racial and ethnic landscape has changed too much in recent years to view it with the same eyes as before. We are looking at a multi-dimensional reality in which race, ethnicity, nationality, culture and immigrant status come together with breathtakingly new results. We are also seeing global changes that have a massive impact on our domestic situation, especially the economy and labor force. For a group of Korean restaurant entrepreneurs to hire Mexican cooks to prepare Chinese dishes for mainly African-American customers, as happened in Houston, Texas, has ceased to be unusual.

The ever-changing demographic landscape compels those struggling against racism and for a transformed, non-capitalist society to resolve several strategic questions. Among them: doesn't the exclusively Black-white framework discourage the perception of common interests among people of color and thus sustain White Supremacy? Doesn't the view that only African Americans face serious institutionalized racism isolate them from potential allies? Doesn't the Black-white model encourage people of color to spend too much energy understanding our lives in relation to whiteness, obsessing about what white society will think and do?

That tendency is inevitable in some ways: the locus of power over our lives has long been white (although big shifts have recently taken place in the color of capital, as we see in Japan, Singapore and elsewhere). The oppressed have always survived by becoming experts on the oppressor's ways. But that can become a prison of sorts, a trap of compulsive vigilance. Let us liberate ourselves, then, from the tunnel vision of whiteness and behold the many colors around us! Let us summon the courage to reject outdated ideas and stretch our imaginations into the next century.

For a Latina to urge recognizing a variety of racist models is not, and should not be, yet another round in the Oppression Olympics. We don't need more competition among different social groups for the gold medal of "Most Oppressed." We don't need more comparisons of suffering between women and Blacks, the disabled and the gay, Latino teenagers and white seniors, or whatever. Pursuing some hierarchy of oppression leads us down dead-end streets where we will never find the linkage between different oppressions and how to overcome them. To criticize the exclusively Black-white framework, then, is not some resentful demand by other people of color for equal sympathy, equal funding, equal clout, equal patronage or other questionable crumbs. Above all, it is not a devious way of minimizing the centrality of the African-American experience in any analysis of racism.

The goal in re-examining the Black-white framework is to find an effective strategy for vanquishing an evil that has expanded rather than diminished. Racism has expanded partly as a result of the worldwide economic recession that followed the end of the post-war boom in the early 1970s, with the resulting capitalist restructuring and changes in the international division of labor. Those developments generated feelings of insecurity and a search for scapegoats. In the United States racism has also escalated as whites increasingly fear becoming a weakened, minority population in the next century. The stage is set for decades of ever more vicious divide-and-conquer tactics.

What has been the response from people of color to this ugly White Supremacist agenda? Instead of uniting, based on common experience and needs, we have often closed our doors in a defensive, isolationist mode, each community on its own. A fire of fear and distrust begins to crackle, threatening to consume us all. Building solidarity among people of color is more necessary than ever—but the exclusively Black-white definition of racism makes such solidarity more difficult than ever.

We urgently need twenty-first-century thinking that will move us beyond the Black-white framework without negating its historical role in the construction of U.S. racism. We need a better understanding of how racism developed both similarly and differently for various peoples, according to whether they experienced genocide, enslavement, colonization or some other structure of oppression. At stake is the building of a united anti-racist force strong enough to resist White Supremacist strategies of divide-and-conquer and move forward toward social justice for all.

My call to rethink the prevailing framework of U.S. racism is being sounded by others today: academics, liberal foundation administrators and activist-intellectuals. But new thinking seems to proceed in fits and starts, or tokenistically, as if dogged by a fear of stepping on others' toes or being seen as a traitor to one's own community. Even progressive scholars of color often fail to go beyond perfunctorily saluting a vague multiculturalism.

Serious opposition to developing a new model also exists. Academics of color scrambling for funds will support only one flavor of Ethnic Studies and to hell with the others. Politicians of one color will cultivate distrust of others as a tactic to gain popularity in their own communities. When we hear, for example, of Black/Latino friction in the electoral arena, we should look below the surface for the reasons. In Los Angeles and New York, politicians out to score patronage and payola have played the narrow nationalist game, whipping up economic anxiety and provoking a resentment that sets communities against each other. White folks have no monopoly on such tactics.

We also find opposition from ordinary people with no self-interest in resisting a new model. African Americans have reason to be uneasy about where they, as a people, will find themselves politically, economically and socially with the rapid numerical growth of other folk of color. The issue is not just possible job loss, a real question that does need to be faced honestly. There is also a feeling that after centuries of fighting for simple recognition as human beings, Blacks will be shoved to the back of history again (like the back of the bus). Whether these fears are real or not, uneasiness exists and can lead to resentment when there's talk about a new model of race relations. So let me repeat: in speaking here of the need to move beyond the bipolar concept, the goal is to clear the way for stronger unity against White Supremacy. The goal is to identify our commonalities of experience and needs so we can build alliances.

The commonalities begin with history, which reveals that again and again peoples of color have had one experience in common: European colonization and/or neo-colonialism with its accompanying exploitation. This is true for all indigenous peoples, including Hawaiians. It is true for all Latino peoples, who were invaded and ruled by Spain or Portugal. It is true for people in Africa, Asia and the Pacific Islands, where European powers became the colonizers. People of color were victimized by colonialism not only externally but also through internalized racism—the "colonized mentality."

Flowing from this shared history are our contemporary commonalities. On the poverty scale, African Americans and Native Americans have always been at the bottom, with Latinos nearby. In 1995 the U.S. Census found that Latinos have the highest poverty rate, 24 percent. Segregation may have been legally abolished in the 1960s, but now the United States is rapidly moving toward re-segregation as a result of whites moving to the suburbs. This leaves people of color—especially Blacks and Latinos—with inner cities that lack an adequate tax base and thus have inadequate schools. Not surprisingly, Blacks and Latinos finish college at a far lower rate than whites. In other words, the victims of U.S. social ills come in more than one color. Doesn't that indicate the need for new, inclusive models for fighting racism? Doesn't that speak to the absolutely urgent need for alliances among peoples of color?

With greater solidarity, justice for people of color could be won. And an even bigger prize would be possible: a U.S. society that advances beyond "equality," beyond granting people of color a respect equal to that given to Euro-Americans. Too often "equality" leaves whites still at the center, still embodying the Americanness by which others are judged, still defining the national character. In her book *Playing in the Dark,* Toni Morrison writes eloquently of this problem from an African-American perspective. Her words resonate for other peoples of color as well: "American means white, and Africanist people struggle to make the term applicable to themselves with ethnicity and hyphen after hyphen after hyphen.... In the scholarship on the formation of an American character [a] ... major item to be added to the list must be an Africanist presence—decidedly not American, decidedly 'other.'

"Other" embraces many communities, many cultures. "Other" could replace the white national character with one grounded in societies whose guiding star is balance between all forms of life rather than domination, interdependence rather than competition. Societies based on these concepts could once be found in pre-colonial Africa, Asia and the American hemisphere. Never perfect, their values could still help define a new U.S. character unshackled from the capitalist worldview that celebrates only hegemony.

The current, exclusively Black-white framework for racism prevails throughout U.S. society, even when it is obviously inappropriate. Everywhere we can find major discussions of race and race relations that totally ignore people of color other than African Americans. President Bill Clinton led the way in the first stages of his "dialogue on race" during 1997, with a commission that included no Native Americans, Asian Americans or Latinos. East Coast–based institutions including academia and the media, our ideological mentors, are especially myopic. Books continue to be published that define U.S. race relations in exclusively Black-white terms, like Simon & Schuster's 1997 volume *America in Black and White: One Nation, Indivisible,* co-authored by Stephan Thernstrom and Abigail Thernstrom. Television programs, panel discussions and conferences on race see only in bipolar terms (does NBC's Ted Koppel ever see more than Black and white in his reports on racial issues?). Major outbreaks of Latino unrest, like the uprisings in Morningside Heights, New York, and the Mt. Pleasant district of Washington, D.C., make little if any dent; Latinos are in the news today and invisible again tomorrow. Except in the arena of electoral politics, much of New York City appears indifferent to the fact that, as of the early 1990s, Latinos totalled 24.4 percent of its population while Asians formed 6.9 percent. New Yorkers often dismiss the need for a new, more complex model of racial issues as "a California hangup."

Not that California is so much less myopic than the East and the Midwestern states. In fact the West Coast has only recently begun to move away from its own denial. In California, this most multinational of states, where Latinos have usually been the largest population of color, it is not rare for reports on racial issues to stay strictly inside the Black-white framework. In San Francisco, whose population is almost half Latino and Asian/Pacific Island-American, the media often use that afterthought phrase, "Blacks and other minorities." Millions of Americans saw massive Latino participation in the April 1992 Los Angeles uprising on their television screens. The most heavily damaged areas were 49 percent Latino; of the dead, 18 out of 50 were Latino; and the majority of people arrested were Latino, according to a 1993 report by the Tomás Rivera Center, a research institute in Claremont, California. Yet the mass media and most people continue to call that event "a Black riot."

For its annual conference held in northern California in August 1997, the American Civil Liberties Union had 18 panelists listed in the program; only one had a Spanish surname. Across the nation, educational resource projects do not include Latinos except in the category of "immigrants." In daily life, to cite several personal experiences, Anglos will admit to having made a racist remark or gesture toward an African American much more quickly than one made toward a Latino. Or they will respond to an account of police brutality toward some Latino/a with an irrelevant remark about the terrible crimes committed by Spanish *conquistadores* against indigenous people. (In other words, "your people" did the same thing, so don't complain.) Or: try to discuss racist acts against Asians, and people of any color will complain about rich Japanese businessmen supposedly taking over everything.

Innumerable statistics, reports and daily incidents should make it impossible to exclude Latinos and other non-Black populations of color when racism is discussed, but they don't. Police killings, hate crimes by racist individuals and murders with impunity by border of-

ficials should make it impossible, but they don't. With chilling regu-
larity, ranch owners compel migrant workers, usually Mexican, to re-
pay the cost of smuggling them into the United States by laboring the
rest of their lives for free. The 45 Latino and Thai garment workers
locked up in an El Monte, California, factory, working 18 hours a day
seven days a week for $299 a month, can also be considered slaves
(and one must ask why it took three years for the Immigration and
Naturalization Service to act on its own reports about this horror).
(*San Francisco Examiner,* August 8, 1995.) Abusive treatment of migrant workers can be found all over the United States. In Jackson
Hole, Wyoming, for example, police and federal agents rounded up
150 Latino workers in 1997, inked numbers on their arms and hauled
them off to jail in patrol cars and a horse trailer full of manure. (*Los
Angeles Times,* September 6, 1997.)

These experiences cannot be attributed to xenophobia, cultural
prejudice or some other, less repellent term than racism. Take the
case of two small Latino children in San Francisco who were found in
1997 covered from head to toe with flour. They explained they had
hoped to make their skin white enough for school. There is no way to
understand their action except as the result of fear in the racist climate
that accompanied passage of Proposition 187, which denies schooling
to the children of undocumented immigrants. Another example:
Mexican and Chicana women working at a Nabisco plant in Oxnard,
California, were not allowed to take bathroom breaks from the assembly line and were told to wear diapers instead. Can we really imagine
white workers being treated that way? (The Nabisco women did file a
suit and won, in 1997.)

No "model minority" myth protects Asians and Asian Americans from hate crimes, police brutality, immigrant-bashing, stereotyp-
ing and everyday racist prejudice. Scapegoating can even take their
lives, as happened with the murder of Vincent Chin in Detroit some
years ago. Two auto workers thought he was Japanese (he was Chinese) and thus responsible for all those Japanese cars that left them
unemployed. Hate crimes against Asians mounted steadily in the
1990s, with a leap of 17 percent nationwide in one year alone—from
1995 to 1996. (*San Francisco Examiner,* October 26, 1997.) A Chinese-American man outside a supermarket was killed in 1995 in
northern California by an unemployed meat-cutter who said he just
felt an urge to "kill me a Chinaman." (*New York Times,* December 13,
1995.) A popular Vietnamese youth, Thien Minh Ly, was stabbed 23
times while skating at the local high school in Tustin, California; the

murderer wrote in a letter, "Oh, I killed a Jap." (*San Francisco Chronicle*, October 22, 1996.) As in the Vincent Chin killing, this case exemplifies the confusion over nationality, another similarity between the experience of Latinos and Asian/Pacific Island Americans: both are homogenized.

In a particularly outrageous case, police killed a young Chinese engineer and father of three young children in Rohnert Park, California, on April 24, 1997. The man had received racist insults while at a bar celebrating a new job, and had gone home furious. Hearing his drunken shouts, neighbors called police, who shot him immediately when he waved a long stick at them that he had grabbed from the garage. Police would not let his wife convince him to go inside their home, as she thought she could, or give him CPR (she is a nurse) after he was shot. Instead, they handcuffed the man and left him to die in his driveway. Their explanation was a racist stereotype: the stick (which was all of one-eighth inch thick) made the officer think the man would use "martial arts" against them. When we hear about this unending list of racist horrors, it is hard to understand how Asian/Pacific Island Americans, like Latinos and other peoples of color, have been excluded from the framework of racism.

We also need to look at the often stunning commonalities of racist experience. When some 120,000 Japanese—most of them U.S. citizens—were packed off to "internment" camps during World War II, this should have rung an old, familiar bell. We have lived with the internment camp under so many other names: reservation, plantation, migrant labor camp. It is not hard to imagine Arab Americans being rounded up someday for imprisonment in "terrorist camps."

Along with African Americans, millions of other people of color have been invisibilized, terrorized, demonized and dehumanized by White Supremacy. Yet up to now, the prevailing framework for racial issues has not included them, except occasionally in books and articles (mainly by people of color). We need to ask: why?

Why the Black-White Model?

A bipolar model of racism has never been really accurate for the United States. Early in this nation's history, Benjamin Franklin perceived a tri-racial society based on skin color—"the lovely white" (Franklin's words), the Black, and the "tawny," as Ron Takaki tells us in *Iron Cages*. But this concept changed as capital's need for labor intensified in the new nation and came to focus on African slave labor. The "tawny" were decimated or forcibly exiled to distant areas; Mexicans were not yet available to be the main labor force. As enslaved Africans became the crucial labor force for the primitive accumulation of capital, they also served as the foundation for the very idea of whiteness—based on the concept of blackness as inferior.

Three other reasons for the Black-white framework seem obvious: numbers, geography and history. African Americans have long been the largest population of color in the United States; only recently has this begun to change. Also, African Americans have long been found in sizable numbers in most parts of the United States, including major cities, which has not been true of Latinos until recent times. Historically, the Black-white relationship has been entrenched in the nation's collective memory for some 300 years—whereas it is only 150 years since the United States seized half of Mexico and incorporated those lands and their peoples. Slavery and the struggle to end it formed a central theme in this country's only civil war—a prolonged, momentous conflict. Above all, enslaved Africans in the United States and African Americans have created an unmatched heritage of massive, persistent, dramatic and infinitely courageous resistance, with individual leaders of worldwide note.

We also find sociological and psychological explanations of the Black-white model's persistence. From the days of Jefferson onward, Native Americans, Mexicans and later the Asian/Pacific Islanders did not seem as much a threat to racial purity or as capable of arousing white sexual anxieties as did Blacks. A major reason for this must have been Anglo ambiguity about who could be called white. Most of the Mexican *ranchero* elite in California had welcomed the U.S. takeover, and Mexicans were partly European—therefore "semi-civilized"; this allowed Anglos to see them as white, unlike lower-class Mexicans. For years Mexicans were legally white, and even today we hear the ambiguous U.S. Census term "Non-Hispanic Whites."

Like Latinos, Asian Americans have also been officially counted as white in some historical periods. They have been defined as "colored" in others, with "Chinese" being yet another category. Like Mexicans, they were often seen as not really white but not quite Black either. Such ambiguity tended to put Asian Americans along with Latinos outside the prevailing framework of racism.

Blacks, on the other hand, were not defined as white, could rarely become upper-class and maintained an almost constant rebelliousness. Contemporary Black rebellion has been urban: right in the

Man's face, scary. Mexicans, by contrast, have lived primarily in rural areas until a few decades ago and "have no Mau-Mau image," as one Black friend said, even when protesting injustice energetically. Only the nineteenth-century resistance heroes labeled "bandits" stirred white fear, and that was along the border, a limited area. Latino stereotypes are mostly silly: snoozing next to a cactus, eating greasy food, always being late and disorganized, rolling big Carmen Miranda eyes, shrugging with self-deprecation "me no speek good eengleesh." In other words, *not serious*. This view may be altered today by stereotypes of the gangbanger, criminal or dirty immigrant, but the prevailing image of Latinos remains that of a debased white, at best.

In his book *Racial Oppression in America*, Robert Blauner, an Anglo and one of the few authorities on racism to have questioned the Black-white framework, looks at some psychological factors as revealed in literature:

> We buy black writers, not only because they can write and have something to say, but because the white racial mind is obsessed with blackness.... Mexican-Americans, on the other hand, have been unseen as individuals and as a group.... James Baldwin has pointed to the deep mutual involvement of black and white in America. The profound ambivalence, the love-hate relationship, which Baldwin's own work expresses and dissects, does not exist in the racism that comes down on La Raza.... Even the racial stereotypes that plague Mexican-Americans tend to lack those positive attributes that mark antiblack fantasies: supersexuality, inborn athletic and musical power, natural rhythm.

In short: whiteness would not exist without blackness to define its superiority, nor does whiteness exist without envy of blackness. But white envy of *mexicanidad*, "Mexicanness," has always been very limited, and even less so white envy of the so-called Oriental. Anglo attitudes toward the Native American combine romanticized envy with racist stereotypes, yet carry too little weight numerically to challenge the existing racist model.

Among other important reasons for the exclusively Black-white model, sheer ignorance leaps to mind. The oppression and exploitation of Latinos (like Asians) have historical roots unknown to most Americans. People who learn at least a little about Black slavery remain totally ignorant about how the United States seized half of Mexico or how it has colonized Puerto Rico. Robert Blauner has rightly commented on the Latino situation that "[e]ven informed Anglos know almost nothing about La Raza, its historical experience, its present situation…. And the average citizen doesn't have the foggiest notion that Chicanos have been lynched in the Southwest and continue to be abused by the police, that an entire population has been exploited economically, dominated politically, and raped culturally."

One other important reason for the bipolar model of racism is the stubborn self-centeredness of U.S. political culture. It has meant that the nation lacks any global vision other than relations of domination. In particular, the United States refuses to see itself as one among some 20 countries in a hemisphere whose dominant languages are Spanish and Portuguese, not English. It has only a big yawn of contempt or at best indifference for the people, languages and issues of Latin America. It arrogantly took for itself alone the name of half the western hemisphere, America, as was its "Manifest Destiny," of course.

So Mexico may be nice for a vacation and lots of Yankees like tacos, but the political image of Latin America combines incompetence with absurdity, fat corrupt dictators with endless siestas. Similar attitudes extend to Latinos within the United States. My parents, both Spanish teachers, endured decades of being told that students were better off learning French or German. The mass media complain that "people can't relate to Hispanics (or Asians)." It takes mysterious masked rebels, a beautiful young murdered singer or salsa outselling ketchup for the Anglo world to take notice of Latinos. If there weren't a mushrooming, billion-dollar "Hispanic" market to be wooed, the Anglo world might still not know we exist. No wonder that racial paradigm sees only two poles.

The exclusively Black-white framework is also sustained by the "model minority" myth, because it distances Asian Americans from other victims of racism. Portraying Asian Americans as people who work hard, study hard, obey the established order and therefore prosper, the myth in effect admonishes Blacks and Latinos: "See, anyone can make it in this society if you try hard enough. The poverty and prejudice you face are all *your* fault."

The "model" label has been a wedge separating Asian Americans from others of color by denying their commonalities. It creates a sort of racial bourgeoisie, which White Supremacy uses to keep Asian Americans from joining forces with the poor, the homeless and criminalized youth. People then see Asian Americans as a special class of yuppie: young, single, college-educated, on the white-collar track—

and they like to shop for fun. Here is a dandy minority group, ready to be used against others.

The stereotype of Asian Americans as whiz kids is also enraging because it hides so many harsh truths about the impoverishment, oppression and racist treatment they experience. Some do come from middle- or upper-class families in Asia, some do attain middle-class or higher status in the U.S., and their community must deal with the reality of class privilege where it exists. But the hidden truths include the poverty of many Asian/Pacific Islander groups, especially women, who often work under intolerable conditions, as in the sweatshops. Many youths are not students but live on the streets or in pool halls. A 1993 U.S. Census study reported that the poverty rate for peoples of Asian origin in the United States ran as high as 26 percent (Vietnamese), 35 percent (Laotian), 43 percent (Cambodian) and a monstrous 64 percent (Hmong). (*San Francisco Examiner,* October 7, 1997.) Just how "model" is that?

The Devils of Dualism

Yet another cause of the persistent Black-white conception of racism is dualism, the philosophy that sees all life as consisting of two irreducible elements. Those elements are usually oppositional, like good and evil, mind and body, civilized and savage. Dualism allowed the invaders, colonizers and enslavers of today's United States to rationalize their actions by stratifying supposed opposites along race, color or gender lines. So mind is European, male and rational; body is colored, female and emotional. Dozens of other such pairs can be found, with their clear implications of superior-inferior. In the arena of race, this society's dualism has long maintained that if a person is not totally white (whatever that can mean biologically), he or she must be considered Black.

This form of dualism also underlies the perception of "race-mixing" as a threat to White Supremacy. In the Euro-American racial hierarchy of the 1840s, as one historian has noted, "Africans, Native Americans, and any nation that had mixed the races—Mexico, for instance—were clustered at the bottom." The amalgamation of races would generate a deterioration of national character in this country and lead to barbarism. (Thomas Hietala, "This Splendid Juggernaut," in *Manifest Destiny and Empire: American Ante-Bellum Expansion-*

ism, ed. Robert Johannsen et al. [Texas A&M University Press, 1998].)

That belief haunts our society today, as David Hayes-Bautista and Gregory Rodríguez have noted: "[A] disdain for mixture haunts and inhibits U.S. culture. Because it does not recognize hybridism, this country's racial framework emphasizes separateness and offers no ground for mutual inclusion." ("Latinos Are Redefining Notions of Racial Identity," *Los Angeles Times,* January 15, 1993.) As the child of Mexican and Anglo parents, I remember growing up haunted by that dreaded word "half-breed," meaning me. Today *mestizaje—* mixing—is still seen by the dominant society as indicating a polluted or at least problematic bloodline, rather than a source of cultural richness. The hybrid is mysteriously "un-American."

The mainstream culture doesn't deal comfortably with complex ideas or peoples, and Latinos are highly complex in every way. In addition to biological and cultural complexity, Chicanos and Chicanas have a complex political identity: they were born from a process of Spain colonizing Mexico, then became colonizers themselves in what is now the Southwest, only to be colonized again by other whites. They are both indigenous and immigrant. For 150 years, people moving north from Mexico did not feel they were going to a foreign country; the land had been Mexico and in many ways it remains so. Nothing spoke of a real border—not the landscape nor the people nor the culture. Only in the 1920s did checkpoints and border control begin to institutionalize a separateness. Psychologically and culturally, the Southwest remains today, for many Mexicans, a Mexican nation within an Anglo nation.

The complex identity of Chicanos/as led poet Bernice Zamora to write:

You insult me
When you say I'm
Schizophrenic.
My divisions are
Infinite.

But dualism prefers a Black-white view in all such matters, leaving no room for a wildly multi-colored, multilingual, multinational presence called "Latino."

A Culture of Color

"If you're white, you're all right; if you're yellow, you're mellow; if you're brown, stick around; if you're Black, get back." As that old saying indicates, color is crucial to understanding racism, and it has a different history for different peoples of color. Latinos and Asian Americans have a commonality here: both say, "I'm not Black or white—but then, what am I?" The relatively light skin of many U.S. Latinos, especially those in the middle class, has meant that they can often "pass," which transmits great privilege in a racist society. The ability to be accepted as white can lead Latinos to deny the reality of racism and thus to discourage solidarity among peoples of color, so that we become our own worst enemy.

This dilemma intensified in the 1970s and 1980s with the rise of a Latino middle class and the use of the term "Hispanic" ("His Panic, Her Panic," as some of us mocked it then). The term supports a racist attitude of "wannabe white/don't wannabe Indian," which has long existed among Latinos who focus on their European roots and deny their Indian and African heritage. Such denial includes failing to see that life is very different for those who look "white" enough to pass and those who cannot even try. Such denial means looking at people of color through White Supremacist eyes.

When Latinos buy into that denial, they sustain the culture of color, the hierarchy based on whiteness. When they express prejudice against Latinos who look *indio,* mulatto or Black, they sustain the culture of color. When they celebrate a newborn Latino child for being *huero* ("fair, light-skinned"), they sustain the culture of color. Latino magazines do it when their editors choose a blonde, never an "Indian-looking" woman, to grace the cover. Latinos do it when they tell their misbehaving children not to act "like Indians." Such color prejudice not only dehumanizes fellow human beings, but also divides our forces in the struggle for social justice. There can be no solidarity if Latinos insist on trying to preserve the advantage of passing.

Latinos need to see how the elite *Californios* lost their "whiteness" when they lost their land and became a laboring population after the 1846–48 war. The broad parallelism of race and class embraced Mexicans ferociously, as they dropped into the lowest ranks of the working class. With the decline of the cattle industry in California, for example, the men could not even have the status of foremen or *vaqueros*; they became plain proletarians, if they could get work at all. Mexican physical features, including color, kept them at the bottom—and the darker they were, the lower. The culture of color was imposed and remains. As with African Americans, color usually undermines any benefits from superior class status; a perfectly tailored suit and Gucci shoes will not save a Latino professional from a racist policeman.

The Color of Culture

If there is a culture of color in these racist United States, we also have a color of culture. That is, cultures have color. In a land where the national identity is white, speaking a "different" language from English or eating "strange food" can make a person "other" as much as having a different skin color. Cultural prejudice is a common form of discrimination against Latinos, yet the Black-white model has no room for this reality because it is not seen as race-related by most African Americans, whites and even many Latinos.

The right to speak Spanish at work or on a school playground has often been punitively denied to Latinos. A Spanish accent (though not a British or French accent) is a liability in many professional situations. For other peoples, speaking Spanish signals immigrant status, which is grounds for immediate scapegoating in the current era. Among Latinos, children's names are Anglicized upon entry into school by most white teachers; Latino children are ridiculed for bringing Mexican lunches; and humiliation is daily fare if their English is minimal. Cultural repression has led to fantastic extremes, such as the 1995 case of Texas judge Samuel Kiser ordering a Mexican woman, Martha Laureano, to speak only English to her daughter or lose custody. Speaking Spanish leads those who are citizens to be denied citizen rights, and non-citizens to be denied human rights. Asian/Pacific-Island Americans face the same.

Cultural discrimination imposes its most deadly effects in education and must be a major reason for the fact that Latinos had the nation's highest dropout (pushout) rate in 1995, according to an Education Department report. (*San Francisco Chronicle,* August 1, 1997.) Linguistic imperialism is sure to create a profound sense of inferiority in young minds and thus encourage such a percentage. Later in life many other examples of cultural apartheid exist, from the mild but nagging frustration of being considered exotic, outside the main-

stream, alien, to no one appreciating the beauty of Spanish or understanding Raza's self-mocking jokes. For artists, the alienation can become ghettoization, and one is forever typecast, folklorized or just
plain excluded. For working-class Latinos, linguistic imperialism can
drive you a little crazy. Consider the two women who were hired by a
Texas insurance company specifically because they could speak with
clients—and then fired in 1997 for talking Spanish with each other.

Today's attack on language rights is becoming a genuine cultural war. For more than ten years the "English Only" campaign has
worked to get laws passed making English the language of the ballot,
the public schools and government functions. More than 20 states
have passed such a law. A new campaign to abolish bilingual education is underway. No end can be seen to such attacks.

Culture combined with nationality makes Latinos especially
vulnerable in the southern borderlands of this nation. California's San
Diego County feels today as Mississippi must have felt for Blacks in
the 1960s. Five years ago in that county a pair of middle-class white
youths spied two young, documented Latinos standing by the roadside; one shot them dead and later explained to the judge that he did it
because he "didn't like Mexicans." Such attitudes are common in that
county today.

"It just ain't chic to be a spic," as poet Gerardo Navarro rhymed
sardonically at a performance in San Francisco, California.

In a land where the national identity is white, cultural or nationality oppression and racial or skin-color oppression function inter-
changeably. Discrimination based on the culture of color is racist, and
so is discrimination based on the color of culture. We cannot separate
them simplistically; they overlap and collaborate constantly. Once
again we see the need to develop a multifaceted rather than bipolar
model of racism.

Racism Evolves

A glimpse into the next century tells us how much we need to
look beyond the bipolar model of race relations. Black and white are
real poles, central to the history of U.S. racism. We should not ignore
them; neither should we stop there. Our effectiveness in fighting racism depends on seeing the changes taking place today and trying to
perceive the contours of the future, which includes defining new
poles. From the time of the Greeks, racism has had certain common

characteristics around the world but no permanently fixed character. So it is today as well.

Racism evolves. If you thought Latinos were just "Messicans" down at the border, wake up. They are all over North Carolina, Pennsylvania and Manhattan, too, although you may not see them on *your* streets. If you thought Asians were just a few old guys chatting in Chinatown, look again at a California mall or the Atlanta, Georgia, airport or a New York state university campus. Qualitative as well as quantitative changes are taking place. With the broader geographic spread of Latinos and Asian/Pacific-Island Americans, policies and attitudes that were once regional have become national. California leads the way: the West is going east and the oldest part of this country is taking on many new colors.

Racism evolves; our models must also evolve. Today's challenge is to move beyond the Black-white dualism that has served as the foundation of White Supremacy. In taking up this challenge, we have to proceed with both boldness and infinite care. Talking race in these United States is an intellectual minefield; for every observation, one can find three contradictions and four necessary qualifications from five different racial groups. Making your way through that complexity, you have to think: keep your eyes on the prize.

Sometimes our task seems so clear. A few years ago, I showed slides on Chicano history at an Oakland high school, with 47 African-American and three Latina/o students present. The images included lynchings and police beatings of Mexicans, along with many depictions of resistance and revolution. At the end one Black student, a young woman, raised her hand and said: "Seems like we've had a lot of experiences in common—so why can't Blacks and Mexicans get along better?"

That was the first step: asking a hard question openly and in a way that said, "Let us solve this problem together." In that same spirit, we can all summon the courage to stretch our imaginations into the next century *de colores*.

chapter three

THAT OLD WHITE (MALE) MAGIC

It took two glasses of wine to prepare for the Approach. Small wonder: I was about to put a rather sticky question to a Lion of the Left, a noted white scholar and writer, at a reception on the campus of a very prestigious university. The moment arrived and my question came stumbling out: "I learned so much from your book, but I was wondering why your analysis of problems facing the U.S. Left didn't include racial issues and women's issues?"

His reply went along the lines of "I wouldn't presume to speak for ..." Wimpily, I murmured, "Well, you could say that in your introduction, so nobody would think you had just ignored ..." But just ignored he had.

Many of us looked toward the 1990s with a dash of hope. The Left appeared to have learned some lessons. The degree of sectarian infighting had diminished. Hoary dogmatism could still be heard at times but usually sounded like chatter from people who needed to hear themselves talk; it commanded little attention. With the abandonment of pretensions to instant state power, our strategic imaginations could be liberated. Yet on issues of race and sex, many liberals and leftists seemed to have learned so little. Our white male intellectuals—if those words ring like a cliché, bear with me a minute—too often resembled members of a club where the Old Boys flag still flew high.

"Honky," "male chauvinist pig" and other shibboleths of the 1960s had a dated ring by the 1980s. But today, when horrendous racist acts can occur without stirring the nation to action, when a woman's right to abortion is under renewed attack, those oldies can take on a grim relevance. Some progressive white intellectual men do combat racism and sexism. But not nearly enough.

Nowhere is such failure more evident than in the books published about "the sixties." This writer reviewed two dozen books purporting to address that era in general terms. That is, they were not specialized studies focusing on one movement, one organization or one person, so you could reasonably expect to find the whole range of 1960s activism, including the movements led by people of color and the women's liberation movement. Instead I found a spectacular level of straight, white middle-class, male centrism.

Here are some observations about the books reviewed, with special attention to the way Latinos/as are treated. These comments don't include an in-depth look at the treatment of the women's or gay rights movements.

When Was "the Sixties"?

The era called the sixties can be said to run from 1955 (the Montgomery bus boycott) to 1975 (when the mass movements had died down and most activists were moving on to new forms of struggle or non-political priorities). But many of the authors of those two dozen books end the era in 1970, not because the decade formally ended then but largely because *that was when male-led, white student protest sharply declined.* This dating negates high points of struggle by peoples of color (such as the Native American armed occupation of Wounded Knee in 1973) and by the women's movement, which reached its heights after 1970. By their dating of the era, our authors impose an overwhelmingly white male definition on it. Other arbitrary limitations follow.

Todd Gitlin exemplifies this definition in *The Sixties*, the most widely noted of such works, when he says about late-1960s activism: "At the hub is the youth movement, principally the white student part of it, and its self-conscious core, the New Left.... For along with the black movement ... the New Left became the dynamic center of the decade." Thus Gitlin ends the era in 1970–71. Another well-praised book, James Miller's *Democracy Is in the Streets*, addresses the question "What was the significance of the New Left?" and proceeds to evaluate it as an all-white phenomenon.

From those two books, and others that examine student activism at length, you would never know that during a single week of 1968 at least 10,000 Chicano high school students in Los Angeles walked out of school to protest racist policies. You would never know there was a "Yellow Identity Movement" of Chinese and other Asian students at universities in California and New York City. You will learn nothing of the potent Third World student strikes of 1968–69 in San Francisco. Gitlin's book does not even mention any movement of color except the Black civil rights movement until page 433. There he speaks of "an amalgam of reform efforts, especially for civil rights (ultimately for Hispanics, Native Americans, and other minorities as well as blacks)." Six words, and in parentheses at that, for the thousands of Asian, Latino and Native American people who lived and sometimes died for liberation and social justice in those years.

Such treatment typifies almost all of the 24 books reviewed, even when they are otherwise well written. Four offer bibliographies, with some 200 titles each. Not a single title listed concerns Asian, Chicano, Native American or Puerto Rican struggles, although many have been published. (Lawrence Lader does include nine footnote references to such works in *Power on the Left;* in general his book gives substantial coverage, albeit with errors.) Three chronologies can also be found, containing a total of two references to struggles by people of color.

And so it goes. The skimpy treatment of Latino activism is perhaps the most astonishing of all, given the movement's size and multifaceted nature. Three books devote from one paragraph to a page to the Chicano/a movement. The rest are totally silent. Although the anti–Vietnam War movement is widely discussed, only one book mentions the August 29, 1970, Chicano moratorium against the war that brought out at least 20,000 people. Only one book mentions the three Chicanos killed by police action that day, and the thousands who were teargassed. And where are the huge, spirited marches against the Vietnam War sponsored by the Puerto Rican Socialist Party?

In two books about the cultural flowering of the 1960s, the many volumes of Chicano poetry, short stories, songs, and skits go unmentioned. In two books on the underground press, Robert Glessing's *The Underground Press in America* and Abe Peck's *Uncovering the Sixties*, you will find no mention of Chicano movement newspapers in the first (except for two listings in its appendix) and two references in the second. Yet there was a Chicano Press Association comprising 60 newspapers and magazines in those years.

Puerto Rican activism can be found in exactly two works. So much for the Young Lords Party in New York and Chicago, which achieved widespread community support, or its martyrs of police abuse, or the alternative clinics and schools it established. Asian-American protest garners a single sentence in two books. So much for the Filipino farmworkers who struck in 1965, even before Mexicans. So much for the Chinatown-Manilatown draft counseling project, the Red Guard community-based youth organization and the eight-year struggle to save the International Hotel for elderly Asians in San

Francisco. Native American activism gets a phrase in three books and from one paragraph to a page in two others. The rest have nothing to say about the 1967–69 occupation of Alcatraz that dramatized the Indian land struggle, the American Indian Movement, the military siege at Wounded Knee or the framing of Leonard Peltier, who has remained imprisoned for more than 20 years.

Omission is only part of the problem; these books also demonstrate their ethnocentricity in what they do include. Several authors apparently can envision Latino struggle only through a prism of white priorities and white experience. For example, Edward Bacciocco Jr. in *The New Left in America* refers to two Latino organizations, but only because they criticized an organization inimical to the primarily white Students for a Democratic Society (SDS). *Turning Point 1968* by Irwin Unger and Debi Unger mentions striking Mexican farmworkers, but only in the context of how young Tom Hayden became politicized when he visited them.

Native Americans receive even more ethnocentric treatment. Their militant struggles ignored, they do surface briefly as victims—that is, via white guilt—when William O'Neill recounts in *Coming Apart* how the hippies "showed sympathy for American Indians" by wearing beads, leather goods and what all. The same book later says: "One of the most genuine and attractive things about Robert Kennedy was his passion for obscure minorities. If there were any Indians in the country he had not spoken to, it was only by accident."

The few mentions of Latino protest show a preference for leaders committed to nonviolence rather than angry urban rebels. The parallel here between César Chávez and Martin Luther King Jr. is striking. Another favorite: internal conflicts. One of the three books that gives a paragraph or more to Chicanos devotes that space to problems between Reies López Tijerina of New Mexico's land-grant movement and Black leaders during the 1968 Poor People's March in Washington, D.C. A second book reiterates how, among the different peoples of color at that event, "the squabbling ... was endless."

There is a striking similarity between the treatment of activism by peoples of color other than Blacks and the treatment of the women's movement. With only two exceptions, authors who ignore the former also downplay the latter. Milton Viorst, the respected author of *Fire in the Streets*, presents 14 interviews with leading figures in the 1960s; not one is an Asian, Latino or Native American—or a woman. Only two authors mention the lesbian (or gay) rights movement.

Also, the women's movement is negated both by total omission and by the kind of attention it gets. In *The Sixties*, for example, women seem to do fairly well at first glance. Gitlin devotes 15 pages to the struggle against sexism in New Left organizations, especially SDS. Unfortunately those pages are plagued by an undercurrent of hostility and a tendency to perceive women's struggle primarily in relation to what men were doing at the time. With incredulous eyes we read that in the late 1960s "[w]hile men ... were miserable with the crumbling of their onetime movement, women were riding high. With amazing speed they spawned ... a web of women's health collectives, clinics, legal centers." Spawn? Web? Gitlin's very language rushes resentfully from his beloved, male-dominated movement to decry the Eggs of the Spider Woman.

Along with the parallelism of color and sex prejudice, there is a possible parallelism of class identification in these books. For example, working-class opposition to the Vietnam War, as in the GI coffeehouse movement, tends to be dwarfed by middle-class student protest. A former member of both SDS and the Student Nonviolent Coordinating Committee (SNCC), Phil Hutchings, sees significant class distinctions in SDS, with a prevalence of graduates from elite universities and academic types among the early founding members (Tom Hayden being a notable exception), and more varied class backgrounds coming later. The founders have remained the spokespeople for the 1960s, through either their own writings or their influence on other authors. So the perspective that dominates our 24 books may well reflect that upper-middle-class component.

The Why of It All

When we try to explain the large blank areas in these canvases of the 1960s, we should first note that all but two of the 24 books have white authors, or so it appears from the jacket photos and biographies. All but six had exclusively male authors or editors. Books by leftists or liberals (four-fifths of the total number) are only a little better than those by mainstream or reactionary authors. At the time of their writing, the authors comprised 18 academics or scholars and six journalists or political analysts (some had more than one profession).

We should also recall the exclusively Black-white model of race relations, which makes all other peoples invisible. It is not surprising that two dozen white writers who have been conditioned to see the struggles of Asian/Pacific Island Americans, Latinos and Native Americans as minor would write their books accordingly. It would be amazing to find anything else.

The relatively major attention given by these same authors to Black protest might seem to prove that their omissions of other struggles can't be due to racism. But what about the quality of that attention? The massiveness, courage and exceptional leaders of Black protest are widely recognized in these two dozen books. You will look long and hard, however, for the concept of that movement as *central* or *seminal*, as a catalyst of the 1960s in general. It is seen as germane only to the problems facing African Americans—a "special interest" group, in conservative idiom—and not as a challenge to the totality of U.S. society. This minimizes Black struggle. Racism, then, does warp the thinking of these authors and explain the omissions.

It is true that nationwide Black protest really did overshadow Latino protest in the 1960s, so that giving less attention to the latter is appropriate. But the absence of information about protest by other peoples of color is too extreme to be explained away on this basis. Do regional limitations explain the neglect of Latino protest? Unlike African Americans, Chicanos are heavily concentrated in one region, the Southwest, and 1960s Chicano activism often took place in rural areas or smaller cities. (The same is true of Native American activism.) With news bureaus concentrated in the Northeast, we might say that the neglect of Latino protest has a simple explanation: the Chicano is geographically in the wrong place. But what about Los Angeles, where the biggest protests took place? And what about Puerto Ricans, who live primarily in large cities such as New York? There is much that regional limits on media coverage cannot explain.

A more helpful explanation—also related to the media—might be that no leaders with the vast, multifaceted, international stature of Martin Luther King Jr. and Malcolm X emerged among Latinos (or Asians and Indians). César Chávez came closest. Knowing that the presence of outstanding leaders often determines the degree of media attention, we can assume that our authors have simply noticed what the mass media noticed. But we are still entitled to ask: why didn't these writers do better?

It does not help that former Latino activists themselves have written so little. At least four leaders of white student protest (Richard Flacks, Todd Gitlin, Tom Hayden and Paul Potter) have published books of history and analysis about the 1960s. Martin Luther King Jr., Malcolm X, activists from SNCC, the Black Panther Party and other

Black groups have done so. But none of the "Big Four" Chicano leaders (César Chávez, Rodolfo "Corky" Gonzáles, José Angel Gutiérrez and Reies López Tijerina) has produced such a work. Participants should move to shine some light on our own histories.

The Sixties as Linkage

Generalizing about the 1960s from a white male perspective also leads to not seeing the linkages between different struggles and learning from them. We cannot afford to let our strategies for the future be skewed by the same narcissistic vision that distorts the past.

In actuality, the 1960s was an era of interconnection across lines of sex and race, time and space. But with rare exceptions, these authors are guilty of fragmenting the movement. George Katsiaficas' book *The Imagination of the New Left* is alone among all the titles reviewed in not "giving" Latinos a sentence and then forgetting them as it returns to the main, white track. Katsiaficas interweaves different struggles, so that Latinos appear and later reappear, as do other peoples. In this way, both their universality and particularity are seen, as they should be.

White radicals of the 1960s—many of them called "the New Left"—learned tactics from African Americans, who had learned some of theirs from Asians (Gandhi) and who also adopted tactics from white workers of an earlier era. Native Americans took tactics from Blacks. Asian-American youths were inspired by young Puerto Rican activists. Chicano organizations copied from the Black Panther Party, as in their breakfast program.

Yet the "New Left" is usually staked out with Eurocentric boundaries in our books on the 1960s. Even many people of color define the New Left as white, and would deny that their activism had anything to do with a new, old or any other kind of Left. The New Left was indeed born primarily white. But its vision of a society in which the exploited and oppressed become an empowered collectivity did inspire people across racial and national lines. That vision generated an international political culture that stirred youth from Paris to Mexico to Tokyo and lives on today. Who cannot be reminded of that New Left ideal, "participatory democracy" (an SDS phrase), when hearing of how 3,000 Chinese students voted on every major decision in Tiananmen Square in May 1989?

Perhaps the obvious needs to be repeated: what frightens U.S. ruling-class circles is the linking of issues, strategies and, above all, people in struggle. What frightens them most is the prospect of grassroots alliances across national or racial lines. Progressives have no business falling prey to the dominant society's common view that the problem of racism is minorities feeling dissatisfied, rather than a lethal poison in the spirit and the body of our entire society. The cure is a whole new world that only a sense of our global linkage, of interdependence, can breathe into life.

An Afterword

Since this study of books about the 1960s was first written, have there been any new books published, or new editions of existing books, that see the 1960s more inclusively? The sad answer is: if such a book exists, it's very hard to find. One possibility appeared in 1996, titled *New Left, New Right and the Legacy of the Sixties* by Paul Lyons. Although it is a polemical work rather than a history, Lyons finds space for ten informative pages about the women's movement, as well as lengthy comments on the Black civil rights and human rights movement and identity politics. But you cannot even find the words "Latino" or "Asian American" in this volume. A 1997 book on that era titled *Reassessing the '60s* and edited by Stephen Macedo appeared; the editor's Spanish surname gave a moment of hope. Forget it. This anthology is so sardonic and essentially anti-1960s that one is almost glad he doesn't include the other struggles of color. In the case of Todd Gitlin's book, a new edition has appeared but contains no changes along the lines we might have wanted.

Most histories continue to teach us not to understand and not to hope. But the struggle for transformation also continues, stubbornly insisting on other stories, other visions. Personal memoirs have helped. A new interest in movement history flourishes today among young people who know that something is terribly wrong with the world they inherited; who know there was a time not long ago when people thought they smelled revolution in the wind; who want to know where, when and how that was possible. The hope persists of grasping lessons from the past to help shape the future.

Books Reviewed

Judith C. Albert and Stewart A. Albert, eds., *The Sixties Papers: Documents of a Rebellious Decade* (New York: Praeger, 1984). Both are former activists; she is an academic, he is a private investigator and journalist.

Philip G. Altbach, *Student Politics in America: A Historical Analysis* (New York: McGraw Hill, 1974). An academic.

Roberta Ash, *Social Movements in America* (Chicago: Markham, 1972). An academic.

Edward J. Bacciocco Jr., *The New Left in America: Reform to Revolution 1956 to 1970* (Stanford, CA: Hoover Institution Press, 1974). An academic.

James Boggs and Grace Lee Boggs, *Revolution and Evolution in the 20th Century* (New York and London: Monthly Review Press, 1974). Authors are Marxist scholars (he has since died).

Wini Breines, *The Great Refusal: Community and Organization in the New Left 1962–68* (New York: Praeger, 1982).

David Caute, *Sixty-Eight: The Year of the Barricades* (London: Hamish Hamilton, 1988). Published in the United States as *The Year of the Barricades: 1968*. British journalist and novelist.

Morris Dickstein, *Gates of Eden: American Culture in the Sixties* (New York: Penguin Books, 1977 and 1989). British professor.

Richard Flacks, *Making History: The Radical Tradition in American Life* (New York: Columbia University Press, 1988). Participant (SDS) and scholar.

Todd Gitlin, *The Sixties: Years of Hope, Days of Rage* (New York: Bantam Books, 1987). Participant (SDS), academic.

Robert J. Glessing, *The Underground Press in America.* (Bloomington, IN: Indiana University Press, 1970). An academic.

Paul Jacobs and Saul Landau, *The New Radicals: A Report with Documents* (New York: Random House, 1966). Jacobs was a researcher and author, Landau a researcher, writer and filmmaker.

Charles Kaiser, *1968 in America: Music, Politics, Chaos, Counterculture, and the Shaping of a Generation* (New York: Weidenfeld and Nicholson, 1988). Journalist and activist.

George Katsiaficas, *The Imagination of the New Left: A Global Analysis of 1968* (Boston: South End Press, 1987). Activist and teacher.

Lawrence Lader, *Power on the Left: American Radical Movements Since 1946* (New York and Toronto: W.W. Norton & Co., 1979). Author an activist.

Phillip Abbott Luce, *The New Left Today: America's Trojan Horse* (Washington, DC: Capitol Hill Press, 1971). Organizer for the Right and the military.

Allen Matusow, *The Unraveling of America: A History of Liberalism in the 1960s* (New York: Harper & Row, 1984). An academic.

James Miller, *"Democracy Is in the Streets": From Port Huron to the Siege of Chicago* (New York: Simon & Schuster, 1987). Book and music critic.

William L. O'Neill, *Coming Apart: An Informal History of America in the 1960s* (Chicago: Quadrangle Books, 1971). Editor, academic.

Abe Peck, *Uncovering the Sixties: The Life and Times of the Underground Press* (Secaucus, NJ: Citadel Underground Press, 1991).

Sohnya Sayres et al., eds., *The 60s Without Apologies* (Minneapolis, MN: University of Minnesota Press, 1984). Editors mostly academics.

Irwin Unger, *The Movement: A History of the American New Left 1959–72* (New York: Dodd Mead, 1974). Historian, academic.

Irwin Unger and Debi Unger, *Turning Point 1968* (New York: Charles Scribner's Sons, 1988). Debi Unger listed only as "wife."

Milton Viorst, *Fire in the Streets: America in the 1960s* (New York: Simon & Schuster, 1979). Journalist and academic.

chapter four

WHOSE CHICANO HISTORY DID YOU LEARN?

 When we read a social studies textbook for fifth graders that refers to slavery as a "life-style," we might think it's some book from the 1940s or 1950s. But such descriptions can be found in the glossy series published by Houghton Mifflin in the 1990s. Even worse, the series was supposed to make a major break with the longtime Eurocentric textbook tradition. Adopted for use in California, among other states, these books provoked a storm of controversy.

California had invited publishers to submit new history texts for kindergarten through eighth grade (K-8) as part of an overall effort to upgrade its instructional materials and methods. Houghton Mifflin was the only house that submitted books for all those grades. It also was the only press that prepared books specifically intended to fit into a new history and social studies "framework," or curriculum, that California had adopted in 1987.

The framework called for pupils to study history much earlier and more extensively than in the past. Recognizing that the majority of California's 3.7 million elementary and junior high pupils were people of color, California education officials also required that textbooks "accurately portray the cultural and racial diversity of our society." The Houghton Mifflin series' main author is Gary Nash, a University of California, Los Angeles, professor with a reputation for advocating multiculturalism.

California's Board of Education adopted the Houghton Mifflin series and an additional eighth-grade history from Holt, Rinehart & Winston despite protests from thousands of people in virtually every racial and ethnic sector (including Muslims, who had been the first to object), as well as gays, lesbians and the disabled. Since local school districts in California are not legally obliged to buy the state-approved books, the struggle continued.

Eventually most local school boards adopted the approved texts, sometimes with supplemental readings. In Oakland, where students of color form almost 92 percent of the school population, both the Houghton Mifflin series and the Holt, Rinehart & Winston title were rejected. In San Francisco, where 83 percent of the student population is of color, the new books were finally adopted on the condition that supplemental readings be used. However, the school district placed only one copy of each supplemental title in each school.

Behind all the highly publicized debate, one can assume some heavy-duty politicking. On the strictly commercial level, Houghton Mifflin calculated that, in California alone, sales of the series could yield $52 million. With so much at stake, Houghton Mifflin for the first time in its history hired a public relations firm to help win state approval.

But much more complex and powerful forces were at work on the ideological and political level. The new California framework was written by Diane Ravitch, a U.S. Department of Education official. She and several colleagues in the education field received heavy funding from the conservative Olin Foundation, which supports right-wing think tanks, according to an exposé in the *San Francisco Examiner* (May 28, 1992). The article described "an interlocking network of educational reformers, their work supported by conservative foundations and [funds from] a Republican administration" that works in the field of education parallel to "a similar network of rightist think tanks and advocacy groups, also funded by conservative foundations, seeking to control the nation's political debate." The goal is a "multi-cultural" history curriculum that ostensibly celebrates diversity but basically celebrates melting-pot assimilationism. Behind this move to co-opt multiculturalism was a web of relationships among academics, government officials and activists.

When the Houghton Mifflin titles implementing the new Ravitch framework appeared, they were defended as a vast improvement over the past, with much more information about people of color and their perspectives. "We have 80 pages on African history for 12-year-olds," Gary Nash pointed out. But a numerical increase in textual references or images doesn't promote multiculturalism if the content leaves a fundamentally Eurocentric worldview in place. The occasional inclusion of dissenting views from people of color may give some balance to isolated passages; it does not alter the dominant perspective.

The worldview put forth in these texts rests on defining the United States as "a nation of immigrants." This view sees Native Americans as the first "immigrants," based on their having come across the Bering Strait from Asia (but isn't this theory rejected by many Indians?). After Native Americans come Africans (but weren't they brought here in chains?) and then Mexicans (but wasn't their homeland seized by Anglo force?). Europeans and Asians round out the list of so-called immigrants.

The immigrant model has usually included the "melting pot" metaphor; the Houghton Mifflin series rejects that now tarnished image in favor of the "salad bowl," which allows different peoples to retain their ethnic identity and culture inside one big unified society. But how different is the bowl from the pot?

Both images liquidate issues of power and domination, such as which groups in society have power and which don't or which groups dominate and which are dominated. Both are molded by a national identity firmly rooted in an Anglo-American culture and perspective. As critics of the textbooks pointed out, the norm to which so-called immigrants are supposed to relate is white, Anglo-Saxon and usually Protestant—in short, WASP. (Thus the Mexican American, for example, is not a "real" American.) The Houghton Mifflin texts hammer home the power and authority of this norm with an extraordinary quantity of U.S. flags: in the K-5 books alone, there are 29 depictions of U.S. flags, compared with zero flags from other nations.

The Eurocentric viewpoint of the series can be found in its treatment of all U.S. peoples of color, exemplified by one sentence in a literature selection in the Grade 5 textbook: "She had blue eyes and white skin, like an angel" (which reduces us darkies to being devils, I assume). Scores of inaccuracies, distortions, sanitizations, omissions and outright racist accounts pepper these books. In reviewing how the Houghton Mifflin books depict Mexican Americans and other Latinos in the United States, we find five major problems, ranging from general perspective to the handling of key events involving people of Mexican origin. The first general question is, do we even exist?

Making Latinos Invisible

Increasing the quantity of references to a people doesn't make a textbook multicultural or non-racist, as we said; at the same time, invisibility definitely hurts. The Houghton Mifflin series gives very shabby treatment to Latinos in this respect.

By the third grade, it would seem reasonable to expect some real awareness of Mexicans in the United States, especially when the textbook *From Sea to Shining Sea* has a 60-page unit called "Settling the Land." Wrong; in the whole book, Mexican Americans appear only as farmworkers, and even then their historic role in producing vast agricultural wealth is not recognized (nor is that of Filipinos). A single photo shows an orchard with a rain of almonds being shaken out of the trees—by machine, not people. Nowhere does the text say that agriculture was made possible in the Southwest by an art that Mexicans and Native Americans taught to Anglos—irrigation.

The fourth-grade book, *Oh California,* offers many Latinos, but they are almost all "explorers" and "settlers," missionaries, or upper-class ranchers. Nowhere can we find the lower-class Mexicans, the laborers of the eighteenth and nineteenth centuries. Nowhere can we find the many Mexicans who were violently repressed and driven off the land—often even lynched—from the Gold Rush days to the 1930s. Nowhere do we read about the massive strikes by Mexican workers in the 1930s or the deportation of thousands who were actually citizens. Chicanos and Mexicans vanish totally from California for 100 pages. Then we find a paragraph on East Los Angeles that includes Mexicans in a listing of all immigrant groups. It doesn't say that they formed the original population of Los Angeles and have continued to be a strong presence for more than 200 years.

Oh California briefly describes the United Farm Workers, led by César Chávez, in the series' only account of Chicano/Mexicano struggle for social change in this country. We find nothing about how the courageous farmworkers stood up to mass arrests, beatings and harassment by the growers and their goons. Nothing about Dolores Huerta—one of the best-known women activists for social justice in the United States today—who headed the union along with Chávez until his death in 1993. Nothing about the ongoing struggle against pesticides. And nothing about other movements of California Chicanos, such as the walkouts by thousands of high school students in 1968 and the anti–Vietnam War march of some 20,000 people on August 29, 1970, that ended with a police riot leaving hundreds of peaceful demonstrators teargassed and three Chicanos dead. A picture of one "Chicano Power" mural is apparently supposed to suffice for all that mass activism.

In *America Will Be*, a basic fifth-grade U.S. history book, Latinos as people do not exist beyond immigration statistics and other lists, with the exception of a single family presented out of context. Even Latinos as governmental figures vanish after three pages on Juan de Oñate, who invaded New Mexico for Spain in 1598. If it is hard to find Mexicans or Chicanos and Chicanas in this series, other Latinos are even less visible. After profiling the great baseball player and humanitarian Roberto Clemente in the Grade 2 text, the series abandons Puerto Ricans. For the millions of Central Americans resident in the United States, Houghton Mifflin includes a single nameless young woman who came from Guatemala for unspecified reasons and lives an undescribed life here (Grade 3 text). In Grades 4 and 5 we get one and two sentences, respectively, referring to refugees from Cuba and Central America—with no explanation of why they had fled.

Eurocentrism and Its Values

The second overarching error of the series, Eurocentrism, begins with the books for kindergarten and Grade 1, *The World I See* and *I Know a Place*. Both include a thematic photo showing several young pupils of color, including a probable Latino, and the K volume has one story about Mexico. But the drawings in the "Long Ago" pages of the K book are overwhelmingly populated by white people for no historical reason. In one case, out of 35 people we see 31 whites; another makes all 20 people white; and so forth. In the Grade 1 book, everyone from the past is white (e.g., a unit called "Grandma's Album" and another called "I Go with My Family to Grandma's"). The message comes across loud and clear: the foundations of our country are Euro-American (or perhaps people of color never had grannies?). Yet Mexicans settled in what is now the United States from 1598 on—more than 20 years before the *Mayflower* landed at Plymouth.

Some People I Know (Grade 2) introduces Teresa Sánchez of East Los Angeles. The text puts a healthy stress on the merits of being bilingual and bicultural like Teresa, but why did they make her a totally Anglo-looking girl? Any Latina—like this writer—who has grown up longing for blond hair and light-colored eyes will know what a bad message this conveys, especially when everyone else in Teresa's family is dark. (She must be one of those angels.)

A special form of the Eurocentric perspective, Hispanicism, flows through the Houghton Mifflin series. Again and again the "customs," "culture" and "traditions" of the Mexican people in the United States are described as originating in Spain. Indigenous, mestizo and African roots go unnoticed. This would be laughable (how many people in Madrid eat tortillas and beans?) if it were not so racist.

The Houghton Mifflin authors actually discuss Eurocentrism (Grade 8), defining it as "the notion that Europe is the center of the world." Then, however, they support that point of view by stating: "And for a long period of time it seemed to be. From the 1500s to the 1900s, European countries controlled a large part of the world." Ignoring the imperialist policies behind that control, the explanation leaves readers with a very Eurocentric view of Eurocentrism. The same book tells us that "U.S. citizens ... tended to look on Mexico as a backward nation, an attitude that has continued to this day." No criticism or alternative view is suggested.

If one of the goals of Eurocentrism is to make U.S. history a more comfortable abode for white people, the fifth-grade textbook shows how. The teacher's edition suggests an exercise in which students are asked to think about what it is like to move into a neighborhood or even a new country: What are the neighbors like? Is it scary? It then says, "Lead them [the students] to understand that the colonists in America shared many of the same experiences and feelings." What a novel way to imagine seizing someone else's land! Other examples of sanitized treatment abound. For example, the often deadly racism practiced against Mexicans in the Southwest is described as "considerable discrimination" (Grade 4) and "prejudice" (Grade 5).

The series is riddled with a Eurocentric vocabulary: "discoveries," "the New World," "the Age of Exploration" and "Moving West." It also manipulates the reader with self-justifying types of word usage. Again and again Anglo-Americans' "belief" in the rightness of their actions is used to justify how Mexican people and Native Americans have been treated historically. One text (Grade 4) even describes as "idealistic" the U.S. belief that westward expansion would help "bring freedom" to the "less fortunate" Indians and Mexicans.

The use of "dreams" serves a similar purpose, as in statements like "The forty-niners had dreams of becoming very wealthy," which we find in the teacher's edition for Grade 4. Such descriptions tend to make young readers identify with men who in fact often robbed, raped and murdered people of color. The text goes on to say of the forty-niners that "they did not feel they had to share those dreams with Indians," a remarkably mild way of describing their actual deeds.

Eurocentric usage of "beliefs," "idealism" and "dreams"—all concepts that many youths embrace—can work wonders. We see this in the series' treatment of three crucial events: westward expansion and the takeover of Texas, the U.S. war on Mexico and the Gold Rush, and Mexican resistance to the U.S. takeover.

I. Westward Expansion and Taking Texas

"United States expansion in the West was inevitable," says the fourth-grade text. One section, "Texas and the Struggle with Mexico" (Grade 5), describes how Anglos obtained land and settled in Texas with Mexico's permission on certain conditions, including that they wanted no slaves and were Catholic. When they broke their promises and Mexico tried to tighten its control, the Americans in Texas "were upset ... [because] Mexican rule ... had become too strict." Being "upset"—a variation on "belief"—apparently legitimizes the Anglo move to take Texas.

The Battle of the Alamo at San Antonio, Texas, in 1836 is the one event involving Mexicans that appeared in every textbook submitted for consideration in California. This Mexican military victory, in which all Anglo fighters died defending the fort—or, some scholars say, were executed—sparked a legendary desire for revenge. The Grade 5 teacher's edition emphasizes that students should see the Battle of the Alamo as "an important symbol of freedom and liberty" where "heroes" fought for Texas independence. From a different perspective, it was a symbol of U.S. land grabbing in which the "heroes" featured an escaped murderer (William Travis), a slave runner (James Bowie) and a gunfighting adventurer (Davy Crockett). But that perspective doesn't appear.

Holt, Rinehart & Winston's eighth-grade book tells how, after losing the Alamo battle, the United States surprise-attacked Mexico at San Jacinto. Confronted by the revenge-hungry Anglos, the Mexican troops "fearfully" called out, "Me no Alamo!" supposedly in hopes of being spared. "In fact," the book says, "these were the very same men who had slaughtered the defenders of the mission." Thus Holt encourages the stereotypes of Mexicans as cowardly, murderous, sneaky, lying buffoons who cannot, of course, outwit the brave, righteous Anglo.

II. The 1846–48 U.S. War on Mexico
and the Treaty of Guadalupe Hidalgo

This sequence of events must rank among the most inaccurately depicted history in all U.S. schoolbooks. "Belief" strikes again in the Grade 4 text from Houghton Mifflin, which bluntly states: "In the 1840s many [U.S.] people believed that their nation should rule all the land between the East and West coasts. Mexico owned much of this land. So the United States decided to go to war with Mexico to try to win this land."

More detail comes in Grade 5: "Mexican officials refused to talk" (that word "talk"—which sounds like little enough to ask—actually meant negotiating with the United States over its demands for more Mexican land), so "President Polk ordered American forces to move down to the Rio Grande. They were now in territory that the Mexican government said was theirs. In April 1846 Mexican troops fought with an American scouting party, leaving 16 dead or wounded. The United States and Mexico were now at war." A teacher's edition section on critical thinking says: "No one really wanted the Mexican War. How could it have been avoided?"

This is a disingenuous, indeed deceptive, version of what even Anglo historians have identified as Polk's deliberate provocation of war with a view to seizing half of Mexico. Polk declared his intent in his own diary, but the Houghton Mifflin text remains silent on that. We also find not one word about the infamous atrocities committed by U.S. invading forces during the war or the fact that General Ulysses S. Grant and other Americans denounced the war. In some apparent gesture to objectivity, the Grade 4 text says about the war in California, "In these battles [Mexican] soldiers fought brilliantly. Stephen W. Kearney, a general in the United States Army, admired their horseback riding." Given the failure to identify the invasion of Mexico as naked expansionism, such compliments are patronizing trivia.

The war officially ended with the Treaty of Guadalupe Hidalgo, which, the text states, provided that "as citizens, the Californios would have the same rights as other United States citizens." There's no mention that this treaty has been grossly violated from the time of signing. The civil and property rights of Mexicans have not been respected as promised by the United States. The land-holding rights guaranteed in a Statement of Protocol accompanying the treaty at the Mexican government's insistence have been ignored.

By Grade 8, the textbook does say that Polk deliberately "provoked" the war and that the treaty was "often not enforced." But at this late stage a few facts about what the United States really did are unlikely to reverse years of conditioning students to identify with this nation's policies, no matter how murderous.

III. The Gold Rush and the U.S. Occupation

The Houghton Mifflin series sanitizes some events and demonizes others. Its treatment of the Gold Rush is wondrous: "Besides the gold they found, what did the forty-niners contribute to California?" The teacher's edition answers, "They contributed the skills, energy, and population increase that would help California grow." One wants to add: not to mention driving out or killing Mexicans and Indians so that California had a white instead of a Mexican majority and could become a state. And what about the crucial skills that Anglos learned from the indigenous peoples, beginning with mining technology? Not to mention that gold was first discovered in California by a Mexican sheepherder, Francisco Lopez Arballo, in 1842. But we hear only about James Marshall in 1848.

Resistance to the U.S. occupation is transformed into sheer criminality: "'Joaquin!' they gasped. No one felt safe.... Who was this Mexican bandit?" Actually, Anglo miners drove Joaquín Murieta out of the goldfields (like other Latino miners) after reportedly raping his wife; as a result, he began a guerrilla-like movement that enjoyed widespread support. Many Mexican people saw him as a resistance hero, but both the Houghton Mifflin book and the text from Holt, Rinehart & Winston call such fighters "bandits."

Confronted by textbooks like these, some California teachers have made special efforts to present the Mexican-American or Latino perspective with other materials. One San Francisco teacher in a largely Latino neighborhood has created a special curriculum around the theme of Manifest Destiny, and another makes minimal use of the adopted textbook at her school. Let's hope many more are taking such corrective steps.

What is the larger, long-range solution? During the textbook battle, Sylvia Wynter, then a Stanford University professor of Spanish, Portuguese, and Black Studies circulated a provocative position paper. The textbooks present a dual problem, Wynter observed. First, they are dominated by a Eurocentric perspective. Second, this perspective is not acknowledged but is camouflaged by a "multiculturalist alternative." The supposed alternative remains entrapped by an assumption that the United States is integrated as a nation on the basis of a single, Euro-American culture. Thus the "multiculturalist alternative" seeks to save the Euro-American nation model by multiculturalizing it. The real solution, however, is to de-imagine the United States as a nation and then reimagine it as a "world": a community of communities relating on the basis of mutual respect and integrity.

Such a goal would require a massive shift in power relations throughout U.S. society. It sounds like a dream, like the idea of textbooks that make real sense out of American history. Still, defining one's goals—no matter how distant they may seem—matters. Honesty about the past can shine the light of freedom on a new kind of future.

chapter five

REINVENTING "AMERICA"
Call for a New National Identity

For some 15 years, starting in 1940, 85 percent of all U.S. elementary schools used the Dick and Jane series to teach children how to read. The series starred Dick, Jane, their white middle-class parents, their dog Spot and their life together in a home with a white picket fence.

"Look, Jane, look! See Spot run!" chirped the two kids. It was a house full of glorious family values, where Mom cooked while Daddy went to work in a suit and mowed the lawn on weekends. The Dick and Jane books also taught that you should do your job and help others. All this affirmed an equation of middle-class with whiteness with virtue.

In the mid-1990s, museums, libraries and 80 Public Broadcasting Service (PBS) stations across the country had exhibits and programs commemorating the series. At one museum, an attendant commented, "When you hear someone crying, you know they are looking at the Dick and Jane books." It seems nostalgia runs rampant among many Euro-Americans: a nostalgia for the days of unchallenged White Supremacy—both moral and material—when life was "simple."

We've seen that nostalgia before in the nation's history. But today it signifies a problem reaching a new intensity. It suggests a national identity crisis that promises to bring in its wake an unprecedented nervous breakdown for the dominant society's psyche.

Nowhere is this more apparent than in California, which has long been on the cutting edge of the nation's present and future reality. Warning sirens have sounded repeatedly in the 1990s, such as the fierce battle over new history textbooks for public schools, Proposition 187's ugly denial of human rights to immigrants, the 1996 assault on affirmative action that culminated in Proposition 209, and the 1997 move to abolish bilingual education. Attempts to copycat these reactionary measures have been seen in other states.

The attack on affirmative action isn't really about affirmative action. Essentially it is another tactic in today's war on the gains of the 1960s, a tactic rooted in Anglo resentment and fear. A major source of that fear: the fact that California will almost surely have a majority of people of color in 20 to 30 years at most, with the nation as a whole not far behind.

Check out the February 3, 1992, issue of *Sports Illustrated* with its double-spread ad for *Time* magazine. The ad showed hundreds of newborn babies in their hospital cribs, all of them Black or brown except for a rare white face here and there. The headline says, "Hey, whitey! It's your turn at the back of the bus!" The ad then tells you, read *Time* magazine to keep up with today's hot issues. That manipulative image could have been published today; its implication of shifting power appears to be the recurrent nightmare of too many potential Anglo allies.

Euro-American anxiety often focuses on the sense of a vanishing national identity. Behind the attacks on immigrants, affirmative action and multiculturalism, behind the demand for "English Only" laws and the rejection of bilingual education, lies the question: with all these new people, languages and cultures, what will it mean to be an American? If that question once seemed, to many people, to have an obvious, universally applicable answer, today new definitions must be found. But too often Americans, with supposed scholars in the lead, refuse to face that need and instead nurse a nostalgia for some bygone clarity. They remain trapped in denial.

An array of such ostriches, heads in the sand, began flapping their feathers noisily with the publication of Allan Bloom's 1987 best-selling book, *The Closing of the American Mind*. Bloom bemoaned the decline of our "common values" as a society, meaning the decline of Euro-American cultural centricity (shall we just call it cultural imperialism?). Since then we have seen constant sniping at "diversity" goals across the land. The assault has often focused on how U.S. history is taught. And with reason, for this country's identity rests on a particular narrative about the historical origins of the United States as a nation.

The Great White Origin Myth

Every society has an origin narrative that explains that society to itself and the world with a set of stories and symbols. The origin myth, as scholar-activist Roxanne Dunbar Ortiz has termed it, defines how a society understands its place in the world and its history. The myth provides the basis for a nation's self-defined identity. Most origin narratives can be called myths because they usually present only the most flattering view of a nation's history; they are not distinguished by honesty.

Ours begins with Columbus "discovering" a hemisphere where some 80 million people already lived but didn't really count (in what became the United States, they were just buffalo-chasing "savages" with no grasp of real estate values and therefore doomed to perish). It continues with the brave Pilgrims, a revolution by independence-loving colonists against a decadent English aristocracy and the birth of an energetic young republic that promised democracy and equality (that is, to white male landowners). In the 1840s, the new nation expanded its size by almost one-third, thanks to a victory over that backward land of little brown people called Mexico. Such has been the basic account of how the nation called the United States of America came into being as presently configured.

The myth's omissions are grotesque. It ignores three major pillars of our nationhood: genocide, enslavement and imperialist expansion (such nasty words, who wants to hear them?—but that's the problem). The massive extermination of indigenous peoples provided our land base; the enslavement of African labor made our economic growth possible; and the seizure of half of Mexico by war (or threat of renewed war) extended this nation's boundaries north to the Pacific and south to the Rio Grande. Such are the foundation stones of the United States, within an economic system that made this country the first in world history to be born capitalist.

Those three pillars were, of course, supplemented by great numbers of dirt-cheap workers from Mexico, China, the Philippines, Puerto Rico and other countries, all of them kept in their place by White Supremacy. In history they stand alongside millions of less-than-supreme white workers and sharecroppers.

Any attempt to modify the present origin myth provokes angry efforts to repel such sacrilege. In the case of Native Americans, scholars will insist that they died from disease or wars among themselves, or that "not so many really did die." At worst it was a "tragedy," but never deliberate genocide, never a pillar of our nationhood. As for slavery, it was an embarrassment, of course, but do remember that Africa also had slavery and anyway enlightened white folk finally did end the practice here.

In the case of Mexico, reputable U.S. scholars still insist on blaming that country for the 1846–48 war. Yet even former U.S. President Ulysses Grant wrote in his memoirs that "[w]e were sent to provoke a fight [by moving troops into a disputed border area] but it was essential that Mexico should commence it [by fighting back]." (*Mr. Lincoln's General: Ulysses S. Grant, an illustrated autobiography* [New York: Dutton, 1959].) President James Polk's 1846 diary records that he told his cabinet his purpose in declaring war as "acquiring California, New Mexico, and perhaps other Mexican lands." (*Diary of James K. Polk 1845–49* [Chicago: A.C. McClurg, 1910].) To justify what could be called a territorial drive-by, the Mexican people were declared inferior; the U.S. had a "Manifest Destiny" to bring them progress and democracy.

Even when revisonist voices expose particular evils of Indian policy, slavery or the war on Mexico, they remain little more than unpleasant footnotes; the core of the dominant myth stands intact. PBS's eight-part documentary series of 1996 titled "The West" is a case in point. It devoted more than the usual attention to the devastation of Native Americans, but still centered on Anglos and gave little attention to why their domination evolved as it did. The West thus remained the physically gorgeous backdrop for an ugly, unaltered origin myth.

In fact, "The West" series strengthens that myth. White Supremacy needs the brave but inevitably doomed Indians to silhouette its own inevitable conquest. It needs the Indian-as-devil to sustain its own holy mission. Remember Timothy Wight, who served as pastor to Congress in the late 1700s and wrote that, under the Indians, "Satan ruled unchallenged in America" until "our chosen race eternal justice sent." With that self-declared moral authority, the "winning of the West" metamorphosed from a brutal, bloody invasion into a crusade of brave Christians marching across a lonely, dangerous landscape.

Racism as Linchpin of the U.S. National Identity

A crucial embellishment of the origin myth and key element of the national identity has been the myth of the frontier, analyzed in Richard Slotkin's *Gunfighter Nation* (1992), the last volume of a fascinating trilogy. He describes Theodore Roosevelt's belief that the West was won thanks to American arms, "the means by which progress and nationality will be achieved." That success, Roosevelt continued, "depends on the heroism of men who impose on the course of events the latent virtues of their 'race.'" Roosevelt saw conflict on the frontier producing a species of virile "fighters and breeders" who would eventually generate a new leadership class. Militarism thus went hand in hand with the racialization of history's protagonists.

No slouch as an imperialist, Roosevelt soon took the frontier myth abroad, seeing Asians as Apaches and the Philippines as Sam Huston's Texas in the process of being seized from Mexico. For Roosevelt, Slotkin writes, "racial violence [was] the principle around which both individual character and social organization develop." Such ideas have not remained totally unchallenged by U.S. historians, nor was the frontier myth always applied in totally simplistic ways by Hollywood and other media. (The outlaw, for example, is a complicated figure, both good and bad.) Still, the frontier myth traditionally spins together virtue and violence, morality and war, in a convoluted, Calvinist web. That tortured embrace defines an essence of the so-called American character—the national identity—to this day.

The frontier myth embodied the nineteenth-century concept of Manifest Destiny, a doctrine that served to justify expansionist violence by means of intrinsic racial superiority. Manifest Destiny saw Yankee conquest as the inevitable result of a confrontation between enterprise and progress (white) versus passivity and backwardness (Indian, Mexican). "Manifest" meant "God-given," and the whole doctrine is profoundly rooted in religious conviction going back to the earliest colonial times. In his short, powerful book *Manifest Destiny: American Expansion and the Empire of Right*, Professor Anders Stephanson tells how the Puritans reinvented the Jewish notion of chosenness and applied it to this hemisphere so that territorial expansion became God's will.

Linking the national identity with race is not unique to the United States. National identity always requires an "other" to define it. But this country has linked its identity with race to an extraordinary degree, matched only by two other settler states: South Africa and Israel. Given its obsession with race and the supremacy attached to whiteness, the U.S. national identity inevitably reserved a special disdain for "half-breed" peoples—above all, Mexicans. "The West" documentary series reflects that disdain with its offhand treatment of Manifest Destiny and the U.S. expansionist takeover of Mexico, violations of the 1848 Treaty of Guadalupe Hidalgo, land robbery, colonization backed by violent repression, the role of Mexican people in building vast wealth in the West, and the West as a reflection of Mexican culture. In doing so the series typifies all the other standard historical treatments of people of Mexican origin. Who could care less? is their message. If anyone in this society remembers Mexicans before the twentieth century, it is usually as "bandits" who fought the U.S. occupation, or señoritas on big California ranchos who had the good sense to marry Anglos. Almost never have we formed part of the origin myth.

Manifest Destiny Dies Hard

The concept of Manifest Destiny, with its assertion of racial superiority sustained by military power, has defined U.S. identity for 150 years. Only the Vietnam War brought a serious challenge to that concept of almightiness. Bitter debate, moral anguish, images of My Lai and the prospect of military defeat for the first time in U.S. history all suggested that the long-standing marriage of virtue and violence might soon be on the rocks. In the final years of the war the words leaped to mind one day: this country is having a national nervous breakdown.

Perhaps this is why the Vietnam War continues to arouse passions today. Some who are willing to call the war "a mistake" still shy away from recognizing its immorality or even accepting it as a defeat. A few Americans have the courage to conclude from the Vietnam War that we should abandon the idea that our identity rests on being the world's richest, most powerful and indeed *best* nation. Is it possible that the so-called Vietnam syndrome might signal liberation from a crippling self-definition? Is it possible the long-standing belief that "American exceptionalism" had made freedom possible might be rejected someday?

The Vietnam syndrome is partly rooted in the fact that, although other societies have also been based on colonialism and slavery, ours seems to have an insatiable need to be the "good guys" on the world stage. That need must lie at least partially in a Protestant dualism that defines existence in terms of opposites, so that if you are not "good" you are bad, if not "white" then Black, and so on. Whatever the cause, the need to be seen as virtuous, compared to someone else's evil, haunts U.S. domestic and foreign policy. Where on earth would we be without Saddam Hussein, Qaddafi, and that all-time favorite of gringo demonizers, Fidel Castro? Gee whiz, how would we know what an American really is?

Today's origin myth and the resulting concept of national identity make for an intellectual prison where it is dangerous to ask big questions about this society's superiority. When otherwise decent people are trapped in such a powerful desire not to feel guilty, self-deception becomes unavoidable. To cease our present falsification of collective memory should, and could, open the doors of that prison. When together we cease equating whiteness with Americanness, a new day can dawn. As David Roediger, the social historian, has said, "[Whiteness] is the empty and therefore terrifying attempt to build an identity on what one isn't, and on whom one can hold back."

Redefining the U.S. origin narrative, and with it this country's national identity, could prove liberating for our collective psyche. It does not mean Euro-Americans should wallow individually in guilt. It does mean accepting collective responsibility to deal with the implications of our real origin. A few apologies, for example, might be a step in the right direction. In 1997, the idea was floated in Congress to apologize for slavery; it encountered opposition from all sides. But to reject the notion because corrective action, not an apology, is needed misses the point. Having defined itself as the all-time best country in the world, the United States fiercely denies the need to make a serious, official apology for anything (I'm not counting the unofficial apologies that Clinton issued as an individual in 1998, so cautiously worded that they were meaningless). To press for any serious, official apology does imply a new origin narrative, a new self-image, an ideological sea-change.

Accepting the implications of a different narrative could also shed light on today's struggles. In the affirmative-action struggle, for example, opponents have said that that policy is no longer needed because racism ended with the Civil Rights Movement. But if we look at slavery as a fundamental pillar of this nation, going back centuries, it becomes obvious that racism could not have been ended by 30 years of mild reforms. If we see how the myth of the frontier idealized the white male adventurer as the central hero of national history, with the woman as sunbonneted helpmate, then we might better understand the dehumanized ways in which women have continued to be treated. A more truthful origin narrative could also help break down divisions among peoples of color by revealing common experiences and histories of cooperation.

A new origin narrative and national identity could help pave the way to a more livable society for us all. A society based on cooperation rather than competition, on the idea that all living creatures are interdependent and that humanity's goal should be balance. Such were the values of many original Americans, deemed "savages." Similar gifts are waiting from other despised peoples and traditions. We might well start by recognizing that "America" is the name of an entire hemisphere, rich in a stunning variety of histories, cultures and peoples—not just one country.

The choice seems clear, if not easy. We can go on living in a state of massive denial, affirming this nation's superiority and virtue simply because we need to believe in it. We can choose to believe the destiny of the United States is still manifest: global domination. Or we can seek a transformative vision that carries us forward, not backward. We can seek an origin narrative that lays the groundwork for a multicultural, multinational identity centered on the goals of social equity and democracy. We do have choices.

There is little time for nostalgia. Dick and Jane never were "America," they were only one part of one community in one part of one country in one part of one continent. Yet we have let their image define our entire society and its values. Will the future be marked by ongoing denial or by steps toward a new vision in which White Supremacy no longer determines reality? When on earth will we transcend the assumptions that imprison our minds?

At times you can hear the clock ticking.

chapter six

FOLLOW ME HOME
The Movie That Makes Magic with Pennies

Falling in love with a movie can happen now and then, but how often does a dazzling film like *Follow Me Home* come along? A film whose aesthetics are marvelously unpredictable and whose politics make the revolution seem possible after all. A film that not only confronts the nightmare of today's dehumanized, racist society but also suggests what is needed to transform it—without denying all the obstacles, including those inside ourselves?

Yet *Follow Me Home,* the first feature film of 34-year-old writer-director Peter Bratt, is a film without a commercial distributor or advertising. In a world where the average Hollywood flick costs $60 million, this one cost $300,000. Its sheer existence calls for thanks to a crew that worked for free and donations from the San Francisco Bay Area's community of indigenous people (Bratt's mother is indigenous, from Peru). Once completed, *Follow Me Home* made its way from theaters in the West to the East Coast primarily thanks to enthusiastic word of mouth. As for reviews, too often they were written by white critics who labeled the film "anti-white" or just didn't get it.

The film's basic story line presents four street artists—two Chicanos (Abel and Tudee), one African American (Kaz) and one Native American (Frank)—who set out in a van from San Francisco for Washington, D.C. They plan to paint a mural on the White House, to re-create that symbolic structure with "our colors and our images," "the faces of our ancestors." Along the way, in Nebraska, the artists pick up an African-American woman, Evey, whose car has just collided with that of a white man costumed as an Indian on his way to a local reenactment of U.S. history. He has died in the accident and the ancient tomahawk in his van full of native paraphernalia has vanished. This leads our group to be attacked by the white man's friends, also on their way to the reenactment and costumed as Civil War soldiers.

Call it a "road movie" if you like, but remember that in Gringolandia there are roads and then there are *roads*. The artists' long drive is a journey of multilayered discovery, exploring both external and internal truths about this nation and its people. Above all, it reaches to the deepest roots of U.S. nationhood—historical roots that include genocide, enslavement and imperialist expansion. Roots that so many of us, especially Anglo-Americans, would deny. One detail speaks to the depths of the film's discovery: those Civil War soldiers wear the uniform of the Union, not that of the Confederacy. They are not caricatures of Southern racism; they speak to an illness afflicting the whole nation.

Nothing is simple about what happens in this film or how it is depicted, or about the characters of color and the white men they meet on the road. Everything is both surreal and all too real. *Follow Me Home* alternates haunting black-and-white dream sequences with full-color ugliness and terror, but the line between reality and surrealism can easily vanish. The racist white men in Civil War costume firing their nineteenth-century pistols sometimes seem like a parody of themselves—yet they can also kill real people. The point of such duality is just that: we confront contradiction everywhere and must search hard for a sense of balance.

Not Just Good Guys and Bad Guys

This is indeed a film about racism, but it's not about good guys (of color) versus bad guys (white). It is indeed a film about privilege and greed, but it's not about poor guys (of color) versus rich guys (white). Among the men of color we have the recovered alcoholic Steve, silently seeking to renew an ancestral pride. We have Abel, the Chicano *cholo* whose sexism, habitual profanity and antisocial aggressiveness veil his internalized racism and self-destructiveness. He changes on the road, especially when Evey talks him into a silent nod of agreement with her strong declaration that "I am not a whore, I am not a bitch, I am a woman." Kaz, the African-American Buddhist, remains the least developed character individually. Yet he emanates a direct knowledge of racism at its most vicious, creating an aura that can be as powerful in its near-silence as words might be.

Then there is Tudee, the group's leader of sorts, whose art patron in dream sequences is an elderly white man dressed to combine Roman emperor and bewigged English colonialist. With his encouragement, Tudee plans to secretly collect for himself all the income from sales of paintings done by the group. In one stunning dream scene, Tudee seems to fully recognize how much he has internalized the competitive value system of the white colonizer and lost the sense of interdependence embodied in indigenous cultures. So much for idealized victimhood.

As for the white men, it is one of the Civil War soldiers (Perry) who rejects his friends' deadly racism with a dramatic action and three words: "It's not right." (The film has even made this good guy a good-looking white man.) When Tudee encounters his former girlfriend and her Anglo husband in a store on the road, the Anglo speaks a decent Spanish and behaves in relatively civilized fashion while Tudee launches insults. As for the short-order cook at the roadside restaurant, shotgun in hand as he demands proper behavior from the group, where did he ever surface before? Racist he surely is, but no redneck dummy.

So the locus of good and evil in *individual* people is not simplistic here. But the power of collective goodness reverberates, like the film's haunting soundtrack. In its most unforgettable scene the folk of color find themselves trapped by racism, facing death itself. Responding to the evil around them, they begin to rhythmically chant what sounds like a child's jump-rope song (actually it's "Rapper's Delight"). The chanting rises insistently, persistently, until the collectivity of their voices and the power of memory make time stop.

In this moment of spiritual triumph we can see why the film begins with a quotation of words by Chief Seattle, when he said that after the last red man was gone the land would still be filled with their spirits: "The white man will never be alone."

Is this a promise (as heard by some people of color) or a threat (as heard by some whites) or simply a truth that we should all heed? Again, *Follow Me Home* is not a mechanical celebration of indigenous peoples and their values. "Our battle," as one character says, "is not just to remember something ancient but to create something new." For that endeavor *Follow Me Home* offers us a splendid strength. It does so without abandoning its basic humility, so luminously captured in the rhyme that Evey made up for her young daughter:

A lost penny isn't tragic
Pick it up and it makes magic.

Meanwhile, Back in Hollywood

The experience of making *Follow Me Home* is a classic case of Americana as known to many artists of color. It was screened at the 1996 Sundance festival and other film festivals without finding a commercial distributor. This has occurred despite the known names in its cast: playing Abel, Benjamin Bratt (brother of the director), a regular on television's "Law and Order" program, who has also acted in *Demolition Man* and *Clear and Present Danger;* Jesse Borrego as Tudee, with *Mi Vida Loca* and *Lone Star* among his credits; Calvin Levels *(Point of No Return)*, as Kaz; Steve Reevis *(Fargo, Dances with Wolves)* as Steve; and the celebrated Alfre Woodard as a compelling Evey. Yet all that talent could not change the minds of mainline distributors, who cater primarily to white males between 14 and 24, according to Jesse Rhines, a professor at Rutgers University and author of *Black Film/White Money.*

We cannot escape drawing a color line of explanation for the distributors' reaction. How else to understand why Alice Walker could call *Follow Me Home* "a work of genius," while most Anglo movie critics blasted away with their biggest Eurocentric guns. White critics may have written some of the better reviews, but not often in the mainstream media. In February 1997, the *New York Times* said that the movie "is peopled with white racist stereotypes who are fully as monstrous as Hollywood's worst B-movie nightmares of black homeboy gangsters"; the *New York Post* hated the "walking stereotypes," "clichés," and "sophomoric, condescending tone"; the *San Francisco Chronicle*'s Sunday movie guide denounced the film's "mean-spirited, caricatured presentation of white middle-American characters"; and in another edition the *Chronicle* told us how the film is taken over at the end by "its paranoid fantasies of racist white behavior."

Tell *that* to Rodney King, among others. Which is, of course, the heart of the matter. The producers, directors, funders and critics of U.S. film, theater and television almost never come in colors. They usually have no knowledge of, or patience for, any culture but their own. At the same time most of the critics are arrogantly quick to denounce any depiction by a person of another culture as "simplistic" or "stereotypical" (remember some of the comments on Gregory Nava's film *Mi familia/My Family*). They cannot wait to indulge their own stereotypes, and at best they are patronizing, paternalistic. Should a person of color be so bold as to depict a less-than-perfect Anglo in action, he or she could get ready for accusations of "caricature," "political correctness" and "glorified victimhood." Along with their straight-up racism, most critics are uncomfortable with symbolism and irony if focused on racial issues and authored by people of color.

I say all this gloomily, as someone who has followed theater, film, television and critics' treatment of non-white stories or characters over the years (for example, watching 50 installments of the television cop series "Hunter" and dozens from the more genteel "Remington Steele"). The racism ranges from subtle to gargantuan. In the more subtle department we have the *Times'* top film critic, Janet Maslin, who reviewed *Lone Star* very favorably but called its main and almost only Latina actor, Elizabeth Peña, "sultry." This seems the least accurate way to characterize her performance, but everybody knows that Latinas are sultry, right? Another criticism said director John Sayles "succumbs to the temptation to make all the Anglo characters nutty, evil or corrupt." (Did we see the same movie?) Also in the area of more-subtle problems: Anglo director Allison Anders' film about Latina gang girls, *Mi vida loca,* had many strengths, but it is hard to believe that a Latina writer or director would have ignored the girls' family relations, as Anders did.

Gangbangers and All That

Not at all subtle is the scarcity of positive Latino characters in current media. Drug traffickers, gangbangers, slimy informers, corrupt cops, hysterical females and Latin American dictators have filled the television screen for years. (To a limited extent, "NYPD Blue" has been an exception, but its Latino detective, my namesake, is patronized, while those smart-ass Puerto Rican criminals manage to be more obnoxious than others.) In movies, the assumption is, the whiter the better. The first choice to play Latinos and Latinas has, again and again, been Italians. The best-known example of this pattern was Luis Valdez casting an Italian-American actress as Frida Kahlo in his film about the artist. Sharp criticism from his own community led Valdez to back off, even as he explained that Hollywood pressure had caused his selection.

With *Mi familia,* Gregory Nava insisted on having Latinos play Latino roles. "This was one of the reasons we had trouble raising money," said Nava in a 1994 interview. "It's tough to do that, but I stuck to my guns." U.S. filmmaking is a capitalist enterprise with little space for people of color as subjects rather than objects. Nor is the problem limited to this country; Mexican television constantly makes its stars blonde, and has thus been just as racist in its assumption of what audiences relate to best.

The film *House of the Spirits*, based on Isabel Allende's fine novel, marked a high point in Latino casting nightmares, with blondish Euro-American actors playing Chileans who couldn't pronounce Spanish correctly. The 1996 movie based on another Allende novel, *Of Love and Shadows,* continued that tradition. Even one Anglo critic was compelled to ask, "Why, with loads of qualified Latin American actresses ... did [Jennifer] Connelly get this part" [as a beautiful Chilean fashion journalist]? Not to mention casting an Italian star as her mother.

The distinguished Chilean author Ariel Dorfman had no problems with Glenn Close being cast in the stage version of his work *Death and the Maiden*; she was "more universal," he said. Anyway, Chile does have many light-skinned people, given its history of European immigration. But the real issue is not whether Chile's population includes enough blondes to justify such casting; it is the fact that the dark ones remain invisible. Class and race call the tune: the kitchen maid is never blonde.

Such are the realities that prevail in show business today. They remain deeply rooted despite such promising developments as a television commercial for Saturn cars that features Mexican mariachis piling giddily into one such vehicle, and the fact that tequila is the increasingly popular drink of sophisticates. It will be a long, long time before such fashions add up to any genuine move away from Anglo-centricity. It will be a long time before a movie focused on people of color can have commercial success in this country if it does not unequivocally center on good white guys.

In the end the experience of *Follow Me Home* shines a glaring light on the degree of stubborn racism in today's society. Anglo insistence on being the center of attention, on denying uncomfortable historical truths, on reacting to any criticism as a mortal attack, can seem frightening. As this nation based on a hateful colorism becomes ever more colored in its population, the stakes rise and the smell of Anglo fear becomes ever stronger. Who will speak to the fears, and who or what will speak to the need for collectively reimagining Las Americas?

Follow Me Home does more than expose ugly truths; it points a way toward one light at the end of today's tunnel: the collective strength of our colors. Its haunting slogan—seen in advertising for the film—will not let us forget that strength: "Remember something ancient, imagine something new."

part two

NO HAY FRONTERAS: The Attack On Immigrant Rights

Nosotros volvimos a aprender
que la legitimidad no la da el gobierno,
la da el pueblo;
y es a él, a ustedes a
quien debemos dirigirnos.

We learned once again
that legitimacy doesn't come from the government
but from the people
and it is to the people, then, to you
that we should direct ourselves.

—*palabras zapatistas/EZLN*
—from the Zapatista movement

chapter seven

IMMIGRANT-BASHING ON THE RISE
1990—94

 It's a pretty train ride from Los Angeles down the coast to Oceanside, California. The outskirts of L.A. give way to vast, anonymous industrial sites and then mostly open country. The train hugs the ocean's edge for about an hour, peaceful and panoramic. Oceanside itself is one of those bland, clean-cut towns that all look like each other, that look like the birthplace of boredom, that look as if they have no past. But it sits next to one of the nation's largest Marine Corps bases, Camp Pendleton. It sits in San Diego County, less than two hours from the Mexican border. It sits in a world of blood and terror for certain people.

When I first went to San Diego County in the early 1990s, Mexicans were being hunted down like animals, and "immigrant rights" for many Latinos meant nothing less than the right to live. Along the border with Mexico it is not unusual for Mexican, Guatemalan, Salvadoran and other migrants to meet death or injury by beating and kicking, drowning, being deliberately run over by vehicles and shooting (usually in the back) at the hands of Immigration and Naturalization Service (INS) officials, the Border Patrol and local police.

It's been going on for years. In late September 1990, for example, 17-year-old Victor Mandujano, trying to escape "La Migra," was pulled off the fence that he was climbing to get back to Mexico and shot point-blank in the chest. Two months later, Eduardo García Zamores was running toward the Mexican side of the border to escape border police when they shot him with hollow-point bullets and left his body hanging on the fence, severely wounded. He was unarmed. Verbal abuse is also common, as when a Border Patrol supervisor parked near the border facing south and for more than an hour shouted over his van's public address system such insults as "Your mothers are all whores."

History thus far has shown that when border officials are charged with crimes, the worst penalty seems to be promotion and transfer to another state. In a canyon area near Nogales, Arizona, Border Patrol agent Michael Elmer must have set a record for impunity. On June 12, 1992, he fired his personal, unauthorized semi-automatic weapon at the back of Dario Miranda Valenzuela, who was running toward the Mexican side of the border. Elmer then dragged the body 55 yards and hid it in a crevice, planning to return and bury it later. Elmer's partner, agent Thomas Watson, reported the shooting 15 and a half hours later, but only after ensuring the safety of his family due to Elmer's threats against him. Local investigators concluded that the shooting was unjustified; forensic experts said the victim might have lived if the agents had summoned medical help.

On the last day of the trial the federal judge reduced the first-degree-murder charge to second degree, sending a strong message to the jury to acquit. And so they did, based on the defense's depiction of the border as a war zone, immigrants as drug smugglers and Border Patrol agents like Elmer as embattled troops doing their duty to guard the nation's security.

They were right about one thing: the borderlands are a war zone today. But the Border Patrol is the army of the war-makers, and the migrant workers are their civilian victims. If it were Vietnam, the migrants would be called "gooks"; here the Border Patrol has dubbed them "tonks," which sounds all too similar. "Tonk," the agents say, is the sound a flashlight makes when it hits the skull of someone being arrested. The borderlands are a lawless area within the United States where the Constitution and the Bill of Rights just don't apply.

Other government officials get the same mild treatment for criminal abuse, like the six Marines stationed at Camp Pendleton who poured kerosene on some farmworkers sleeping in lean-tos and other makeshift shelters. The Marines intended to climax this "beaner raid," as they called it, by setting the workers on fire. They failed because the matches were wet. Five of the Marines were tried and acquitted; the leader was sentenced to spend a year in an honor camp.

Civilian attacks in San Diego County have included sniper shootings at the "greaseballs" and other "filth." Such crimes are a major agenda item of the Ku Klux Klan, Nazis, violent skinheads and similar groups. A few years ago even high school students had a paramilitary hate club, the "Iron Militia," to intimidate border crossers.

The actions of all these organizations as well as the Border Patrol have been documented starting in 1980 by Roberto Martínez of the American Friends Service Committee's (AFSC) U.S.-Mexico Border Project. Martínez notes the important role in spreading anti-immigrant hatred played by Tom Metzger, who headed the White Aryan Resistance and lived just outside Oceanside when I visited there, and his son John, who heads the violent skinhead movement. It was Tom Metzger who masterminded the skinhead murder of an Ethiopian in Seattle, Washington.

Much of San Diego County's immigrant-bashing can be credited to relatively affluent whites from recently developed neighborhoods located in areas traditionally populated by poor migrant encampments. Their most spectacular action to date has been the "Light Up the Border" campaign. In November 1989 more than a thousand whites repeatedly parked at sundown on Dairy Mart Road—the last San Diego County street facing the border—and trained their headlights on the Mexican hills where immigrant workers gathered to enter the United States. Their message: it's fine for Mexicans to clean our homes and tend our gardens, but not to live in, or even pass through, our communities.

After some months of this, Roberto Martínez organized counter-demonstrations in which activists held up mirrors and aluminum foil to reflect the lights back. Martínez has received death threats for years. So has Victor Clark Alfaro, a human rights activist on the Mexico side of the border. (Abuse by Mexican officials, immigrant smugglers and bandits is a long story in itself.)

Along with the hate crimes are long-standing forms of economic exploitation and working conditions that add up to slavery. One typical example: a flower rancher north of Los Angeles hired 150 workers, shaved their heads military-style upon arrival and compelled them to buy on credit from the company store. Forced to work 16 hours a day, six days a week, these *mejicanos* were kept at the ranch by threat of physical harm and locked gates.

Women immigrants face special dangers in addition to those known to men. Violent rape or the demand for sex as the price of safe passage to *el norte* is an old custom. It happens on both sides of the border so often that one Mexican woman told Arnoldo García of the National Network for Immigrant and Refugee Rights, based in Oakland, California, that women headed north would start using birth-control pills because they anticipated such treatment. Another ugly problem came to light when many women complained that in order to file a joint petition for legal entry based on marriage to a U.S. citizen, they were having to stay with wife-beaters and risk serious harm or even death. (The joint petition requirement has since been waived if the woman can establish that a good-faith marriage occurred.)

So many stories can be told by women. Alicia Lambert, a U.S. citizen living in El Paso, Texas, went on a shopping trip across the border in 1991 and was stopped when returning. Without explanation, border agents put her through a series of repetitious interviews and physical searches. Finally telling her she could leave, the main agent held out her driver's license, withdrew it when she reached to take it, held it out again. Finally she grabbed for it. He shouted that he had been assaulted; three other agents beat her repeatedly and jailed her. After four months in jail she was found guilty.

Children are not exempt from the violence and harassment. Two Mexican boys, ages 11 and 12, were shot by U.S. border officials—in Mexican territory, at that. In June 1990, the U.S. Court of Appeals granted the INS sweeping power to jail children alleged to be deportable. Boys and girls as young as three years old have been separated from their parents and detained. A 36-year-old woman named Perla, who lives in Juárez but commutes almost daily to El Paso to sell fruit and candy door to door, speaks of what happened one day to her nine-year-old daughter, Lily. Two Border Patrol agents caught her and Lily at the river. A young Mexican on the other side was cursing the agents, so they fired machine guns at him for five minutes. "Lily was hysterical, she thought we'd all be killed. The agents were laughing," Perla told journalist Debbie Nathan.

Nor are borderlands the only places where anti-immigrant hatred reigns. One image speaks to the attitude you can sometimes find in the North. Irma Muñoz, a young woman who immigrated from Mexico, became a successful engineering student at the University of California, Davis. She began working as an intern for State Senator Richard Polanco, who advocated less reactionary immigration policies. In April 1993, two white male students at UC-Davis, punched her, cut her hair, then scrawled on her arms and her back with a black Magic Marker the words "Wetback" and "Go home you illegal." If she told anyone about the attack, they warned, she would be killed along with "your wetback friends" like the legislator.

The largest number of immigrants, 40 percent, settle in California, with Texas the destination of the second-largest number. In Texas the inhumane smuggling of Mexican laborers often leads to death. North of Laredo in July 1986, 26 Mexicans were locked in a metal boxcar in 103-degree heat by a labor smuggler. Two died. The following year, near El Paso, 18 Mexican youths suffocated to death in a boxcar where a *coyote* ("smuggler") had locked them in with no escape possible. Near Victoria, Texas, four Latinos died of asphyxiation in a fumigated trailer in 1991. A year does not go by without reports of migrant workers being found—dead or still alive somehow—in locked vehicles.

Texas is also the place where "Operation Blockade" went up in September 1993: 650 armed Border Patrol agents stood in a 20-mile-long line facing the Juárez–El Paso border to stop anyone who tried to cross. This tactic was replicated in the San Diego area. However, somebody there fretted that the word "blockade" implied an act of war, so the San Diego operation became the "Enhanced Enforcement Strategy." That does sound nicer, more laid-back—California-style.

Let there be no doubt about the racism that poisons U.S. immigration policy, about the fact that its primary target is Latinos. People from at least 72 nations crossed the U.S.-Mexico border in 1990. Only a small part of this flow, which went in both directions, were immigrants. People crossed for family, business or other reasons. Yet migration and immigrants became synonymous with criminal activity. Agents would detain fruit vendors with "Whatcha got there? Come on, where's the dope?" The civilian population of the borderlands was and still is harassed by agents carrying out surveillance, "routine questioning," checkpoint stops, detention. In 1992, 90 percent of the people arrested were Mexican nationals. Undocumented Mexican male teenagers were most likely to be violently attacked and/or killed. Of 367 victims of abuse, including murder, in 1990, 91 percent were Latinos and more than half were "legal" residents of the United States. As María Jiménez of the Immigration Law Enforcement Monitoring Project of the AFSC in Houston stated flatly: immigration law discriminates overwhelmingly against Latinos.

Still, it would be a mistake to think only Latinos are targets of anti-immigrant attacks or that such attacks take place only in the Southwest. New York, the third main destination of immigrants, saw a tidal wave of hatred (particularly anti-Arab and anti-Muslim) after the World Trade Center bombing in 1993. Add to such hysteria the racist depiction of Chinese refugees assaulting U.S. shores by the boatload. The stabbing of an Asian on the subway by a man yelling "Hey, egg roll!" was not so surprising (the attacker didn't seem to know about that model-minority image). Attacks on Asians also occur in scattered locales like Fall River, Massachusetts, where 12 white men murdered a Cambodian American and severely beat his friend on August 14, 1993, while racially taunting both. As elsewhere, violence against Asian immigrants is not just the work of individuals.

One last example of what Asians can fear: at the University of Nevada in Las Vegas, a student from India died after being set on fire by two men—one white, one African-American—who said they didn't want any more foreign students on campus.

The United States hardly stands alone as a hotbed of anti-immigrant attacks. Most European countries have also witnessed sometimes fatal attacks. One of the worst occurred in Germany on May 29, 1993, when neo-Nazi firebombs killed five Turks—three young girls and two women. Chancellor Helmut Kohl refused to attend a memorial service for the victims and threatened any Turks who might defend themselves. Of Germany's two million Turks, many went there 30 years ago as invited guest workers; many were born in Germany. France, Italy and Spain are not far behind, their victims usually African. In France a series of anti-immigrant laws written by Interior Minister Charles Pasqua made it harder to obtain legal residency or asylum and easier to impose forced deportations. Under the Pasqua laws (modified in 1997 by a new government) thousands of immigrant worker were expelled. Britain's victims tend to be Indians and Pakistanis, called "Blacks" in that country. Hungary has seen gypsies beaten to death by skinheads; elections in Austria and Switzerland, as in France, show increasing animosity toward immigrants, cultivated by opportunistic right-wing politicians.

Chilling commonalities surface when we look at anti-immigrant actions in Europe and the United States. First, in almost every country anti-immigrant sentiments coincide with a rapid growth of neo-Nazi and far-right groups. Second, the attacks are frequently sparked by "respectable" conservative politicians, who have campaigned with anti-immigrant rhetoric in several countries. Also, liberals often join reactionary forces in denouncing immigrants. In the United States, some major environmentalist forces have been loudly demanding curbs on immigration for its supposed ecological damage and excess population. ("Immigrant women have high fertility rates.") It seems that 2 to 4 percent of the U.S. population causes every evil from pollution to traffic jams.

Finally, the attack on immigrants is usually racist (and often anti-Muslim). Paris's conservative mayor, Jacques Chirac, minced no words: "they even have smells" of their own, he said about immigrants. The very word "immigrant" means people of color to most Americans today; forget the English nannies, French chefs or people from the former Soviet Union who have come.

In Gov. Pete Wilson's California we have seen a tidal wave of anti-immigrant laws and programs. Wilson pushed outrageous proposals that included denying citizenship to children born here of undocumented parents. He got four of his laws passed in October 1993, among them a ban on giving driver's licenses to the undocumented; requiring state and local agencies that provide job training and placement to verify a person as a legal resident; and increasing penalties against getting MediCal benefits "fraudulently" or helping others to do so. His great triumph, of course, would be Proposition 187 in November 1994.

Not to be outdone by a Republican, California's two new Democratic women senators offered their own measures. Even the erstwhile liberal Sen. Barbara Boxer urged sending the National Guard to defend the U.S.-Mexico border against my relatives. Sad to say, the Hispanic Congressional Caucus has taken a mix of positions on these issues.

At the federal level, President Clinton quickly broke his campaign promise not to return Haitian refugees. We should also recall how in the negotiations over the North American Free Trade Agreement (NAFTA) an anti-immigrant attitude prevailed on the U.S. end. The U.S. government never let immigration issues be addressed—a strange omission from a treaty supposedly intended to open up economic relations and make trade "free." In pushing for NAFTA to be accepted by the U.S. public, politicians tried to play on anti-immigrant sentiment, arguing that NAFTA would diminish the number of workers coming here by providing more jobs in Mexico.

In the face of all the laws, policies and actions directed against immigrants in the United States, too many people remain blind to the need for solidarity among Latinos, African Americans and Caribbean Blacks, Asian/Pacific Islanders, Arab Americans and others—not to mention progressive whites. In Los Angeles during the 1992 uprising, longtime Mexican-American residents could be heard to say, "We're not the ones rioting, it's those immigrants"—meaning Mexicans and Central Americans. It is not rare to hear Chicanos sneer "Mexican!" at day laborers waiting on the street for work.

At a San Francisco rally for women's reproductive rights in 1992, Dolores Huerta was speaking when a middle-aged African-American woman in the front row stood and shouted at her angrily: "Go back to Mexico! We need our jobs!" Both Latinos and Blacks may refuse to protest the bombing of an Asian civil rights center, as happened in Sacramento, because "those people didn't have it hard like us." Today's basic message is: don't blame greedy corporate interests, don't blame the savings-and-loan banks, don't blame politicians, do blame immigrants!

We all need to understand the reason for Operation Scapegoat and how it functions. Scapegoating calls for the U.S.-born to see immigrants as individuals who have freely chosen to leave their homes. But most people migrate under the pressure of economic, political or social forces. Most migrants are victims of contemporary economic restructuring, intended by capitalists to restore their profit rates by using many more low-paid, unskilled workers, and to hell with millions of skilled steelworkers, autoworkers and others. In other words, globalization has made Mexican and other migrant labor—especially when undocumented—key to restructuring the U.S. economy. Scapegoating these same workers for U.S. economic problems is thus an act of supreme hypocrisy and political opportunism.

We also need to understand the role of the border in guaranteeing the supply of cheap labor from Latin America, and why we hear so much about efforts to prevent workers from crossing. For many years, Mexican migrant labor in particular has carried great advantage for the U.S.-based capitalist. It is almost totally vulnerable, especially when undocumented and disenfranchised. The historic function of the border has been as a mechanism for defining and maintaining control over workers and their wages according to whether they possess or lack "legal" status. U.S. history is packed with examples of how low wages and terrible working conditions have been accepted because complaints could mean deportation; of undocumented workers being deported just when their wages were due to be paid, or when workers began to organize for their rights. Crippling controls make the undocumented worker a very special kind of wage slave, in Marxist terms—and more enslaved than waged.

Today, in the light of intensified global economic integration, questions about the function of the border have been raised by mainstream forces. Why did the *Wall Street Journal* call for a totally open border, even as other voices from center to right demand tighter control? It seems possible that the *Journal* understands that today countries belong to an interdependent collectivity shaped by global trends and that the role of borders is uncertain in an era of galloping economic integration. Why try to regulate immigration with border controls at a time of energetic efforts to open up national economies and create trading blocs like NAFTA?

Saskia Sassen of Columbia University, a longtime expert on immigration issues, has written about such contradictions. She points out, for example, how overseas operations of firms have an impact on migration. People move when investment moves. The real migrant, then, is capital, traveling where it will and attracting labor as it goes.

Another truth about immigration that is usually ignored rests on the view of the country that receives migrant workers as a passive victim of invading hordes. In fact, its policies may well "pull" migrants. The United States sent $6 billion in aid to El Salvador's government during the 1980s to crush the popular insurgency. Almost 500,000 destitute, frightened Salvadorans moved to Los Angeles, mostly during the 1980s. Could there be a connection? Did those Salvadorans make independent, personal decisions to leave their country? Other examples of how international developments and foreign policy cause migration would include the disintegration of Yugoslavia and the Soviet Union.

Instead of considering such realities, many of us get derailed by all the hostile myths about immigrants. When Governor Wilson of California was heating up his campaign for Proposition 187, which would deny health care and schooling for any child or adult who could not prove legal status in the United States, we heard a constant din about immigration as an economic burden: politicians told us that immigrants use services but don't pay for them, and thus drain local and state resources. Numerous studies show the opposite: immigrants, including the undocumented, pay more in taxes than the cost of most services they use. (This truth is masked by the fact that much of the tax money goes to the federal government, not the state providing the services.) Also, immigrants use fewer services than the native-born; the undocumented, always fearful of deportation, use even less.

As for Social Security taxes, since most immigrants are young, they pay a disproportionate amount of the taxes to support an increasingly aging population. All over the world, countries are coming to realize that, as more people live longer and birthrates drop, migrant workers will be crucial to covering the cost of support for the aged. For this and other reasons, migrants not allowed to vote because they lack documents should be demanding, "No taxation without representation!"

Another argument favored by politicians supporting Proposition 187 was that immigrants were taking away jobs. This claim did not stand up against the facts to any serious or permanent extent, except at the lowest levels of mostly service-type employment. Where there is some displacement, reports said, new jobs are soon created by the presence of new immigrants with their needs for basic goods and services. Also, immigrants mostly work under terrible conditions for terrible pay, in sectors like the garment industry, in the fields or as nannies—jobs that few native-born workers seek today. Even "legal" immigrants work two to five hours more per day than the general population, and the undocumented may work a 16-hour day, six or seven days a week. How many native workers would put up with such conditions?

Still, we can't ignore the issue of job competition, particularly as it affects African Americans. This debate would get even hotter in the late 1990s, as we discuss later in chapter nine, "It's a Terrorist War on Immigrants 1995–Present." The point here is that in the Proposition 187 battle, its proponents used the job-loss argument in a totally opportunistic way, to divide African Americans from Latinos and Asian/Pacific Island Americans. How could anyone believe that those politicians and the right-wing propagandists really cared about working-class Black people?

Instead of blaming immigrants for the deprivation experienced today by millions of the native-born, we should protest the true causes of the crisis. That means the global restructuring by capitalists to sustain profit margins, with the accompanying attack on social services and labor. The very concept of collective responsibility for human well-being is under attack by neo-liberalism all over the world.

In the long run, we need global changes in today's economic policies and the supra-national agencies like the World Bank and the General Agreement on Tariffs and Trade, that determine them. For the short run, we need to define immigrant and refugee rights as a civil rights issue around which all of us should unite. At the same time, immigrant rights are broader than civil rights. Malcolm X once pointed out that the Black movement of the 1960s was a struggle for human rights, not just civil rights. In a similar way, we need to see that the struggle for immigrant rights is in fact a struggle for both civil and human rights.

That struggle points to our need for a politics that recognizes the globalization of racism that today accompanies economic globalization. Does anybody really think the best way to deal with more than 100 million migrants wandering the planet today is by locking doors in the spirit of nineteenth-century nationalism? It is profoundly backward to go on seeing countries primarily as bordered nation-states that can resolve issues like immigration policy unilaterally. It is not only backward but monstrous to think of the world's people as divisible into those who should be dehumanized at will and those who should not. Once again, it must be said: *¡No hay fronteras!*

chapter eight

FOR WHOM THE TACO BELL TOLLS

Listen up, all you Chickanos and Chickanas out there! Call yourselves Hispanics if you like, but it will do *no* good when Taco Bell gets you. Time to catch on, fellow spics, this land is *not* our land—it belongs to the *gringotes* and their Border Lights. We got the word, loud and clear, during the 1995 Super Bowl.

Picture this as a commercial you happened to catch while the Super Bowl is on break: it's night, a young man and woman in a pickup truck are looking for a quiet place to make out. They pull over in a dark, deserted spot and start doing their thing. Just then a blinding searchlight hits them, all kinds of lights flash. Helicopters whir overhead. What is this shit, they are wondering. Then the message: BORDER LIGHTS ARE COMING!

("Border Lights"—as in "Lites"—were Taco Bell's new menu of supposedly nutritious, low-calorie Mexican food.)

For lots of us *cucarachas* (Cuckoo Roaches), that commercial was a creepy reminder of the truly *gacho* "Light Up the Border" campaign in southern California. Concocted by Muriel Watson, the widow of a Border Patrol officer, the campaign had Anglos park their cars at a site facing the border, at night. They would turn on their headlights with the supposed goal of revealing "illegals" trying to sneak into Gringolandia. Sometimes up to 600 cars would do this. So "Border Lights" doesn't sound so good to many of us who have this weird idea that California used to be part of Mexico. (In other words, we didn't cross the border—the border crossed us.)

The Taco Bell commercial drew complaints from the Mexican American Legal Defense and Education Fund that it was a subtle attack on Latinos and exacerbated anti-immigrant sentiment. The *New York Times* Business Section had its doubts about the ad. On January 31, 1995, the "Advertising" column carried a round-up on Super Bowl commercials, commenting that the Taco Bell spots "stirred unpleasant associations by juxtaposing the Taco Bell theme 'Cross the Border' with helicopters ominously shining searchlights." Taco Bell itself just couldn't understand all the fuss; a company spokeswoman said the ad had no relation to the anti-immigrant furor.

Tell that to the INS.

The commercial was the creature of a $75 million advertising campaign for Border Lights food such as the Border Light Taco Supreme, available at the Bell's 4,500 locations. We've also had the "Run for the Border" campaign, one version of which was immortalized in a Taco Bell paper mat placed upon a serving tray. Pictured on the mat is a tiny Taco Bell restaurant seen from afar. A highway runs down the middle of the picture, heading straight for the eatery. On both sides appear freeway-type signs bearing such phrases as "Jump it!" and "Crash it!"

Taco Bell's parent company is Pepsi, which also has solid racist credentials. It owned Frito-Lay, creator of Frito Bandito, who advertised its chips back in the 1960s. Señor Frito was a gun-toting, wildly mustachioed, rotund little guy under a gigantic sombrero. His silly appearance, together with his hands outspread in a helpless "Who, me?" gesture, assured Anglos he was no threat. Strong protests during the 1970s finally retired this particular version of a well-worn stereotype. Taco Bell has a reputation for racist advertising that reaches beyond Raza. The company once put on a notorious commercial showing some scantily clad Black folks in supposed tribal costume dancing around a fire, going "wild" (the voice said) for a Taco Bell burrito.

"A culture reflects a society's anxieties," says painter Yolanda López, who has made a revealing video *When You Think of Mexico: Commercial Images of Mexicans in the Mass Media*. As Yolanda commented, "The Taco Bell border ads provide a safety valve in a time of fear. They soothe Anglos afraid of demographic change, afraid of losing their majority control. Such commercials play on this fear and then exploit it by telling you to 'experience the adventure of the border.... Eat a new 59 cent taco!'"

Raza, today we face a ferocious, complex, divisive assault on immigrant rights along with affirmative action, bilingualism and other hard-won gains. Sometimes the attack will be direct hatred and destructiveness. In other cases, the attack will be indirect: a racism that plays games with us and our food, belittles us to the point of dehumanization and then says, "It's just a joke—don't be so serious!"

Both direct and indirect ideological warfare are real. So remember, we don't need no Border Lights. A veggie burger with lots of green chile is more what Raza needs, *qué no?*

chapter nine

IT'S A TERRORIST WAR ON IMMIGRANTS 1995–PRESENT

In the spring of 1997, a Latino immigrant who had worked legally in the United States for 40 years committed suicide after receiving a letter saying that under the new welfare law his Supplemental Security Income (SSI) might end. Not long afterward, a wheelchair-bound Russian immigrant threw himself off his balcony from the same fear. Shouldn't we call them victims of a monstrous new terrorism?

What we once called immigrant-bashing should be called immigrant-smashing. It's an outright war, waged at the highest levels of government, as immigrant-rights leader María Jiménez of Houston has long said. Like many wars, this one utilizes vicious divide-and-conquer tactics to prevent a united resistance: divide immigrants and the U.S.-born; the so-called legal (documented) and the illegal (undocumented); recent and established arrivals. The war cabinet has a very busy Department of Propaganda, its purpose being to convince the public that some overwhelmingly poor, exploited and vulnerable people are the enemy. Other tactics include a barrage of new laws whose goal is to legalize the war and consolidate the foundation for anti-immigrant terrorism.

Those laws, passed since 1994, show that the war-makers include not only upfront reactionaries like Gov. Pete Wilson of California but also the president. When Clinton was running for re-election in 1996, he supported a fat package of anti-immigrant legislation. It passed, followed that same year by so-called welfare reform legislation, whose victims include millions of migrant workers—a more accurate term than "immigrant." The 1994–97 legislation was fed by electoral competition and the politicians' goal of winning votes through scapegoating. Such campaign opportunism explains a host of horrors, including Wilson's promising a few days before the November 1996 election that he would end prenatal care for "illegal" immigrants—which he did, on January 1, 1998. (This act was then appealed.)

One of the worst anti-immigrant laws of 1996 was the Anti-Terrorism and Effective Death Penalty Act. It contains semi-fascist clauses attacking immigrant rights, tucked into the act by Clinton and supporters. Among them is what amounts to *the abolition of due process.* Previously, long-term permanent residents could obtain a waiver to block deportation for minor criminal offenses, and thus have a chance to prove they had been rehabilitated. Although technically this right has not been abolished, the new law makes it next to impossible to meet the requirements. Also, it is now permissible to jail anyone on the spot who reports to apply for citizenship and is then found to have a criminal record.

Another clause *authorizes police to perform tasks outside their normal duties.* Local police can "cooperate" with the Immigration and Naturalization Service (INS) by making arrests for supposed violations of immigration law. Even before this new law passed, local police had already been using false or nonexistent warrants and engaging in physical and verbal abuse. Yet another clause in the anti-terrorism act provides for *spying on dissidents.* Any foreign group would be designated a "terrorist organization" if it "threatens the national security," and this designation could be made without revealing the evidence for such allegations. Groups that defend immigrant rights could obviously be made prime targets. Whatever happened to civil liberties?

Yet another law with semi-fascist overtones, which even conservative attorneys found shocking, passed in 1996. It said that the INS could single-handedly decide the fate of an immigrant—for example, to be given political asylum or not—and the person would have no right of appeal for judicial intervention. The INS can legally pick up people, deny them asylum as refugees, along with the right to an interpreter or attorney, and deport them—all with impunity.

When we consider how the anti-terrorism act and other laws passed in 1994–97 have imposed fear and suffering, we have to ask: who are the real terrorists? If terrorism means the systematic use of intense fear as a means of coercion, we can look at Latino immigrants (not to mention others) and find appalling examples of such victimization. To mention only one: uncounted Latino families have not gone to clinics for health care or sent their children to school out of fear of deportation. California's Proposition 187 said children and adults must be able to show documents proving legal residence in order to receive such services. Isn't there something surreal, indeed monstrous, about little children having to be sure they are carrying a certified birth certificate in order to go to school?

Proposition 187, which was later declared unconstitutional, frightened many in California. But even without it, Latinos and others are stopped anywhere and everywhere to prove their legal status. Often the INS announces new restrictions that suggest mass deportations in the minds of immigrants, some of whom remember "Operation Wetback" and similar expulsions in the past. Once again, after the new laws passed, lines formed around the block at INS offices, with people trying to find out what was happening and when deadlines would take effect. "People are panicking" became a commonplace description.

In the summer of 1997, 50,000 Nicaraguans would have faced deportation from three states if a provision in one of the new laws had been applied retroactively. A judge ruled against this at the time, but the fight went on. Many live with similar unrelenting insecurity, fear for themselves and their families. Again we must ask: who are the real terrorists?

The one law that should have passed but didn't in this period is H.R. 2119, which would have established an Immigration Enforcement Review Commission. The commission would have investigated complaints about the Border Patrol—the largest and least accountable police department in the United States, which has resisted oversight for years. Thus the message rings out clearly from the halls of Congress and the White House: it's open season on migrant labor, which means anyone who looks "foreign"—especially Latinos, the main focus of this essay.

To speak in terms of hunting seasons is no exaggeration. Check out the February 1995 issue of *Outdoor Life* and find an exciting article called "Manhunter." It's the story of a Border Patrol agent named Mike Calvert who loves to use his "extraordinary tracking skills" to hunt "that most elusive trophy of all—man." The article appeared with a drawing of a hunter staring intently at a map showing the U.S.-Mexico border.

And so:

- When we hear that 13 migrants were killed or injured along the San Diego border during just one month, April 1996, in high-speed chases by Border Patrol and highway-patrol officers, we should think of the INS's Operation Gatekeeper. Established by Clinton in

1994 supposedly to stop unauthorized immigrants and illegal drugs from entering San Diego, the operation is equipped with millions of dollars in sophisticated military hardware and high-tech viewing devices. As of spring 1997, there were 2,000 Border Patrol officers and 250 National Guardsmen in the San Diego area.

- When we hear about the May 1996 video-taped beating in Riverside County, California, of Alicia Soltero Vásquez and her companion when the Border Patrol stopped their truck, we should think about the ferocious immigrant-bashing that went on during that national election year. (Later, the two received a $740,000 settlement.)

- When, in November 1996, a group of ten people, including children, were swept away by a wave and drowned on the Texas border in an area known to be dangerous (they had hoped it would be less commonly used and thus less patrolled), we should think of how the number of such deaths will surely rise. A 1996 law said that the INS should hire at least 1,000 Border Patrol agents for the U.S.-Mexico border in each of the next five years, to have a total of 10,000 by the year 2000. Even the INS has said it cannot responsibly absorb more than 500 new agents a year; also, no plans to improve the screening, training and accountability of INS agents are required.

- When we read that a University of Houston study reports that 1,185 people drowned, died of exposure or dehydration or were hit by automobiles while trying to cross the border away from designated checkpoints during 1993–97 (*San Francisco Examiner,* August 24, 1997), we should consider the racist attitudes toward these victims. Many of the bodies found are never identified; sometimes no autopsy is performed and no death certificate filed. "They're not from here. They don't matter" is often the attitude. The report included only cases that could be documented and focused only on certain counties.

- When 17 migrants perished in freezing weather near San Diego between January 7 and 24, 1997, because they tried to avoid the Border Patrol by passing through isolated mountains, we can ask ourselves, "Don't they matter, either?"

- When we hear of the May 20, 1997, murder near the Texas border of 18-year-old Esequiel Hernández by a U.S. Marine during a drug patrol, we should realize just what the growing militarization of the borderlands can mean. Hernández was tending his goats near his home at the time. His death provoked an uproar but no action by the state. In February 1998, it was announced that the federal government would not charge the Marine with a civil rights violation, either. Involvement of the military in civilian law enforcement is as dangerous today as it was when it was banned in the United States more than 100 years ago.

Along with the specifically anti-immigrant laws, Clinton combined immigrants and welfare recipients in one big package for super-convenient scapegoating. His so-called welfare reform bill ended 60 years of federal responsibility for helping the nation's poor. Among various provisions, it denied benefits to "legal immigrants," including food stamps and SSI. It also abolished AFDC (Aid to Families with Dependent Children) and replaced it with TANF (Temporary Assistance to Needy Families), which is time-limited and which states have the option of denying to documented immigrants. Under the new welfare law, states may also deny Medicaid to documented immigrants. As for those so-called illegals, they are ineligible for *all* federal programs except some select emergency medical services and some immunization programs.

What will all this mean? The Urban Institute announced in late 1996 that of the 1.1 million children predicted to fall into poverty from the new law, 450,000 will be harmed by the immigrant provisions. Other damage includes an estimated half-million documented immigrants losing access to SSI income and about 900,000 losing food stamps. (People can continue to receive SSI only if they are veterans, *can prove* they have worked in the United States for ten years, can prove refugee status or become citizens.) In California alone, more than 200,000 seniors and disabled people will lose their SSI, as feared by the two men who killed themselves. Confronted by sharp criticism, Clinton later promised to restore some of the welfare benefits.

Even if Clinton's package of new legislation is modified in small ways, the damage has been done. Open season on migrant workers continues nationwide. One of the worst cases of abuse exploded on June 18, 1995, at the Elizabeth, New Jersey, detention center where immigrants with papers deemed questionable were taken, usually directly from airports. That day, inmates demolished much of the center's interior and barricaded themselves inside for five hours.

They rose up against conditions that investigators had criticized harshly for months before the uprising: being held in large dormitory rooms where, according to a Catholic official, they "eat, defecate, sleep, and remain for 23 hours a day." Sometimes, if there was a shortage of guards, inmates would be shackled for hours. Many were applicants for refugee status who had been awaiting a decision too long, like the man from Sudan expelled from his country for pro-democracy activism who stayed locked up at the center for seven months. Two years after the uprising, the center reopened under new management and with many inmates discharged (investigators said they never should have been detained in the first place) but without real improvement in center conditions, one attorney said.

INS raids dramatically increased during 1996–97 from Maryland to California and at workplaces from construction sites to garment factories to nightclubs. Most of the workers arrested—sometimes as many as 97 percent, for example, in New York City—were Latino. The raids are utilized as a tactic to maintain an abusive working environment and push the immigrant economy even further underground, where it will be even more vulnerable.

Collusion between the INS and employers often occurs for different reasons. On one hand, garment-factory owners in New York asked the third-ranking INS official to curtail its raids—perhaps because they wanted to keep the low-wage workers they had trained?—and the INS complied. On the other hand, bosses use the INS to police their employees, particularly when they suspect workers may be preparing some collective action such as a union drive. An especially notorious case involved Mediacopy, the world's third-largest video-tape duplication company, located in San Leandro, California. In early 1997, one day before workers planned to launch a unionization campaign, Mediacopy locked its doors and then brought in the INS. Almost 100 workers, some of them documented, were arrested. The International Longshoremen's and Warehouse Workers Union (ILWU Local 6) brought a case on their behalf. (After a long struggle, workers won union recognition along with a wage increase and full medical benefits in 1998.)

How long does the arm of the INS reach, one wonders, when hearing that the Ohio Highway Patrol has repeatedly stopped organizers of the Farm Labor Organizing Committee, a 25-year-old union? In a federal suit filed last year, members reported being stopped on the highway and detained for hours without a ticket or warning ever being issued. Not infrequently, they are U.S. citizens.

Incidentally, the INS was sued in 1995 by some of its own. More than a dozen Latino agents who gave their names and 13 anonymous ones charged discrimination so widespread that it damaged their daily work as well as their careers. Another 40 agents wanted to be included if the case was certified as a class-action suit. Their complaint is not that the INS fails to hire enough Latinos but that too many of those hired end up sweeping the floor and shuffling paper. Latino agents can be as brutal as anyone, but these agents say that many of the INS white employees are racist toward Latinos in general—which makes the likelihood of abuse even greater when Anglos are in charge.

Building a United Resistance

Where is the resistance movement to the war on migrant workers? Many groups, networks, coalitions and workers' centers exist across the country and have been holding protests. In some, disagreement about strategy and tactics runs deep. Liberals have often bought into the distinction between "legal" and "illegal" immigrants, which has divided the immigrant rights movement in California and nationally. Such a distinction fails to recognize that the new laws can devastate both groups and that the instruments of repression make no such distinction. Race and class link the documented and undocumented tightly, negating legalistic differences. When a cop or *migra* agent arbitrarily arrests a dark-skinned Latino who looks poor, he or she doesn't really care whether the person has the right piece of paper or not.

The treatment of Latino (and other) immigrants tells us that if one freedom is curtailed today, others will be at risk tomorrow. Anti-immigrant laws and procedures threaten the civil rights of everyone. Thus we all, whatever our legal status, have an interest in maintaining the rights of all migrant workers, whether documented or not. In the end, those rights are no less than democratic rights as well as workers' rights.

Another debate centers on whether to utilize various reputable reports showing that, nationwide, the amount that immigrants pay in taxes is greater than the cost of services they receive. Therefore, immigrants are not parasites, contrary to the propaganda about pregnant Latinas who come to the United States just to have babies and collect welfare, or similar myths. Those facts are true enough, but this argument also falters. Do we really want the public to focus primarily on the net financial worth of a human being rather than on the need to provide human rights for everyone? Do we normally evaluate the life of a child or elderly person according to the value of what they produce or how much they pay in taxes? The argument that immigrants are not a financial burden to taxpayers can be useful, but it becomes depoliticized and liberal if we don't add that a person's economic contribution is not the main issue; we must look primarily at the importance of human and civil rights.

A third strategic problem is lack of understanding about the reasons for migration. There is a tendency to speak of "the immigration problem," which has come to mean unwanted foreigners imposing difficulties on the citizenry. That phrase reduces a global movement of displaced human beings to a U.S. national security issue called "defending our borders." That phrase denies the fact that "immigration" actually reflects a set of economic forces at work that we need to understand.

Promoted by transnational corporate giants, globalization integrates the economies of poor nations into a world system created and controlled by such giants. That integration causes people who should be called migrant workers to whirl from one space to another in search of subsistence. In this light we can see that the anti-immigrant laws of 1996 were in fact an anti-labor bill.

Sometimes, though rarely, the truth appears in the U.S. mass media, as in the special report titled "Illegal in Iowa," published by *U.S. News and World Report* (September 23, 1996), with its simple cover statement that "American firms recruit thousands of Mexicans to do the nation's dirtiest, most dangerous work." Which is, of course, hardly news.

For the immigrant rights movement and progressives in general, winning the support of U.S.-born workers calls for much work. Among the huge variety of Asian/Pacific Island communities, complex relations exist. Even people of the same national background can be divided, as conflicts between Chicanos/as and newly arrived Mexicans indicate. Among people of the same racial or ethnic background, division can also be found. The majority of Puerto Ricans (who are citizens by birth) reportedly want stricter controls over immigration, including that of other Latinos. They see it in terms of job competition and other threats. Some Puerto Ricans actively support civil and human rights for immigrants, and see those rights as inextricably intertwined with Latino empowerment in general and Puerto Rican rights in particular. Howard Jordan, who edits the Puerto Rican publication *Critica* in New York, has written eloquently about this.

The vast majority of immigrants are people of color, for whom racism is the daily diet served along with immigrant status. Thus a potential for coalitions exists in Black communities. Alongside the commonality of racial oppression we also have the commonality of displacement—in the past or present—resulting from economic forces. But strong disunity has developed. Although often cultivated by divide-and-conquer tacticians, it must be taken seriously. We cannot ignore the issues of job and wage competition, with particular reference to Latinos and Blacks.

For several years, African-American communities have believed that immigrants—meaning Latinos and Asians—are taking away jobs once available to Blacks. Defenders of immigrant rights have sometimes made the mistake of dismissing this concern arbitrarily. African-American scholars cite such evidence as a 1993 *Wall Street Journal* study of the impact of the last recession, which found that Blacks had lost 59,479 jobs across the United States while other groups had a net gain, and that the worst losses were in states with the highest immigration rate, such as Florida and California. Further, wages had gone down for Blacks in some sectors where unionized Black workers once prevailed. Localized studies also encourage the sense of loss. For example, a study of the garment and hotel industries in New York City in 1940–90 found that immigrants' share of employment grew as natives' share of employment fell.

Other scholars, usually white, have maintained that a very small amount of absolute job loss for African Americans may indeed occur in a few sectors. However, they say, immigration generates new jobs, which are then available to all. For example, in a particular city immigration may cause an increase in jobs at government agencies that offer services used by immigrants. Often African Americans, and rarely immigrants, are hired for such work. In other words, one must look at the total employment picture.

Two massive studies released in 1997, one by the National Research Council and another by the international Organization for Economic Cooperation and Development, provided new data on the job-competition issue. The first agreed that there can be job loss, usually for less-skilled native-born workers competing with migrant workers (also less-skilled). Thus African Americans and also low-income native Latinos are the main groups affected. The OECD report found job competition mainly between different immigrant workers, not with native-born workers. (*Wall Street Journal*, November 25, 1997.)

But there is another factor in Black anti-immigrant attitudes: people's perceptions. Rarely, if ever, do reports and statistics examine the impact of personal experience on the debate about job loss. In evaluating how serious such loss is for African Americans, we cannot ignore reality as seen by a people for whom centuries of enslavement and the worst kind of brutalization will almost inevitably condition their perspective. When an African American goes to a hotel in the East where the service workers have always been Black and sees mostly Latino faces, the impact is powerful. The word spreads. Even if only a few jobs are involved—and poor jobs at that—the visual reality strikes home. "Don't tell me immigrants aren't taking jobs from Blacks," they might say. (Similarly, a Latino might go to a gas station in San Francisco's Mission District and find that the gas-station workers, once Latino, are now Asian.)

It is true, as the 1997 National Academy of Sciences report says, that immigrants represent only about 8 percent of the population, and so losses for any native group would have to be statistically huge to appear significant. Again, this fact doesn't undermine the psychological effect on communities that have been under racist and classist siege for centuries. That effect is aggravated, in the case of African Americans, by the fact that they will soon become the second-largest U.S. population of color—no longer the first—if current immigration rates continue. The feeling of losing whatever power comes from numbers, in a society that has constantly disempowered you with its racism, can be overwhelming. It must seem like becoming a minority twice, once in the past and now in the future, with the present an unending struggle for survival.

Framed by those realities, the issue of job-and-wage competition must be faced with honest dialogue and a commitment to creating understanding—not more divisiveness. In the end, the question is not whether job loss really happens or not, and how much. The question is: do we let it divide African Americans and migrant workers, or do we acknowledge the problem, join forces to offset division and work to win more jobs for everyone?

In answering that question, we all need to recognize how effectively division has been fostered, deliberately in some cases and out of ignorance in others. During the campaign for Proposition 187 in California, the right-wing Federation for American Immigration Reform ran radio spots in Black communities that blamed their problems on those foreign hordes coming across the border. The large Black vote in favor of that proposition was facilitated by such propaganda.

On the Latino or Asian/Pacific-Island American side, negative reactions to Black attitudes toward immigrants should also be discussed. Latinos know all too well that migrant workers have suffered greatly and even lost their lives by trying to come to this country. So it did hurt when the National Association for the Advancement of Colored People initially refused to take a position against employer sanctions. Imposed by the 1986 Immigration Reform and Control Act, these sanctions were supposed to penalize employers for hiring undocumented workers. As a study by the U.S. General Accounting Office showed, their main effect has been discrimination against job-seekers based on appearance or accent, with many victims being citizens. In other words, racism.

The Congressional Black Caucus opposed sanctions early on, but the NAACP supported sanctions for a decade until Latino civil rights organizations threatened to resign from the National Civil Rights Leadership Conference. Finally the NAACP joined the opposition to sanctions. What should count here, from a Black/brown alliance-building perspective, is the NAACP's eventual support. Latinos and Blacks should also recall that the NAACP once worked together with the League of Latin American Citizens against segregation in the South at a time of intense Klan activity.

Another real issue that comes up in relation to Black-Latino views of immigration is language. Too often in a workplace we hear the question from an African-American employee, "Why don't you speak English? You're in America now!" Again, it can help to understand that being denied the right to speak Spanish is an old form of racism that has plagued Latinos for decades. To speak Spanish represents defense of one's culture in a Eurocentric, racist nation that doesn't want to remember that Spanish—not English—was the common language in much of the Southwest for 250 years. (We can also note that some of the worst racist stereotypes about Asians are based on a hateful mockery of speech like "tickee" and "laundree" that homogenizes everything Asian as Chinese.) At the same time, other peoples facing racism—such as African Americans—may feel excluded by the use in their presence of a language they don't know. Sensitivity to these feelings is needed, too.

Relations between African Americans and Latinos (or other peoples of color) on immigration issues can be problematic in areas beyond work and culture. They come up in other aspects of urban life: neighborhoods changing, housing, equitable political representation, gangs. Whatever the arena of conflict, the goal needs to be greater cooperation and solidarity in opposing common enemies. Black Americans have sometimes called for such unity, like Joe Williams III, an African American writing in the *Los Angeles Sentinel* on September 9, 1996. Williams compared the current attacks on the undocumented to the harassment of Blacks during the 1950s and 1960s, when many moved north or west as Southern agriculture declined. "They were accused of taking the jobs of the white man. They were accused [by whites] of undermining the salaries of union workers." It's even worse today, Williams concluded, because mainstream Black politicians as well as segments of the Black and Latino communities join the attacks.

We need Latino voices like that, people who will offer honest self-criticism about our attitudes toward African-American concerns. We need more Latinos condemning the racist attitudes toward Blacks often found in our communities, along with African Americans coming to understand the Latino perspective and our commonalities. This kind of openness will take courage on both sides, not to mention all the other colors that must also communicate.

We can look across the seas for examples to inspire us in the difficult struggle for immigrants' human and civil rights. In 1997, an organization of immigrant African men, women and children made history in Paris. The group, Sans Papiers ("Without Papers," meaning undocumented), organized openly despite threats of instant deportation. They occupied a church and held a 50-day hunger strike there; confronted the passage of laws similar to anti-immigrant legislation here; and did not retreat in the face of severe repression by 1,000 military police who attacked with tear gas and clubs.

Support for Sans Papiers by France's largest labor union, which called for amnesty for everyone without papers, was crucial. Also, many white French citizens participated in demonstrations against scapegoating immigrants. All these efforts, beginning with Sans Papiers' organizing, paid off. On June 11, 1997, France's new government promised to review tens of thousands of requests for residence papers previously denied, and announced it would revoke anti-immigrant laws passed by the previous government.

Here in the United States we have seen a united commitment to fight the war on immigrants being built across the country. In spring 1997 people of color and Anglos protested in Los Angeles, Newark,

New Jersey, and Sacramento, California. In Providence, Rhode Island, protesters stopped the cut in food stamps and SSI for documented immigrants with a large, multi-racial demonstration and other actions. Spurred by the severe cut-backs in welfare, new nationalities have been joining the protests; Asians in particular came out, often for the first time. A new militancy filled the air at Sacramento; protesters did not simply request consideration but affirmed what they are *entitled* to, as immigrants and as human beings.

We must do still more. We need to be constantly moving beyond a short-range definition of needs, and not be deceived by scapegoating campaigns or driven into new fights over crumbs. Instead of pursuing a nationalist agenda, people of color must build a transnational movement for civil and human rights, a movement that will empower working-class people everywhere. Such a movement requires all of us to educate ourselves about our histories and commonalities, including our experiences of working together, so as to break the mythology of inevitable division and domination.

Why should we do all this? Because we have to, if we want to overcome massive disempowerment. Because we have to, period: it is simply decent and righteous for all people to be treated with respect and humanity. If we lose that vision, we lose immigrant rights and far, far more.

part three

FIGHTING FOR ECONOMIC AND ENVIRONMENTAL JUSTICE

Que no haya uno solo de nuestros deseos individuales
que nazca sin la conciencia
de que somos dé lulas de una araña de cinco patas
llamada tierra.

Let not a single one of our individual goals
be born without awareness
that we are all part of a great spider with five legs
called the earth.

—*palabras zapatistas/EZLN*
—from the Zapatista movement

chapter ten

"LEVI'S, BUTTON YOUR FLY— YOUR GREED IS SHOWING!"

When ten decorous, mostly middle-aged Latinas shout such words at the international headquarters of the world's largest garment manufacturer, one suspects that something's shaking. These unpretentious ladies from Texas were holding a protest on the pretty plaza facing Levi Strauss' benign-looking, red-brick office building in San Francisco. Yuppies streamed by at the end of their lunch hour as usual. But it felt as if something new was in the air, and so it was. And so it still is.

In 1990 those Latinas had become the first to carry out a major protest against a plant shutdown by Levi's (between 1981 and 1990, the company closed 58 plants, putting 10,400 people out of work). In November 1997 Levi's announced it would lay off 6,395 more workers at 11 plants, and Fuerza Unida launched a new protest. Whatever happened to the stereotype of the docile *mexicana*? The story of Fuerza Unida is a story of transformations.

Their struggle dates back to January 16, 1990, when Levi's summoned the workforce at its South Zarzamora Street plant in San Antonio, Texas. Over a loudspeaker, workers—the vast majority of them Latina—learned that Levi's was moving to a country with cheaper labor so the company "could compete." Everyone had heard rumors, but in November the plant manager had told employees their jobs were secure, and his reassurances continued. Instead of the usual $500 Christmas bonus, he had said, they would receive a raise in January. But suddenly their world collapsed. Forget that January raise—now you see it, now you don't. This whole sleight of hand was only one of many shabby Levi's maneuvers; more would follow.

By April the South Zarzamora Street plant, which made Dockers pants, had moved its Dockers production to Costa Rica. There it would pay $3.80 a day—roughly half the average hourly wage of San Antonio workers at the time. The move left 1,150 people—92 percent Latino and 86 percent women, including many single mothers—out of a job.

Two years later, 279 of them had obtained jobs in the two other Levi's plants in San Antonio—with decent pay, thanks to a nine-month struggle by Fuerza Unida. The rest were still unemployed, working elsewhere at minimum wage or for limited hours only and not retrained by Levi's as expected.

As a result of what many called intimidation and coercion, the Zarzamora workers had not been unionized (some other Levi's plants in the United States do have unions). Still, they mounted a protest against the closing less than a week after that fatal announcement, and on February 12, 1990, they launched their organization, Fuerza Unida ("United Force"). Membership zoomed when Levi Strauss announced sales totalling $3.6 billion and record profits of $272.3 million for 1989. One reason for such profits was the success of Dockers pants, which accounted for almost $400 million in sales—more than triple the year before. "So why did they have to close the plant?" workers asked.

Fuerza Unida members struggled to get emergency aid from the city, state and federal governments, as well as practical classes in English as a Second Language and for Graduate Equivalency Degrees. They carried out protests in ten cities in the Southwest plus Seattle, Portland, Chicago, Albany and New York, and in Mexico as well as France; several hunger strikes; and a series of community tribunals to judge Levi's actions. Along with filing two lawsuits, they maintained a food bank and set up a small seamstresses' cooperative, both of which continue today.

Everywhere this group of working-class Latinas, many of whom spoke little English, was exposing nasty truths about a world-famous company that cultivates a glowing, liberal image to veil its exploitation. They testified at congressional hearings, developed media contacts, spoke to unions and raised funds. They launched a national boycott against Levi Strauss clothing, urging those who already owned Levi's products to cut off the label and mail it to the company as a sign of support for Fuerza Unida's ten demands. These included increased pension benefits, extended severance pay and special compensation for disabled workers.

Somehow Fuerza Unida women managed this kind of schedule with warm smiles and powerhouse energy. Somehow their chants didn't sound tired, their slogans didn't go stale. Somehow they held their meetings in San Antonio every week, every month, with 50 to 100 to 200 people attending. How to explain three years of such energy and commitment?

One answer is surely the anger and feelings of betrayal by Levi's. Such anger was palpable at the November 1992 tribunal in San Francisco, when ten women fasting in protest against Levi's found the strength to speak out loud and clear. As Ernestina Mendoza testified, *"No tenemos hambre de comida, tenemos hambre de justicia"* ("We are hungry for justice, not for food"). Others wept as they described that moment on January 16 when Levi's suddenly announced the shutdown. "We cry because we still hurt." Emma Davis, who worked a computer at Levi's, was also suspicious: "In my opinion they had all the paperwork ready in July. It takes a lot to get ready for a closedown." Making workers falsely believe their jobs were secure (and just before Christmas, with extra expenses for many of them) was part of one Fuerza Unida lawsuit.

Another suit charged that Levi's avoided medical costs from on-the-job injuries suffered by at least 25 percent of the workforce. At the tribunal one woman after another spoke about such injuries, beginning with their years at the Santone Manufacturing plant, which Levi Strauss bought in 1981 and renamed Levi's in 1983. Rosa Salas told a chilling tale of developing carpal tunnel syndrome (a painful ailment of the wrist) after working for 12 years. It got worse when Levi's began to emphasize making Dockers—considered the right pants for "aging baby boomers" with expanding waistlines—instead of jeans. The Dockers pants required working with heavier material and performing more operations.

Rosa remembered how, as the carpal tunnel problem intensified, workers were told *not* to report injuries. In her case, she finally went to a doctor on her own, and was quickly hospitalized to have surgery on both hands. Ordered to do "light duty," she still worked 12 hours a day dropping off pants to other workers. Eventually the doctor said she could not do work of that type either. After the layoff, "I tried to work in a beauty parlor, but I can't. So I ask Levi's, 'What are you going to do about this?'"

More than one worker talked about being used to make profits and tossed out like an old, unwanted shoe. Severiana Moreno, a 15-year employee who can't work anymore, had traveled to the tribunal from San Antonio in a van—lying on her back. Bertha Suárez, who worked for Santone/Levi's for 22 years, has a bad back but "I'm getting only $85 a month pension and there are more like me. I'm just another face on the welfare line. Where is my pension?" What happened to workers' pension money, including what they had accumulated at Santone before it became Levi's, remains a mystery.

Throughout the tribunal, workers talked about the psychological effects of layoff as much as the material damage: loss of a sense of family (one's coworkers), strains at home with spouses and children, loss of self-esteem and identity in a society that defines a person according to their work or lack of it, and many other forms of depression.

Anger is one reason behind the women's persistence. There is another, even more important, one expressed in Fuerza Unida's beautiful, untranslatable slogan: *La mujer luchando, el mundo transformando.* It says, literally: "Women struggling, the world transforming," in the sense of "Women in struggle transform the world." Whose world? Ah, the world outside and the world inside themselves, I think.

This consciousness shows in the way Fuerza Unida women have built alliances with other groups of women and workers, here and in other countries. Among these are the Southwest Public Workers Union based in San Antonio; Mujer Obrera (garment workers in El Paso); the Southwest Network for Environmental and Economic Justice based in Albuquerque, New Mexico; Mujer a Mujer ("Woman to Woman") in Texas and Mexico; and the Seamstresses' Union in Mexico. Workers organizing in the *maquiladoras* (assembly shops for U.S. companies) along the border are important sisters in the struggle. Networking with other organizations is not merely tactical; Fuerza Unida sees the political and economic links between their experience and other plant closures, other women's struggles.

Fuerza Unida quickly understood that their experience was a precursor of the North American Free Trade Agreement (NAFTA): "We were early victims of the NAFTA," members often say. They soon moved into the forefront of grassroots organizing against NAFTA with the slogan "We don't want free trade, we want fair trade." Or, as their famous chant put it, "Give NAFTA the shafta!"

Locally Fuerza Unida has used a form of the labor-community organizing strategy that argues: corporations that have built great fortunes on the backs of a community owe that community. This means not just their employees but also those who provide the schooling, medical care, fire protection, stores—the whole infrastructure. In San Antonio, much of the Chicano/Mexicano community stands with Fuerza Unida in this spirit. Rubén Solís—veteran of the 1960s Chicano movement, now a Southwest Network leader and longtime adviser to Fuerza Unida—pinpointed its worldview when he told me: "Fuerza Unida's strength has not been simply to capture the moment as Levi's victims but to capture the essence of class, gender and national solidarity. That adds up to a movement."

The story of Fuerza Unida is about women workers of color becoming empowered in many ways. Members speak of having experienced personal transformations. Petra Mata, one of Fuerza Unida's two coordinators, says:

When we used to work for Levi's they would lecture us, blah blah, blah. And we would say, "Yes sir, whatever you say, sir." Now we say, "Wait a minute, is that fair? Is that right?" At the beginning of the boycott we tried to hide our faces behind the picket signs. Now we show our faces proudly. After losing our jobs we discovered a big world out there. We met so many good people who care about us and our struggle, just as we care about them and their struggles.

Since its founding, Fuerza Unida members have acquired faith in their ability to make a plan and then carry it out. They have grown strong in technical knowledge; Irene Reyna, a Levi's machine operator for seven years and one of three Fuerza Unida coordinators until 1996, could run down Levi's corporate tricks like a seasoned labor lawyer. Members have learned how to take part in city council meetings.

In all these ways, external and internal, Fuerza Unida represents a genuinely empowering form of organization. Its humanistic response to inhuman treatment includes such nitty-gritty matters as how internal problems are handled. Their method: hold a meeting immediately so that a conflict does not become a matter of gossip or individual backbiting. *"La mujer luchando—el mundo transformando."*

In response to Fuerza Unida's charges, Levi's claimed to have given the laid-off workers 90 days' notice with pay—30 more than required by law. But Fuerza Unida says 300 women were sent home permanently on the day the closure was announced; instead of giving 30 days extra, the company broke the law. Levi's also stressed its generosity in providing three months of extended, post-layoff health benefits. But it dated that extension from the January 16 closure announcement, which conflicts with its own claim of 90 days' notice. It boasted of giving $1 million for job retraining and other emergency services—but that money went to the city of San Antonio as a whole, not the Zarzamora plant workers. Apparently Levi's was certain that its version of reality would be believed, not that of some Mexican women.

Then came November 3, 1997, and Levi Strauss' announcement that it would close 11 plants in New Mexico, Arkansas, Tennessee and Texas, laying off a total of 6,395 workers. That represented one-third of its total manufacturing workforce in the United States and Canada. Newspaper reports emphasized the "generous severance package" being offered by Levi's. In fact, the company included what it denied Fuerza Unida, and more. In the new layoffs it offered eight months' notice (instead of less than 24 hours); three weeks' pay for each year of service (instead of one week's); and 18 months of continued health benefits (instead of 3 months).

A Levi Strauss spokesman from Dallas said, according to the *Albuquerque Journal* of November 11, that "because of some of the lessons learned in San Antonio, you see what we have here today.... There's no denying that San Antonio in 1990 had something to do with the development of these benefits in 1997." He added that Levi's had failed to anticipate in 1990 how much criticism they would receive from the San Antonio community.

The Fuerza Unida women, while happy that the newly laid-off workers would receive a better severance package and hoping they would not have to go through the same suffering, demanded that Levi's reopen negotiations and pay the San Antonio workers an equivalent severance package. "Now is the time to correct the errors they have admitted making" was their message. Meanwhile, in Brussels, Levi's CEO for Europe (where the company employs 7,500 workers) said on November 4 that closures of certain facilities there could be expected in 1998. European workers have already held emergency meetings and demonstrated.

For years, Levi Strauss has been associated with philanthropy as a major donor in education and the performing arts. The Levi Strauss Foundation has made grants to labor groups and community organizations around the United States as well as in many foreign countries. As an employer, its wage scale, vacation periods and other benefits are often better than elsewhere in the garment industry (a comparison that means little when we consider prevailing standards in that business).

What is the truth behind the Levi Strauss image? This company's 139-year history is said to have begun with the man who created some sturdy pants for miners during the California Gold Rush (but could it have been a *mexicana* who actually sewed them?). In 1985 the company switched from public to private with a leveraged buyout by the Haas family. The $1.6 billion debt that resulted from the buyout was reduced to $475 million by the end of 1989, putting repayment seven years ahead of schedule.

Levi Strauss' road to cheap offshore labor was paved by more than $30 million in federal money. After closing the South Zarzamora plant, it first began buying Dockers from a Honduran contractor whose workers had been trained in a program funded by the Agency for International Development (AID) with $6.3 million, according to the *Journal of Commerce*. Later Levi's shifted to Costa Rica. Documentation presented by Rep. George Brown (Democrat of California) revealed that AID funding of the Honduran training program also enabled Arrow Shirt to move offshore and close several plants in Georgia and Alabama during the late 1980s. This use of taxpayer money to help shops cut labor costs was a pillar of Bush administration policy.

The garment industry makes huge profits off the backs of working-class women, mostly Latinas and Asians. Often the big-name manufacturers contract out sweatshop work to subcontractors. That practice has led to staggering exploitation behind some very fancy labels. For example, on the island of Saipan—which is U.S. territory, some 7,000 miles from California—teenage Chinese girls were imported by a garment subcontractor. This made it possible for manufacturers to get dirt-cheap clothes labeled "Made in the U.S.A." The young women on Saipan worked up to 70 to 80 hours a week under prison-like conditions and for pay ranging from $1.63 to $1.75 an hour. Their passports were confiscated on arrival, so they could not leave without approval. From their hands came goods for companies that included The Gap, Esprit, Christian Dior, Van Heusen, Perry Ellis—and Levi Strauss. After widespread exposure of this scandal in April 1992, U.S. mainland contractors pulled out.

Levi's will tell you that, in the aftermath of the Saipan scandal, it formed a task force to create international guidelines covering the use of foreign contract labor. Scratch deeper and you learn the guidelines included such proposed terms as "Contractors will be favored who schedule employees to work 60 hours or less a week." Sixty hours? Explained Levi's: they don't want to "impose" U.S. values (the 40-hour week) on foreign businesspeople. Well, you can't accuse Levis of being "politically correct." That attitude continues, despite pressure to improve the guidelines and enact some changes.

Establishing global guidelines for eliminating sweatshops goes back to a special presidential task force in 1997, which established a workplace code. *Sweatshop Watch*, a San Francisco newsletter, says the code institutionalizes indecent wages and inhumane hours. A later scheme, launched by Avon, Eddie Bauer and Toys "R" Us, provided for sufficient wages and a 48-hour week; but its auditing system allows for violations to be masked, since the companies paid the auditors. Other problems continue.

Fuerza Unida set a shining example for other workers to expose the crimes of the garment industry and its sweatshops. In the years since that day in January 1990 when managers at the South Zarzamora plant announced the imminent close-down and Fuerza Unida was formed, thousands more garment workers have gone into action. Kathy Lee Gifford's well-publicized admissions of abusive practices by her manufacturers, scandals about Nike plants in Indonesia and revelations of abuses by Guess? and other companies have shed light on sweatshop conditions as never before. The slave conditions imposed on Thai and Latina garment workers, who were forbidden to leave a guarded compound where they worked from 7 a.m. to midnight for a contractor in a Los Angeles apartment complex, became infamous in 1995.

At times it seems as though there is no limit to the horrors that can surface. To give one final example: a Levi's contractor in Indonesia that had been approved by a company inspector was found to be strip-searching female workers to determine whether they really were menstruating, as they claimed, and thus entitled to a day off with pay under Muslim law. Levi's canceled the contract, but the problem remains: it took complaints by workers to an Indonesian rights commission to bring out the truth.

Whether they win any specific demands from Levi's, Fuerza Unida can take a certain satisfaction from the fact that five workers at Levi Strauss plants in El Paso, Texas (where Levi's is the city's largest employer), won $10 million in punitive damages in September 1997. A jury found Levi's guilty of "willful and malicious" discrimination against them. The five Latina/o workers, who suffered carpal tunnel syndrome and other job-related injuries, had been in a re-entry program supposedly to learn less taxing work. They testified that while in the program they were exposed to humiliation and harassment; their wages had been cut, sometimes in half; they received almost no training but were assigned to clean bathrooms; and Levi's said their injuries "were in their head." (*San Francisco Examiner*, September 5 and 10, 1997.) A total of 110 El Paso workers have sued Levi's, stating that the re-entry programs were created to get rid of employees receiving workers' compensation for job-related injuries.

Fuerza Unida members are not the first garment workers to put their lives on the line for social and economic justice. Their roots include struggles as old as the shirtwaist strikers of New York in the early 1900s. Latina garment workers can look back to the Farah pants strike of 1972–74 in Texas, and Latina workers in general have a militant history throughout this century: in the cotton industry, pecan shelling, tortilla production and other fields.

Fuerza Unida has also met the difficult challenge of how to keep going. It has created a center for low-income women and continued its earlier programs, as well as teaching grassroots organizing, building leadership and business skills for women, and teaching them workers' and civil rights. With its overall goal of empowering working-class women and women of color, Fuerza Unida has grown to be an invaluable resource in that Texas city named for the patron saint of the poor.

Outside Texas, Fuerza Unida formed a historic alliance with Asian Immigrant Women Advocates (AIWA) in Oakland, California. This organization conducted a long fight against Jessica McClintock, manufacturer of expensive dresses for weddings and parties. She had refused to accept responsibility for wages owed the workers by a subcontractor who went out of business. After years of struggle, AIWA—with support from Fuerza Unida and many others—won a significant, precedent-setting victory. AIWA and Fuerza Unida stand together as an example of what cross-racial solidarity can be.

Internally, Fuerza Unida carried out a reorganization with stimulating results. Today, many former members who left are coming back, and new people have joined. At the risk of sounding ridiculous, let me just say that to converse with a Fuerza Unida stalwart like co-coordinator Petra Mata is to be left with the thought: she sounds so *happy*. How can that be, unless she loves her life of energizing struggle?—as she should.

She and her sisters in this long fight know they can already count on a place in history for creating a consciousness of garment-worker exploitation that was not there before. Fuerza Unida has helped put on the map one of the major issues facing labor today, a major issue facing women and a major issue facing people of color all over the globe. It has brought us all that much closer to justice. *La mujer luchando, el mundo transformando.*

chapter eleven

WALKING WITH CÉSAR

It was late at night, and I was driving back to San Francisco from the funeral for César Chávez in Delano, California, and thinking about an unforgettable day. Would it bring more widespread recognition of his work, of Raza struggles, of the farmworkers?

When César died in his sleep at the age of 66 on April 22, 1993, most people in the United States were unaware that his life had set an unsurpassed example of persistent struggle for human rights, day after day, week after week, year after year. Most people would not understand, for example, why César Chávez was compared to Gandhi and Martin Luther King Jr. by more than one speaker at the April 29 funeral, including Rep. Ron Dellums, who said: "César stands with the giants of this planet as an advocate of nonviolence as a way to challenge the powerful." Most people shamefully underestimated a heroic figure in the twentieth-century struggle for social justice, and an extraordinary labor leader.

César Chávez (pronounced "CHA-vez") died long after the height of the struggle he led. The farmworker cause, like the entire Chicano movement, had been forced to spend much energy defending its small gains of the 1960s. Though César himself never slowed down, the United Farm Workers (UFW) union did. The big growers had managed to undo many UFW contracts won after great struggle, and membership had declined. But the 35,000 people who marched three miles through Delano to the funeral service on April 29 carried a different message. Their presence was an outpouring of respect to Chávez. It also said that in death he had rekindled an idealistic energy that had gone out of style in the larger society—and among many progressive people—somewhere during the last 20 years. The heart of that idealism is the struggle for social justice as a moral imperative, together with a belief in the possibility of achieving significant social change regardless of setbacks.

The march reminded us that at one time 17 million Americans boycotted grapes not picked by unionized farmworkers. In response, the Pentagon bought almost half a million pounds of the fruit for the troops in Vietnam, which helped to keep the growers going. But even that could not break the boycott's power, and finally the growers yielded. *La Causa* was a movement and it could move mountains. Throughout the April 29 events you could feel a celebration of people power and of a goal that was social justice, not just a piece of the American pie or even some vague, sanitized "empowerment."

Would the sense of a rekindled idealism last, I remember wondering. Would it reinvigorate the California farmworkers' struggle, which faces grave problems today? Would it help bring us out of a very cold time? Or was it just the "last gasp of a bygone 1960s-type politics," as one cynical observer said?

A powerful legacy exists to answer that last question with a loud No. For the farmworkers and their supporters, Chávez had planted a dream in people's hearts that will live on. A whole generation of activists had emerged from the grape and lettuce boycotts, from picketing, from working on the UFW newspaper *El Malcriado*. Chicanos went to law school in the 1960s specifically to defend the farmworker cause when they graduated. Thousands did things one would have thought impossible. I remember cheerfully asking a New York liquor store owner—on New Year's Eve!—please not to sell certain wines.

That generation, and new ones in the making, would not go away.

On the march people saw friends after 20 years apart, and a major activity was peering at a nearby face, then asking, "Didn't we meet ...?" Countless reunions took place. A magical feeling of knowing all 35,000 people present, of having crossed paths at one time or another, created that sense of community that makes social struggle beautiful. The reason was obvious to my friend María Elena: "César grounded us with the land and the people, and there are no stronger forces."

The night before, 10,000 people had paid their respects to César at an all-night wake that moved even my most anti-Catholic friends; the next day's march was for celebrating his life and the farmworkers struggle that he led. The marchers seemed mostly older farmworkers—Mexican and Filipino—plus a large number of African Americans (many from unions), celebrities and other supporters. Many of the politicians and entertainers were scattered through the crowd, not all gathered at the front in VIP formation. There was former Gov. Jerry Brown hiking along, actor Cheech Marin in a cap with the world printed on it, and Dellums. A splendidly costumed Aztec dance group from San Francisco performed in bare feet on the asphalt road all the way, while members of the American Indian Movement sang and drummed.

In a beautiful condolence to Chávez' widow, Helen, thousands of people carried white gladiolas, her favorite flower. Thousands more carried the UFW's black eagle flag. And of the many images from that march, none is more haunting than the elementary school we passed where grinning, shouting children of almost every color had lined up at the fence facing the street. Waving UFW flags, conversing with passing marchers, really connecting with the adults, these kids knew their chants and slogans. *"¡Sí se puede!"*—"We can do it!"—they shouted, and behind them those words had also been painted big on the school wall. *"Gracias, César,"* they called out, echoing a sweetly Mexican theme of the day.

So, yes, a nostalgic "last gasp" may be at work in creating the sense of a reinvigorated idealism. But something else could be happening with youth, especially Latino youth. A striking number marched in Delano; the next day in San Francisco lots of young Latinos and also whites could be seen at a lively, noisy Safeway picket line ("Boycott grapes!"). "If some of them weren't gangbangers, they could have been," one picketer noted. Even if the young Latinos knew little of farmworkers or Chávez, even though many at a San Francisco high school originally thought it was the boxer Julio César Chávez who had died, they knew this was a prideful struggle of their community in the hot present.

"I think César died to wake us up," one farmworker told UFW vice-president Dolores Huerta.

But the whole country still has to wake up. After Chávez' death, people in towns and cities all over the Southwest campaigned to rename schools, libraries, streets and other public institutions for him. Renaming a San Francisco elementary school in the city's largely Latino Mission District was no problem. When the campaign began to rename a neighborhood street for the labor leader, a nasty opposition campaign was organized along that street where it ran through a mostly Anglo neighborhood. A new street was chosen; this time the campaign succeeded, but the city still hasn't changed the major signs. The narrow, racist message is unavoidable: the Latinos can honor Chávez if they want, but he's no national hero. "It would spoil the atmosphere of my neighborhood to have the street named for him," said one letter of protest.

The struggle for justice continues, in death as in life.

Walking with César's Strengths

As we marched on April 29 through flat, dusty farmland and past almond orchards, we were walking with Chávez' strengths. We walked with someone who fought for 40 years to gain labor rights and human rights for the most disenfranchised and impoverished workers in the United States. Under his leadership, they ceased to be faceless immigrants whom the dominant society dismissed as subhuman, disposable. Never again would the public be so unaware of farmworker poverty and exploitation.

We also walked with the struggling farmworker that César was himself, born in 1927 to a Chicano family that lost its Arizona farm during the Depression. To the end of his life he lived on about $5,000 a year, free from material corruption like few labor or movement leaders in modern times. The man's own frugality and self-sacrifice made it easier for so many people to join the UFW staff and work countless hours for a salary that was originally $5 a week (rising to $20 by the mid-1980s) plus $20 for food.

His prolonged fasts combined with a relentless work schedule made him a martyr to his *causa*.

We walked with a fighter who, as a very hoarse Dolores Huerta said in her strong funeral statement, did not know the word "quit." Under César's leadership the farmworkers won union recognition for the first time in U.S. history. A few years later, after a major victory against grape growers in 1970, California adopted the Agricultural Labor Relations Act that established collective bargaining for farmworkers.

Over the years, the union improved working conditions for millions of workers long accustomed to expect no bathrooms, drinking water or other basics on the job. The growers invited the Teamsters to organize farmworkers, and a new battle started that ended when the Teamsters made a truce with the UFW in 1977. Then the growers launched new attacks. Most recently Chávez was fighting a $5.4 million damage judgment won by a big grower against the UFW for waging a boycott judged illegal. On the day of his death in San Luis, Arizona, he had testified in the union's appeal against this potentially fatal blow.

During 12 years of reactionary rule in the United States, the union had lost much of its strength and membership. By the mid-1980s, for example, only 3 percent of all California grapes were union-grown. Enemies of the UFW include some of the most powerful forces and politicians in this country. Among them was President Nixon, who enjoyed strong support from big growers and reciprocated by getting laws passed favorable to them. Others were then-Governor Ronald Reagan, who in effect declared open season on farmworkers, and, later, Gov. George Deukmeijan, who stacked the Agricultural Labor Relations Board with his ilk.

Meanwhile the big growers have not been renewing contracts. They have been hiring labor in ways that circumvent the UFW, aided in this by the huge pool of totally vulnerable, often undocumented immigrating workers. "The growers are more powerful than ever, and just as vicious," commented a former farmworker who went on to college and UFW support work.

We need to remember these realities. Many people do not know that UFW members have faced frequent physical attacks by the big growers' goons, scabs and friends on the police force or at the courthouse. The union has had five martyrs, farmworkers murdered in the struggle over the years: from 1973, when Nagi Daifullah, a young Arab, and 60-year-old Juan de La Cruz were killed within days of each other, to 1983, when René López was shot in the head.

So we walked with the stubborn fighting spirit of Chávez, as seen in those long fasts he endured to call moral attention to the farmworkers' struggle. We also walked with his organizing genius and creativity. César originally worked for Saul Alinsky's Community Service Organization, trained by Fred Ross. On the march, longtime UFW staff members told stories about how César could go into an unfamiliar town and mobilize people. Another union leader noted how César built a national coalition of labor, church, community people and college students around an understanding that the UFW was fighting for justice as a social principle, for human rights and respect.

Dolores Huerta recounted a telling anecdote of how César, then beginning to organize, sent her out to collect $3.50 in union dues from farmworkers at home. She returned saying she couldn't demand that money from people living on dirt floors, with orange crates for furniture. "Go back and get it," he told her. "If they don't pay that $3.50, they'll never get out of poverty." He knew that no dues meant no commitment, no faith and ultimately no fighting union.

Walking with the Shadows

We also walked through Delano with the other side of those strengths, the shadows that accompany any light. United Farm Workers supporters remember mistaken politics and positions on various issues, which were sometimes, though not always, corrected later. These include a distrust of leftist agendas and fear of communist infiltration that may have been aimed at unprincipled, opportunist staffers but sometimes ended up hurting the principled. Also, the pressure to balance movement politics with being a trade union and an AFL-CIO affiliate inevitably generated contradictions. Criticism can be heard about a lack of internal democracy and the fact that César, a brilliant organizer, did less well when he shifted in later years to being more of an administrator. One boycott director who personally experienced some of these problems told me, "Nobody should be in charge 25–30 years. It's deadly for everyone involved, no matter how good the leader."

The criticisms cannot negate basic truths about César: he never sold out, he was never bought off and he never gave up in his profound commitment to *los de abajo*—the underdogs. But as the union searches for new leadership and restructures, it needs to learn from past mistakes—to see what lessons they hold about how to build an organization and then apply those lessons, as my boycott director friend said. Learning from mistakes includes opening the past to fearless analysis, a process that doesn't come easy but could be the most valuable tribute of all to César Chávez. The UFW's long history has much to teach us all.

<<< >>>

When the funeral march reached the old union headquarters in Forty Acres, people filled the space inside two gigantic tents, red, white and green like the Mexican flag. The funeral program—called a memorial celebration—offered a lengthy mass, mariachis, song, poetry, performers and tributes from a spokesperson for Bill Clinton, Joe Kennedy, Dellums, Jesse Jackson, Edward James Olmos and many others. Comedian Paul Rodríguez won a vigorous cheer from the mixed crowd when he talked about the rising population of Latinos and added, "That doesn't mean competing with other people—it's awful when Black and brown kids fight each other." The program included no one speaking as an ordinary farmworker, too few women and too many dignitaries making sure to tell about meeting César. Yet these problems could not break the mood of celebratory dignity.

Several speakers, including Olmos and the influential black California politician Willie Brown (now mayor of San Francisco), called for a national holiday named after César. Celebrated with heart and mind, César Chávez Day could be an educational tool. It could help to break the deadlock of ignorance, indifference and even hostility of many people, especially in the eastern United States, toward Mexicans, agriculture and California in general.

The second call of the memorial celebration for César was to strengthen the campaign to end the use of deadly pesticides like Captan, Phosdrin and Parathion that attack the central nervous system. Spraying with these has created places like "Cancer Alley" near McFarlane, California, where farmworker family babies are being born deformed and children develop leukemia and cancer at an abnormal rate. César fasted for 35 days in 1988 to call attention to these deadly conditions. One-fifth of the nation's farmworkers are children; too many are dying or sick from poisons in the fields. To support this campaign, the call went out for a renewed grape boycott.

When César died, farmworkers were struggling not only in California but in other parts of the country as well. Other farmworker leaders have shown long-lasting commitment. In the Midwest, the 25-year-old Farm Labor Organizing Committee (FLOC) led by Baldemar Velásquez continues its struggle for the right to organize and other basic labor rights. In 1990, FLOC used collective bargaining to end sharecropping for the first time in U.S. history, at 52 farms. Also that year, Mexican agricultural workers of the Pineros Campesinos Unidos del Noroeste (Northwest Treeplanters and Farmworkers United, PCUN) in Oregon forced growers to pay the minimum wage. On March 31, 1998, PCUN signed the first collective bargaining agreement with a grower in the history of Oregon. Latinos, Haitians and other nationalities have come together in the Farmworkers Association of Central Florida. In New Jersey, Puerto Ricans, Mexicans and Cambodians formed the Comité de Apoyo de los Trabajadores Agrícolas.

There are many heroic people out here. A former staffer on the march spoke true words that day: "César was one of those pebbles that land in the water and set off ripples of hope." The march itself said to the powers that be: never underestimate the power of the people—it can pop up just when you think all's quiet.

Postscript

And so it did. The years since César's death have seen a striking resurgence of successes by the UFW under its new president, Arturo S. Rodríguez, who committed the union to new organizing drives. Having reached a low of about 15,000 members in 1993, it added 5,000 new ones within three years. It won 13 straight union representation elections during the same period. Still ahead was a reversal of nearly 12 years of pro-grower actions by the Agricultural Labor Relations Board, dominated by Republican appointees.

Nevertheless, by 1997, farmworker wages had fallen 20 percent (even more in California) during the previous two decades, after accounting for inflation *(New York Times,* March 3, 1997). Working conditions had improved somewhat, thanks to a long, long struggle, but the big growers still did not want to talk wages and such facts as: only about eight cents of the cost of a head of lettuce that retails for $1 goes to the workers, so a 25 percent wage increase would raise the labor cost for each head only two cents (from eight to ten).

The UFW launched an organizing campaign in Watsonville, California, strawberry capital of the world, in 1996. It became the biggest organizing campaign in the nation, of some of the most exploited workers in the nation: an estimated 20,000 strawberry pickers laboring by hand (the work cannot be mechanized) for a $600-million-a-year industry. Along with the union drive, the UFW charged the growers with exposing workers to methyl, a cancer-causing fungicide, with support from many environmental groups.

A high point of the organizing effort came on April 13, 1997, with a march through Watsonville that brought at least 30,000 and possibly 50,000 participants. Labor from all over the country and many Latino students demonstrated with thousands of others, all in bright colors and high spirits. Within two months, the biggest strawberry grower, Gargiulo, had agreed to union elections, a tremendous victory. Gargiulo (now known as Coastal Berry) also agreed both to pay back wages to hundreds of workers who had been forced to work unpaid before their shifts began and to hire back workers who had been blacklisted for union organizing.

The UFW kept up its pressure, sending organizers to Mexico to inform potential migrant workers about the struggle in California before they later went north. Meanwhile, a company union was established that won the July 1998 election. The UFW charged intimidation, strawberry workers walked out in a wildcat strike, and the fierce struggle continued.

Once again we can see, hear, and feel how the spirit of César Chávez and so many workers lives on today in all its stubborn beauty. Problems remain, both inside and outside. But when it comes to a renaissance of commitment at the grassroots level, that spirit soars like the farmworker eagle itself.

chapter twelve

WHEN PEOPLE OF COLOR ARE AN ENDANGERED SPECIES

 The San Jose parish church in Albuquerque, New Mexico, filled as people gathered to hear what the city councilors, county commissioners and other officials would say. The audience was mostly residents of Mountainview, a low-income Chicano neighborhood, who had grown tired of having dangerous chemicals, bad smells and pollution dumped on them. They were angry at the military, the most likely source of poisons in their drinking water for the past 25 years. They were angry that the city, which had already put a smelly sewage plant within a mile of their homes, now planned to locate a garbage transfer station in their midst. Tonight they planned to speak out.

Facing the people, officials in jackets and ties sat at a table covered by a white cloth. The mayor of Albuquerque had been invited but did not come, with no regrets or reason given. A hand-lettered sign on the table said "Mayor Louis Saavedra"; nobody sat behind it. In the mayor's place was a large, neatly trussed turkey—very bare, very white, very visible.

The director of Albuquerque's Solid Waste Management Department rose to speak, looking unhappy. "It's too bad this kind of disrespect ..." he told the crowd, inclining his head slightly toward the turkey. But Mountainview's people had seen their very lives treated with disrespect for years. One resident watched her six-month-old son almost die in her arms after drinking formula made with tap water. A few days before, the area had to be evacuated because of a chlorine leak.

So nobody moved the turkey. It just sat there, through the whole meeting.

That was a while ago. Today people are fighting bigger turkeys, like the billion-dollar computer giant Intel. But the same organization with the same defiant spirit has been in the forefront. It's quite a story.

<<< >>>

For decades, radioactive uranium tailings, lead and chlorine poisoning, asbestos and pesticides have sickened and killed untold numbers of Latinos, African Americans, Native Americans, and other people of color. Yet no one called it environmental racism. The "environment" had long been defined by the dominant society as flora and fauna that white men worried about conserving. Then, in 1982, officials decided to put a PCB disposal site only 15 feet above the water table (instead of the 50 feet generally required) in Warren County, North Carolina—whose residents were 60 percent Black and 4 percent Native American. A series of protests, with more than 500 people arrested, failed to stop the PCB dump.

Soon after, a General Accounting Office survey confirmed the coincidence of hazardous-waste landfills and poor Black communities in the southeastern United States. In 1987 a much broader study, "Toxic Wastes and Race in the United States," was prepared by the United Church of Christ's Commission on Racial Justice, then under Ben Chavis Jr. After examining 25 cities, the report found "a striking relationship" between the location of commercial hazardous wastes dumps and the racial identity of nearby residents. Class also played an important role—the victims were almost always poor or working-class, and included many whites—but "race still proved to be more significant." Hair-raising examples abounded, such as:

- The nation's biggest hazardous-waste landfill, which serves 45 states plus several foreign countries, was located in Emelle, Alabama (Sumter County)—78.9 percent black.

- The predominantly African-American and Latino South Side of Chicago had the greatest concentration of hazardous-waste sites in the nation.

- In Houston, Texas, six of the eight municipal incinerators and all five municipal landfills were located in predominantly African-American neighborhoods.

And that is not to mention the poisoning of Diné (Navajo) Indians by uranium mining, or the 300,000 cases of pesticide-related illness among Latino farmworkers, or the widespread pollution of Puerto Rico, or the massive amount of radiation illness in numerous Pacific islands ruled by the United States. All those people enjoyed less federal protection than the blunt-nose leopard lizard (admittedly a rare creature).

How to explain this? Poor people and those of color have historically been driven into the worst jobs in agribusiness and heavy industry; they often end up living in areas of heavy pollution. Areas where residents do not appear to have a high degree of political clout are often preferred for hazardous- or uncontrolled-waste facilities. Further, as Rev. Leon White, a prime organizer of the Warren County, North Carolina, protests, said: "As long as there are poor and minority areas to dump on, corporate America won't be serious about finding alternatives to the way toxic materials are produced and managed." The pattern of environmental racism is sustained by economic extortion—a process of convincing depressed, often non-white communities that they should accept the presence of hazardous-waste landfills and poisonous industries because of the jobs that come with them. When pollution shows up, the companies threaten plant shutdowns or cutbacks to cover the cost of cleanup.

Recognition of environmental racism and its tactics has been a long time coming. An organization that did much to pave the way in the 1980s was the SouthWest Organizing Project (SWOP) of Albuquerque, New Mexico. Here is a state where the nuclear energy cycle runs its complete course, from uranium mining to radioactive waste, leaving a full array of contamination. It is a state where the economy remains overwhelmingly dependent on the federal government, especially the military, whose needs usually go unquestioned no matter how much environmental damage it does. But it is also a state with a majority population of color and a long history of Chicano-Indian resistance to European incursion. Those conditions, among others, make New Mexico a likely battleground for the struggle against environmental racism.

Born in 1981 and funded primarily by church groups at that time, SWOP is a multiracial, multi-issue community organization working "to empower the disenfranchised in the Southwest to realize social, racial, and economic justice." Its main founder was Richard Moore, a community activist of Puerto Rican background whose work began with the Chicano movement of the 1960s and included leading the militant Black Beret Organization in Albuquerque. Moore and activist Jeanne Gauna served as SWOP's first co-directors. SWOP became involved in fighting pollution when it started organizing in the Sawmill barrio of Albuquerque in 1984 and heard families complain of health problems they attributed to a particle-board company in the area. Ponderosa Products Inc. was polluting the groundwater, generating sawdust everywhere, and making intolerable noise.

In the struggle that followed, and the victory it produced, we can see key aspects of SWOP's general strategy.

A first, basic goal was to demystify policymaking. "Have you ever wondered how decisions are made as to which streets get paved, how our community is zoned, or who receives loans to purchase homes? Who plans the way our neighborhood is developed? Everyone, it seems, makes plans for our community except sawmill area residents!" Those were the headlines—in both English and Spanish—on one of many leaflets. They set the tone for a process that included door-to-door surveys of residents' complaints; community meetings to inform people about the technical and legal aspects of the struggle; setting up a neighborhood organization (in this case, the Sawmill Advisory Council); and voter registration so that residents could hold elected officials accountable.

In 1987 Ponderosa Products finally signed an agreement to pump out bad water and reduce noise emission. That document stands as the first urban cleanup agreement between industry, government and the community in New Mexico—and probably in the whole Southwest. Then the Mountainview-San Jose area of Albuquerque became a major focus of SWOP activism. For years its problem of bad well water remained a mystery. Slowly but surely the finger pointed increasingly at Kirtland Air Force Base as the source of nitrate/nitroglycerin contamination. Again SWOP surveyed, educated and helped set up a local body, the Mountainview Advisory Council, in 1987.

Above all, SWOP helped combat the military's efforts to exclude affected residents from the investigation of Kirtland. As usual the generals preferred to investigate themselves. Every time one commanding officer seemed to agree to let residents participate, he was replaced by a new face; at least five commanding officers came and went. Finally Kirtland signed a contract to allow community participation, as did the federal EPA, the state Environment Improvement Division, and the Mountainview Advisory Council. SWOP refrained from signing until February 22, 1991, in order to assure Kirtland's agreement on a large public ceremony to formalize the agreement. There would be no deals behind closed doors.

The struggle against environmental racism became linked with labor struggle in 1990 when 70 workers went on strike at the Montana de Fibra fiberboard plant in Las Vegas, New Mexico. The workers, routinely exposed to dangerous levels of formaldehyde and other poisonous chemicals, demanded better wages and working conditions. Father Bill Sanchez, a courageous local priest, called for help, and SWOP came with information, experience and bodies. But it stayed to learn.

Given an ultimatum by the company to return to work, the Las Vegas strikers refused: "We don't want the damn jobs back." In one of the poorest areas of a very poor state, where few jobs pay the Montana de Fibra top salary of $6 an hour, this refusal was extraordinary. Richard Moore, then co-director of SWOP, explained the workers' response by the fact that they had become too knowledgeable about the deadly chemicals they saw being dumped behind the factory and contaminating the water. "They were not the same people as when they went on strike," he said. Under difficult conditions, they stood up to economic blackmail.

SWOP has long been aware that in New Mexico people need jobs more than anything else, that it has to be proactive and can't just denounce industry. For this reason SWOP worked to make BetaWest Properties, a developer in Albuquerque, comply with conditions attached to a $10 million federal urban development grant that required creating 1,582 jobs with half of them going to people of color and 75 percent to people of low-to-moderate income. "A climate has been created in this city where people will call industry on its shit," Moore commented. "The reason we've had success, when we've had it, is our multi-issue approach," he added. Exposing the problems and educating the public has been essential in all of SWOP's efforts. For example, SWOP and the National Council of Churches' Eco-Justice Task Force co-sponsored hearings in 1989 where a dozen New Mexicans and borderland Mexicans told personal stories of being sickened in their workplaces. Unforgettable testimony came from Virginia Candelaria, one of many workers exposed to poisonous solvents and wastes in Albuquerque's General Telephone and Electronics (GTE) plant. Candelaria suffered severe damage to her central nervous system after nine years of cleaning circuit boards. Other women had children with birth defects, and eventually 465 workers filed suit. When asked if GTE had changed the process, Candelaria had difficulty speaking; her attorney replied for her, "Most of the dangerous processes, most of the dangerous chemicals, have been moved to Juárez, Mexico. There is a plant across the border now." All too often such transfers have been the so-called solution to a pollution problem.

As Virginia Candelaria's testimony indicated, women workers of color are especially vulnerable to contamination. For example, women in the high-tech industry have been poisoned by chemicals they use in producing equipment for the military; because such equipment is manufactured in parts, for future assembly, they often do not know what they are actually making. This and other problems make it difficult to establish the links in the process. But at least one worker at Motorola in Albuquerque had been identified by early 1991 as suffering from exposure to fumes from solvents used in producing weapons components. In another case, a woman worker at Honeywell was given a poisonous fluid to clean computer chip boards for the instrument panels of fighter planes.

Those who attended the hearings where Candelaria spoke were taken on tours to see the contamination by Albuquerque paint factories, gas refineries, sewage treatment centers and a dog food factory where unused animal parts were heaped outdoors to rot. It became nauseously evident that communities inhabited by people of color are targeted for toxin-producing industries and facilities that wouldn't be allowed in other neighborhoods. For people of color, then, environmental issues are issues of social, economic and racial justice.

A myth exists that people of color don't care about the environment because they are too concerned with mere survival. If anything, their survival is an environmental issue. "This may not be traditional environmentalism, but it's the kind that has concerned people of color for centuries," Richard Moore commented in an interview. "Some says there is more awareness now among people of color about environmental problems. But there was plenty before. In 1968, 1970, we marched—Brown Berets and Black Berets, with Mexican flags flying—against that sewage plant in Mountainview. In Kansas City, in the 1960s and 1970s, Brown Berets marched against a slaughterhouse. So it is not new for Latinos to be concerned.

"The problem is, environmentalists don't see those problems as environmental issues. That's because they don't live in our neighborhoods. At any community meeting, just ask, 'How many people here have lived near a chemical plant? Please stand up.' Then ask, 'How many have lived near a slaughterhouse?' Then, 'How many have lived near a sewage plant?' And pretty soon everybody in the room will be standing. We are getting past the perception of environmentalism as a middle-class, white movement that excludes the human factor."

SWOP became widely known when it took on ten major U.S. environmental organizations in March 1990. It sent them a sharply critical letter signed by more than 100 community activists charging "a clear lack of accountability ... toward Third World communities." The criticisms ranged from the Sierra Club's and the Wilderness Society's support of the creation of a tourist-attracting national monument on sacred Native American land, to the almost total lack of people of color in the Big Ten's decision-making positions.

Nine of the Big Ten environmental organizations have committed themselves to participating in dialogue. A first-time "National Minority Environmental Leadership Summit" meeting was convened by the United Church of Christ's Commission for Racial Justice in October 1991 in Washington, D.C. This historic gathering, which the SWOP letter helped stimulate, aimed to create a national agenda focused on race, poverty and the environment, with a view to diversifying the policies of mainline environmental organizations.

SWOP and other groups have also struggled against the way environmental and other advocacy organizations exclude the people for whom they supposedly advocate. Such paternalism can be found all over Las Americas, especially toward the millions of indigenous peoples who believe that recognition of their land claims and lifestyle models is crucial to defending the biosphere.

At home in Albuquerque, SWOP has recognized the primacy of Native American land rights, often overlooked by Chicano activists pressing the land claims of their own people. It also has an international program formulated over the years that ranges from adoption of a Nicaraguan child-development center to activism against U.S. policy in the Persian Gulf and support for the Zapatistas in Chiapas.

SWOP's growth is closely linked to another kind of growth: the out-of-control expansion of the Albuquerque metropolitan area, which has become a major international production center for the electronics industry over the past 25 years. Big companies have demanded more and more water—that vital resource, all the more precious in a state composed primarily of desert. Among them stands the Intel Corporation, which reported profits of almost $6.95 billion on sales of $25 billion in 1997 (*New York Times,* March 27, 1998) and controls 85 percent of the world market in chips for personal computers.

Intel opened its first factory in Albuquerque in 1982 and expanded its facilities to the point that managers said the New Mexico "fabs" (chip-making factories) generated 70 percent of Intel's profits. By 1992 it was using three million gallons of water a day for production (about 3,400 acre-feet per year). In 1995 Intel gave public notice that it planned to purchase more than 2,000 acre-feet of water rights from large and small holders in Socorro County, 70 miles south of Albuquerque. With this purchase, the current owners would be prohibited from using the surface water and Intel could drill its own wells to obtain a cheaper supply of water for production use. The result would be to transfer water from its current, traditional role in agriculture to municipal and industrial use. The lure, as always, was the promise of jobs, to justify bleeding massive public subsidies and natural resources from a poor state.

SWOP has worked together with urban and rural-based social justice and water-user groups to block Intel's new move. "Once the tax breaks and the water dry up," said Jeanne Gauna, now co-director of SWOP with Michael Guerrero, "these electronics industries will leave, and leave us with major problems." In November 1997 a major victory was won when the state engineer denied the Intel request to transfer 1,148 acre-feet of water from Socorro County.

But the relentless drive for corporate expansion means such struggles will continue, although the Federal Trade Commission announced June 8, 1998 that it would sue Intel for violating anti-trust laws. At the same time, New Mexico's Anglo population has been increasing steadily, leading the Republican Party to have hopes of taking over some traditionally Democratic towns like Santa Fe. Reactionary forces have been gaining on many fronts; for example, in 1998 bilingual education came under attack although New Mexico is officially a tri-cultural state where any "English Only" law would be prohibited by the state constitution. In the current, nationwide reactionary age, when Manifest Destiny rides again, the need is greater than ever for effective community organizing everywhere—and cooperation between organizations.

Today the turkeys are fatter and whiter than ever. But the people are smarter, faster and harder to fool. Watch out, all you corporate gobblers.

chapter thirteen

WEAVING A NET THAT WORKS

It was lunchtime in a dusty barrio near Tijuana, Mexico, where the Southwest Network for Environmental and Economic Justice (SNEEJ) had come to meet in July 1993. The schedule called for us to march to a transfer station for hazardous waste, one of many plants poisoning the area, and picket it. I asked how long the march would be. "Oh, very short," I was told. "It's only a quarter of a mile."

But the quarter of a mile was straight up.

That march to the top of a long steep hill could symbolize the challenges facing the Network as it has worked to build a binational movement led by people of color for social, racial and economic justice. The Network was formed in Albuquerque in April 1990 at a People of Color Regional Activist Dialogue on Environmental Justice initiated by the SouthWest Organizing Project (see "When People of Color Are an Endangered Species"). At the time, observers had said "it won't last a month, there are too many cultural and racial differences."

They were extremely wrong. By 1992 the Network embraced 70 grassroots organizations in six states, working together on such issues as lethal pesticides used in agriculture, dangerous chemicals in the high-tech industry, lead poisoning, and how these hazards affect communities of color. It brought together African-American, Asian/Pacific Island, Latino and Native American groups to develop a common agenda. As an organization of organizations, SNEEJ has always been more than a coalition. Intended to become multi-issue and permanent, it serves as a vehicle for sharing local strategies and victories as well as providing training and leadership development to its affiliates.

During its early years, the Network focused on consolidating its elected leadership (the Coordinating Council), formalizing membership and working on other aspects of organizational development. It held annual gatherings (and still does) where Network members evaluated past work and planned for the next year. Then came 1993, when 20 grassroots community, human rights and youth organizations from Mexico's border states attended the first cross-border Network gathering. That weekend in Tijuana/San Diego, you could see the dream of a binational Network beginning to come true. The next few years would show just how bold the dream is, and why Richard Moore insists on calling the Network "a *developing* binational organization." In short: we're not there yet.

By March 1998, when I attended a Coordinating Council meeting, SNEEJ had completed eight years studded with accomplishments. With a staff of six at its regional headquarters in Albuquerque, it had found ways to coordinate with more than 70 groups in six U.S. states plus three Mexican states (Baja California, Chihuahua and Coahuila) plus more than 15 tribes and other indigenous formations.

One of the most striking organizational accomplishments to me was the continuing reality of women's leadership. Even in its second year, the Network already had a core of strong women like Rose Augustine, a Chicana from Arizona; Patsy Oliver, an African-American woman in Texarkana, Texas; Odessa Ramirez, a Native American from Nevada; and, by the third year, several exceptional Asian American women like Pam Tau Lee and Pamela Chiang of California. The addition of working-class Mexican feminists from the *maquiladoras* has expanded the Network tradition of powerful female leadership. This can be seen in its revised "Mission Statement," which acquired a new emphasis on gender issues in 1997, and the proposal for a women's caucus at a 1998 Network meeting.

In its daily work, SNEEJ has taken on county, state and federal governments as well as industry, agribusiness and the military. It has won some amazing victories, starting with the Environmental Protection Agency (EPA). At a time when deregulation has become a global trend, SNEEJ has compelled the EPA to take regulation more seriously.

The Network's EPA Accountability Campaign was originally launched on July 31, 1991, with simultaneous demonstrations at EPA regional offices in Dallas, Denver and San Francisco. Each office received a copy of SNEEJ's long letter detailing many examples of EPA inaction or opposition in the face of environmental abuse harmful to people of color. The letter asked for several reports on EPA actions, a meeting between the EPA and the Network, and new policies to address past discrimination. I had the pleasure of seeing that letter delivered at an Albuquerque ceremony in which the EPA gave awards for "Environmental Excellence" to two companies known for contaminating water, as SNEEJ pointed out. The EPA representative on hand looked uncomfortable.

Eventually the EPA agreed to negotiate, sending numerous rep-
resentives to various meetings and visiting some of the affected areas
reported by the Network. Richard Moore's testimony before a congressional committee on a children's cancer cluster resulting from
pesticide spraying in California had added to the pressure. So did the
publicity about children in the Brownsville, Texas, border area being
born with all or parts of their brains missing as a result of industrial
pollutants. Throughout the negotiations, the Network stood firm on
two tactical principles: meeting with EPA administrators, not public
relations mouthpieces, and direct representation of the affected communities—no brokering.

Since then, Network-led actions have forced the EPA and other
federal bodies to begin addressing environmental justice concerns all
over the Southwest. SNEEJ has won major victories, including a dramatic increase in the enforcement of EPA regulations in communities
of color and an overhaul of U.S. environmental policy. On the national level, the Network played a key role in organizing an ongoing
dialogue between EPA leadership under both Bush and Clinton and
environmental justice organizations. It compelled EPA visits to 18
contaminated sites in the Southwest. With Clinton's election, SNEEJ
was promised participation in his transition team; when later shut out,
it managed through colleagues to help assure that environmental and
economic justice concerns would be heard. Such efforts led to Clinton's 1994 Presidential Executive Order No. 12898 on Environmental
Justice, issued to all federal agencies. Also, the National Environmental Justice Advisory Committee to the EPA, chaired by Richard
Moore, was established as a vehicle to ensure an official voice for
Network and other grassroots organizations.

On the local and regional level, the EPA campaign has racked
up too many accomplishments to list here. Just to suggest their range,
we can recall that the Network helped stop the world's largest toxic
waste disposal company from placing an incinerator in Kettleman
City, California (95 percent Latino). It helped pave the way for the Is-
leta Indian Pueblo of New Mexico to win formal recognition by the
EPA as a state, which allowed the pueblo to develop precedent-setting regulations over water usage by cities, industries and federal facilities. It pressed for the fining (and later closure) of a southern
Arizona recycling facility responsible for releasing dangerous levels
of chemicals into nearby communities. And when the EPA stepped up
its efforts to make Chevron abate emissions from a plant in the primarily Black/Laotian community of Richmond, California, that was

in no small way thanks to the Network; a $5 million grant for community programs and worker training in Richmond also resulted. Today the EPA campaign has somewhat shifted its aim to the state environmental agencies. The federal EPA has institutionalized its recognition of environmental racism to an important degree, as a result of efforts by the Network and other forces, but not the state bodies. Recently, state governments have been fiercely opposing lawsuits based on Title VI of the 1964 Civil Rights Act that say locating hazardous waste facilities near communities of color is racial discrimination. Many giant corporations, with good friends in state government, see use of Title VI as a serious threat to their freedom to pollute—which it is. In 1998, this became the latest battlefront for SNEEJ in its EPA campaign.

Among the Network's other efforts, the Sovereignty/Dumping on Native Lands Campaign stands out as a rare example of joint work by Native Americans with people of color (a term many indigenous people do not use to describe themselves). It began as an internal education project of the Network but has become increasingly external, with such actions as supporting the Western Shoshone fight to stop missile testing in Nevada; helping Diné (Navajo) groups seeking to end mining by Peabody Coal at Black Mesa; and working with the Havasupai people, who live at the bottom of the Grand Canyon, in their struggle against uranium mining.

In 1998, José Matus became one of two Sovereignty campaign chairs. He represents the Alianza Indígena Sin Fronteras (Indigenous Alliance Without Borders) in which four border nations—the Yaqui, Tohono O'odham, Kickapoo, and Cocopah—work together on human rights abuses, border-crossing issues, land claims and preservation of their heritage. Over the years SNEEJ has also developed working relations with the Indigenous Environmental Network, one of several environmental justice networks that address the needs of particular communities.

The Network's Youth Leadership Development Campaign, which is internal to the Network, has established an internship program; held several trainings that focused on organizing and leadership skills; and ensured the participation of hundreds of youth from affiliate and guest organizations. For all the talk in progressive movements about involving youth, SNEEJ seems to be one place where this really happens. Young people have been integrated in its decision-making and leadership. The Network's ongoing commitment to strengthen youth involvement is reflected in the 1997 addition to its mission statement of "generational injustices" as another target. At the March 1998 Coordinating Council meeting, 21-year-old "Che" Lopez sat at the table as an equal, with no problems in presenting his ideas; at the end of that meeting he announced his plan to run for City Council back home in Hondo, Texas.

The Border Justice Campaign has been growing steadily in its efforts to pressure government and private industry to provide safe working and living conditions in areas around the twin plant industries found in the U.S.-Mexico borderlands. Since 1993, it has convened meetings of representatives from many grassroots organizations on both sides of the border to discuss strategies and collaboration. It has been working closely with the Mexican Action Network Against NAFTA.

Struggling for justice on border issues often coincides with the Worker Justice Campaign. Worker justice involves a broad spread of groups such as Asian Immigrant Women Advocates in the Bay Area and Fuerza Unida in San Antonio. With the Network expanding into Mexico, the *maquiladoras* on the border have become increasingly central to both campaigns. Again and again, the Network has demonstrated the close connection between environmental issues and labor struggles. Network members often say that all worker issues are environmental issues, if we see environment as meaning lifestyle or, more precisely, the cycle of life.

In this spirit of linkage, SNEEJ began meeting with the Oil, Chemical and Atomic Workers Union (OCAW) at the union's invitation. Traditional environmentalist groups have often found themselves at serious odds with labor, hounded by the image of middle-class, privileged "tree-huggers" whose goals threaten the livelihood of hardworking loggers—or whatever the industry might be. "Green" picket lines outside a factory's doors have come to symbolize the clash. Conflict is seen as inevitable, with no possibility of compromise, and the notion that workers and environmentalists might form alliances against common enemies has rarely been articulated.

In 1997, OCAW adopted a resolution recognizing that it often has the same corporate opponents as the environmental justice movement, and is often working for the same goals. Therefore, said the resolution, OCAW would make every effort to form partnerships and coalitions with environmental justice groups around common goals. In February 1998, OCAW and SNEEJ signed a historic agreement based on "our collective desire to move a progressive agenda." In essence it said: let's talk before declaring war on each other. OCAW would try "to avert divisiveness beween communities and workers at facilities represented by OCAW by agreeing to facilitate meetings at the point of controversy to permit representatives to develop a common agenda and to agree, where that can't be done, to mutually respect the mandates of each organization."

In talks before the meetings that produced the agreement, the Network had stood fast on certain principles. It insisted that not only SNEEJ but all the environmental justice networks be present, including the Indigenous Environmental Network, Asian Pacific Environmental Network, Southern Organizing Committee and North East Environmental Justice. OCAW accepted this, but then asked that they agree not to picket factories whose workers belonged to OCAW when dialogue was taking place between the union and any of those groups. This SNEEJ had to refuse; it would be like a union giving up the right to strike, and also SNEEJ couldn't commit its affiliates to such an accord. But the agreement to negotiate in cases of conflict was finally adopted.

In the same meetings, OCAW and the Network discussed the "Just Transition," a strategy to cushion the job loss that often occurs when a corporation must phase out environmentally harmful production. OCAW had resolved in August 1997 that it would support policy initiatives to eliminate extremely harmful substances so long as dislocated workers and their communities were helped during the transition to sustainable production. This set the stage for joint efforts by SNEEJ and OCAW from Alabama to California. In Oklahoma, for example, an indigenous tribe reported problems with the products of a facility where the workers belonged to OCAW; the Network and the union went there in April 1998. The strategy of demanding a "just transition" could be applied in many situations, as Ruben Solís told the Network's Coordinating Council. It could be applied to Levi Strauss, to Intel, and to fight the effects of NAFTA. Any "just transition" should have its terms defined by the people affected.

The concept of "just transition" gives us an example of why making the Network truly binational requires constant two-way translation, ranging from U.S. and Mexican environmental laws and policies, to the structure of tribes in the U.S., to the fact that in Mexico labor has a much more massive presence than here, to the comparative wealth of the United States including the fact that Mexico lacks that whole U.S. world of non-profits and grant-making foundations. On another level, there are differences in decision-making styles and methods to be understood, as well as assumptions of political and theoretical knowledge. The list goes on, down to translating unfamiliar acronyms.

In daily practice, there is the need to translate into at least English and Spanish all discussion at meetings, the minutes of meetings, conference calls (crucial to Network functioning) while in progress, letters and memos, faxes, "Action Alerts," proposals and other documents. This is work whose necessity is not questioned but whose cost can be huge. To sit through a totally bilingual, two-day meeting of 20-plus people discussing complex subjects is to feel a great respect for the Network's effort to create genuine binationalism. Many U.S. organizations working on environmental problems at the border do not seriously integrate Mexican members; paternalism often defines the relationship. As Teresa Leal of Nogales, Mexico, pointed out, "They may organize tours to show the impact of the *maquiladoras*, but often the agenda has been imposed from the U.S. side." Other Mexicans say, "We are never part of their decision-making process."

If the Network has succeeded where others have failed, this must be partly because from the beginning it sought to establish a tradition of mutual respect and cooperativeness. In December 1996 this goal was formalized as the "Jemez Principles for Democratic Organizing" during a meeting of various national groups in Jemez, New Mexico, to discuss international issues. The six principles included being inclusive, doing "bottom-up" organizing, letting people speak for themselves and having a commitment to self-transformation—changing from operating in an individualistic mode to one of community-centeredness. "We must be the values that we say we're struggling for."

It is natural, then, that Network meetings have always included a strong spirituality. They usually begin and end with a circle—often to hear a prayer, given by an indigenous repesentative, or a remembrance, a thought. The spiritual presence is one reason why an annual Network gathering often feels like a vibrant multi-colored family in action.

The need for resources, including people, has always been a basic issue for the Network. Sometimes a project has had to be put on hold for lack of resources or other limitations. This happened to the Hi-Tech Campaign, which worked on making the Intel Corporation accountable to the communities where it operates in New Mexico, and helped expose Intel's water usage. The campaign also teamed up with the Labor Occupational Health and Safety Program at UC

Berkeley to train people in occupational health and safety related to the electronics industry; that program continues today.

Along with its campaigns, SNEEJ maintains several training projects for affiliates on a wide range of issues—for example, environmental law and how to use it. Again, the demands of communication can be intense; for example, the annual workshop on worker health and safety is conducted in five languages: English, Spanish, Korean, Chinese and Laotian. The Network also engages in "partnerships," by which SNEEJ raises funds to help a particular organization in the Network obtain special training, equipment or other necessities. Today the Network has become increasingly consolidated, without losing its grassroots essence and style of work. As the Network's coordinator, Richard Moore, said in the early days, "We may be poor people, but we're professional poor people!"

There is no way to speak of the Network's accomplishments without reference to the coordinator's leadership (although he would not like this himself). Richard Moore somehow combines caution and fearlessness. His history reveals the qualities of a brilliant, often low-key organizer together with a personality that doesn't hesitate to make seemingly outrageous demands on unfriendly forces (and often winning them). Again and again, I have heard him emphasize the need to build the Network slowly but surely, "from the bottom up," and not to rush. He keeps his ear close to the ground, in touch with people and any problems they perceive. Richard plans to step out of the coordinator position in the near future, and who knows what will happen then—but whatever difficulties develop will not result from the Network having been run in a one-man, top-down leadership mode that fails to prioritize training and development. Richard Moore is a fighter on several fronts, both external and internal, and a unique leader in today's struggles for social justice.

On the scenic west side of Albuquerque, more than 17,000 documented works of indigenous rock art known as petroglyphs can be found. Native Americans hold the area sacred, as a place where items are placed for the deceased to begin their journey into the next world, and it is still in use by Pueblo Indians. In recognition of its significance, the Petroglyph National Monument was established in 1990.

In April 1997, Republican Senator Pete Domenici announced intentions to push through federal legislation (Senate Bill 633) that would hand over land so that a six-lane highway could be built through this area. The goal: to facilitate access by real estate developers. They include men like John Black, whose 6,700-acre Black Ranch is slated for development.

Protest against such desecration has been led by the Petroglyph Monument Protection Coalition. On March 20, 1998, in conjunction with the Network Coordinating Council's meeting, Native American, Chicana/o, Mexican, African-American, Asian/Pacific Island and Anglo demonstrators picketed the Albuquerque office of Sen. Jeff Bingaman, who supports the highway. Called a "Youth Speak-Out and Prayer," it featured drumming and native prayers, followed by speakers. I couldn't help counting: of the half-dozen Native American, Chicano, Asian/Pacific Island and African-American speakers, five were in their 20s. The bad guys just might lose this fight.

It is so clear today that we need global movements to answer the ever more globalized assault on people and the planet. The Southwest Network stands as a model for how that answer might be constructed. One thing is sure: the answer must express inter-dependence, like a circle, like the earth. Like life itself, as our native sisters and brothers tell us.

part four

RACISM AND THE ATTACK ON MULTICULTURALISM

Una sonrisa, un llanto, un gesto de revuelta
representan todas las revueltas,
sin unas y otras no seria posible esta pequeña
esperanza que estamos construyendo.

A smile, a sob, a gesture of rebellion,
they represent all the rebellions
without this one and that one it wouldn't be possible
—this small hope that we are constructing.

—*palabras zapatistas/EZLN*
—from the Zapatista movement

chapter fourteen

WILLIE HORTON'S GONNA GET YOUR ALMA MATER
The War on Multiculturalism

They really came out swinging. The March 1991 issue of the *Atlantic* magazine carried an inflammatory drawing on its cover that showed an elderly white man in cap and gown being attacked. His arms and legs had been grabbed by colored hands—black, brown, red and yellow—which were tearing the poor man limb from limb. On his right appeared the words "Hey hey, ho ho, Western culture's got to go!" and on his left books were being set afire. In the background a Greco-Roman temple marked "Veritas" ("Truth") was crashing down. The professor wore a sign saying, "Behind campus controversies over quotas and curriculum lies a larger battle over the very meaning of 'knowledge,' 'diversity,' 'standards' and 'education'—and an assault on the foundation of Western culture."

Inside, the *Atlantic* offered a slick, 21-page diatribe with more drawings, including one of a fierce-faced woman professor flexing her biceps as she flew through space—presumably to pulverize yet another straight white male. The whole package warned: a dictatorship of darkies and dykes is taking over academia. It's a "victims' revolution" that will bring "a fundamental restructuring of American society." The author of this prophecy was Dinesh D'Souza, who came to the United States from India, was a founder of the notoriously conservative *Dartmouth Review*, later became a domestic policy analyst for Reagan and then moved to the right-wing American Enterprise Institute, where he has been a "scholar-in-residence" for several years.

The *Atlantic* article was not alone. In spring 1991 the *New Republic* devoted an entire 48-page issue to an all-out attack on what has come to be called multiculturalism or diversity. *Harper's*, *Newsweek*, the *New York Review of Books*, *Time* and a stream of other national publications chimed in. Newspapers fired daily volleys, my favorite being a column in the *Dallas Morning News* that said, "Their plot is to overthrow the tyranny of Western civilization by replacing Shakespeare, Hobbes and Jane Austen with books preaching the plight of the oppressed and the moral superiority of the Third World. They intend to destroy all standards of achievement and excellence." And who is "they"? Well, "disaffected radicals of the 1960s ... Peter Pans who decided to gnaw at their wounds in ivory towers and take vengeance on a world that rejected their peculiar views by seducing young minds to their fractured version of history." (Cited by Molly Ivins, "Oh, those 'differently visioned' dead white males," *San Francisco Examiner,* April 25, 1991.)

Such rhetoric was almost as poisonous as the infamous campaign ad used by George Bush when he ran against Gov. Michael Dukakis of Massachusetts for president in 1988. It featured an African-American convict named Willie Horton who had been released by Dukakis and who then committed a new crime. The racist implication: vote for Dukakis and those Black criminals will come get you.

When the current demand for diversification of curriculum and faculty first became an issue on university and college campuses, my own reaction was to belittle it. In the 1960s we fought for Chicano power, for Chicano Studies. We wanted a r-r-r-revolution, we didn't want some wishy-washy "diversity." Diversity would offer a few crumbs of recognition for non-Western cultures, I originally thought, in order to forestall confronting systemic racism. Later the attack on multiculturalism showed the inadequacy of that analysis: there's a serious war on.

The anti-diversity war rages not only in academia but in the whole society. Like the anti-affirmative action campaign, it is profoundly racist and sexist. Both represent much more than a backlash: they are tactics for solidifying a rightist ideology to sustain the Right's political hegemony, to guarantee that a racist, sexist and capitalist agenda holds the center of U.S. political culture. This in turn calls for demonizing progressive ideas and people that might impede right-wing domination over ideological space. It calls for blocking the study of U.S. history as a history of racism, sexism and imperialism at work. The U.S. political culture must be kept ahistorical, even anti-historical. The war on multiculturalism parallels the way in which reactionaries sought to use the Gulf War to regenerate patriotism and thereby annul the Vietnam War syndrome with its national self-doubt.

The assault on "diversity," which seemed to be mainly ideological during the early 1990s, took concrete political form within a few years. The state of California led the way, with laws to abolish affirmative action and bilingual education. Soon after, a rightwing campaign to challenge Ethnic Studies was launched in June 1998 by UC Regent Ward Connerly, godfather of the attack on affirmative action. On the national front, Congress blocked the first appointment of an Asian

American to the position of Assistant Attorney General for Civil Rights. Racism and political opportunism have been marching hand-in-hand to the tune of "racism is dying in the United States."

It's risky to view the anti-diversity war as only an extreme-right project. Support for aspects of the war can be heard from liberals, even progressives. And there are other complexities. For example, at about the same time that the attack on multiculturalism reached blitzkrieg intensity across the nation, the Bank of America installed bilingual (Spanish-English) instructions on the monitors of its ATMs. Or: at about the same time that the media relentlessly attacked advocates of racial sensitivity as self-styled "politically correct" thought-police, white managers of big corporations were attending workshops on how to understand employees of color with a view to more minority hiring. Confronted by these and other seeming contradictions, one is tempted to plead: will the real ruling class please stand up? As usual, however, that class may speak with more than one voice. Given the complexity of the issue, we need to look at several realities in turn: (1) the current war on "diversity" or "multiculturalism" and how it's waged; (2) why liberals and even progressives would support it; (3) ruling-class perspectives on multiculturalism; and (4) battles won and lost, and why the war is important. This discussion will focus on issues related to White Supremacy, but sexism and homophobia are also very much involved.

Anatomy of the War on Diversity

New only in its intensity, the current campaign against multiculturalism and for rightist control over ideology began with attempts to turn back the clock on 1960s movement gains. In 1973, for example, a committee of the American Library Association countermanded an earlier decision that libraries should re-evaluate children's "classics" in light of new consciousness about the oppression of Third World peoples and women. This was censorship, said the ALA group, ominously presaging today's rightist vocabulary.

All-out opposition to diversity mounted when Allan Bloom fired a major salvo with his 1987 bestseller, *The Closing of the American Mind*. That same year, the National Association of Scholars in Princeton, New Jersey, was founded to defend "excellence" from extinction with the help of intellectuals like D'Souza and magazines like the *Atlantic*. The Anglo generals in the war soon had a few lieutenants of color, like African-American professor Shelby Steele of California State University in San Jose (and later Ward Connerly, also of California). Steele attacked affirmative action, saying it represented over-reliance by minorities and women on "the power of being victims." In its place we should follow the Horatio Alger formula for attaining success through individual responsibility and hard work. Not long after came a few Chicano academics who also advised Raza students to forget affirmative action; just stop whining, study hard and help your mom sell more tamales, you too could be Hispanics.

Among Anglos, the attack on both multiculturalism and affirmative action accelerated in the early 1990s for two reasons: economic crisis and the expanding population of color. Downward mobility threatened Americans in the middle and working class. Among white academics, massive cuts in university funding encouraged the fear of losing out to teachers of color on jobs, grants and other increasingly scarce resources. Males feared female competition in the same areas. New multicultural curricula threatened the status of faculty untrained in these fields. (Even though economic conditions have improved since then for some people, we can wonder just how long that will last and how much such improvement will reduce racism.) Along with economic anxiety came the other big bogey: those hordes of colored people rushing our borders with millions behind them. Demographic disaster was just ahead for the once-majority, about to be minority, white population.

Some of the anti-diversity warriors claim to have no problem with expanding the canon to include more works by persons outside the Western tradition or women. They insist, however, on the centrality of Western culture in U.S. education, philosophy and values. They may tolerate a little ethnic spice, but the European experience remains the main dish, bonding all Americans. The alternative is "balkanization" or "tribalism"—two buzzwords of the anti-multicultural war.

To bolster Eurocentrism, they often trot out this convoluted charge: "Multiculturalism's hard-liners damn as racism any attempt to draw the myriad American groups into a common American culture," as Fred Siegel wrote in the *New Republic*. They're still trying to melt us in that old racist pot, it seems, and then they snarl if we don't want to jump right in.

Writers like Siegel really do believe that Western values of Reason, Neutrality and Objectivity are intellectual tools serving to establish an abstract truth—not to justify white privilege or power. Without those tools, the very concept of values is lost, they tell us. Such "truth" supposedly exists outside any historical, political or sociological contexts. The anti-diversity warriors denounce those who say all literature is political, that its production, interpretation and

teaching are political acts. At the same time, they tell us that literature must be seen as part of the culture that unites this country and
bonds us all—in other words, it does have a political function. Their
real concern is not with the introduction of politics but with the
wrong kind of politics. They want literature to serve a very political
function indeed: to sustain, not criticize, the status quo.

As this line of misthinking shows, the anti-diversity warriors con-
coct their arguments from a jumble of demagoguery, contextual tricks,
false analogies and furtive rationales. They also specialize in straw
men—adversaries created to be easily demolished. For example, they
claim multiculturalism demands that students cease to study Western
culture. Not true. Vassar faculty dean Nancy Dye wrote in response to
such claims: "The great books are alive and well on college campuses."
The rightist forces also veil their true meaning in various ways; for example, they do not simply believe Western culture is what Americans
have in common. They also think it is superior to all other cultures.

The "PC" Stigma at Work

The biggest gun in the current war on multiculturalism is the accusation of "political correctness." "PC"-baiting fans the flames and bil-
lows clouds of confusion over the debate.

Multiculturalism often advocates that history, literature and other
areas of the humanities be studied with reference to how they reflect
people's real life experience. This includes encounters with the class in-
equality, racism, sexism, homophobia and other oppressions in the society under study. To anti-diversity warriors, that is its greatest crime.
They claim the humanities today are tyrannized by people who view
U.S. society as dominated by heterosexual white males. A so-called PC
movement supposedly forces anti-racist, anti-sexist, anti-homophobic
language and thought on everyone else.

Terrorizing those who might accidentally say "chairman" instead
of "chairperson," this movement is said to constitute a new McCarthyism. The *New Republic* found its goal to be "a chorus of voices all saying the same thing"—an intolerant, repressive orthodoxy.

A term originally created by leftists in humorous self-mockery,
"PC" is now used to evoke Stalinist demands for conformity. Thus PC-
baiting has become a post–Cold War substitute for anti-communism,
and a dangerously reactionary political expression. Another pet term of
the anti-diversity warriors is "the party line": it's "the party line," they
say, to criticize our educational system for being Eurocentric. By equat-

WILLIE HORTON'S GONNA... 123

ing anti-racism, anti-sexism and other progressive politics with intellectual tyranny, both terms strike vicious blows for rightist ideology. Both
serve to demonize progressive thought.

"PC" has almost become a household word. In the 1991 Academy
Awards pageant, a commentator joked that *Dances with Wolves* was
"politically correct" (it shows Native Americans as decent and most of
the white troops trying to exterminate them as bad guys). Since then,
movie critics have sneered at films with anti-racist content, like *Follow
Me Home* or *Amistad,* for their "PC" essence. The term has even inspired a major television show, Bill Maher's "Politically Incorrect"
talkfest. Progressive people use the term without thinking twice about
its reactionary function.

Do I mean to say that those who speak for anti-racist, anti-sexist
and anti-homophobic politics never exaggerate, never slip into dogmatism? Or that people of color cannot make mistakes under the banner of
exposing racism? Or that aspiring academics of color have never used
multiculturalism to advance their own careers? Of course not. There
have been times when a Black student, for example, felt peer pressure
to major in African-American Studies instead of medieval literature for
race reasons; or someone insisted on attributing an incident to racism
when it really had a different cause; or white students felt intimidated
about criticizing a professor of color. Campuses do exist where Ethnic
Studies are taught uncritically. Such situations encourage opportunism
and cynicism; they can become very serious and even damage lives.
They should not be defended.

But we also need to see the straw men at work again. Do such
incidents mean that campuses are being turned into "authoritarian
ministates," as George Will warned? (*Newsweek*, May 6, 1991.) Do
they prove that power relations between the races have been in-
verted? What do these incidents, which occur on relatively few campuses, tell us, compared with the message coming from hundreds of
racist actions by Anglo students nationwide (as discussed in my essay "Campus Racism," page 131)? The supposed evidence of PC
atrocities adds up to yet another straw man intended to breed confusion in the anti-diversity war.

The bitter legacy of White Supremacy means an incident that is
denounced as racism might not really be—but probably is. It means that
only occasionally will a criticism of racism be raised if people of color
don't do it. When white people denounce racist deeds and policies as
energetically as the victims of those acts, then we can imagine a truly
new day in which being politically correct is the norm and not a cynical
accusation.

How the War Confuses Liberals

The war on multiculturalism can also confuse liberals because, unlike conservatives, they usually do not perceive or accept the connection between racism and domination. They fail to see that racism has never been just a matter of negative attitudes but rather an institutionalized set of power relations. This truism seems to need repeating today, when PhDs sometimes insist on putting *institutionalized racism* in quotation marks, reducing its existence to an opinion. They deny the need to look at social relations historically and see how the experience of people over centuries in the United States has created group identities that form the context for individual identities. The group identities have to be understood, or today's social relations make no sense. But the anti-diversity warriors recognize only one group identity as valid, then they justify this exclusively in the name of cultural "unity"—a unity that really means domination by People Like Us.

The rightist war attracts liberals and others not on the Right by combining fearful self-interest with an idealistic appeal to the desire of many Americans for a sense of wholeness as a nation instead of fragmentation. Thus they seek to capture the moral high ground, the most flagrant example being the use of Martin Luther King Jr.'s dream of a de-racialized society to justify their denial of the need to combat ongoing racism.

In this spirit, liberals are comfortable with integrationism as the key to ending racism and mechanically reject any alternative approach that might be called separatist. They echo the devious Right with their talk of eliminating "racial politics" in favor of "unifying politics" and fail to examine what either term really means or whom it serves. They too *equate progress with transcending a racially conscious view of society* (meaning "color-blindness"). They too refuse to recognize that the usual meaning of "color-blind" continues to be "seeing white." They denounce "identity politics" as if such politics were the cause, rather than evidence, of a crisis. They fail to understand that progress in moving away from racist policies is not synonymous with achieving equality.

In short, denial of racism as an ongoing problem, more serious than ever in many ways, became the main ideological weapon of the anti-diversity war during the late 1990s.

In defending the legacy of White Supremacy, the PC-baiters have tried to make freedom of speech an issue—another argument to confuse liberals. While rejecting their opportunism, we need to defend this right. The answer to hate words is not speech codes but strong protest and educational efforts when we hear them. Don't ban bigoted language, but let those who use it know what to expect—severe public criticism, spontaneous demonstrations—and why. This may be the liberal American Civil Liberties Union position; so be it, for history shows that limits on one person's freedom of speech make it a non-freedom for others. In failing to take this stand, progressives and leftists also aid the PC-baiters by giving them the moral high ground of being "anti-censorship."

The use of confusion as a weapon of the anti-diversity warriors multiplied in the 1990s. Deceptive wording of electoral propositions became a California specialty, with the November 1996 law to abolish affirmative action being called a "civil rights" initiative and the 1998 initiative to abolish bilingual education called "English for the Children." The targeted audience was not only Anglo liberals but also people of color. One of the most vivid examples has been the effort to convince Latinos that, for their children to learn English and succeed in this society, they should forget their original Spanish, forget biculturalism.

The Ruling Class: Who's on First?

Not all the voices of capital harmonize with the racist rejection of multiculturalism.

Even Federal Reserve chair Alan Greenspan told a conference at the World Trade Center in January 1998 that racism was bad for business and this country had a long way to go. Many voices of capital express concern that the United States will not be able to meet its workforce needs in the twenty-first century unless domestic policies are changed. The alarm has sounded repeatedly, as in *U.S. News and World Report:* "Inferior schooling and other forces could put a lid on growth" and the nation must "boost the capabilities of those in the bottom half of the 125 million-member labor force"—mostly people of color.

Significant sectors of the corporate elite may be appalled at the current cuts in education spending. They might find the assault on multiculturalism stupid. They have reason to look favorably on affirmative action as a means of achieving the diverse workforce they need. They may also find ridiculous the campaign to make English the "official" language of the United States. One need only walk through any Spanish-speaking neighborhood and look up at the billboards, telling people to buy Salems or Miller Lite—in Spanish. When recent statistics say 48 percent of Latinos in the United States speak Spanish at home, and the Latino market is deemed worthy of $1.4 billion in advertising (an increase of 17 percent in 1997 alone) (*New York Times,* January 19, 1998), who's to say "learn English and shut up"? Better to work on ads in Spanish for baby powder that don't say baby "dust" by mistake, as the *New York Times* financial news once reported.

The corporate class also recognizes the cultural price of intensified globalization. Busy executives take time out to learn such questionable advice as: when you do business with an Asian, don't be put off if he doesn't look you straight in the eye; it's the culture. At home, organizations offer their services in recruiting talented minority youth. "In the corporate boardrooms, the need to acquire minority personnel—and to prepare white managers to relate to them—is widely discussed today, especially in the industries that make consumer products, retail banking and telecommunications," a coordinator of one California program told me. Many companies hold awareness training programs for white managers, with names like "Multicultural Diversity," "Managing Diversity" and "The New Workforce." White managers, said the coordinator, "must become a little more sensitive to minorities and women so that they won't totally turn off these new employees and make them leave the company for one with a better reputation. They are concerned with competing."

Does all this mean that capitalism, out of self-interest, will facilitate our entrance into a new stage of race relations? Not a simple question. We can look at some of the concessions made in the struggle for multiculturalism to see how the wind is blowing.

Battles Won or Lost and What We Must Do

A 1992 study of 196 colleges and universities, including both public and private, two- and four-year institutions, showed that 34 percent had a "multicultural general education requirement" (which means different things on different campuses, as we will see). At least a third offered coursework in Ethnic and Gender Studies. More than half—54 percent—had introduced new material into existing course offerings to make them more multicultural but far fewer had mounted new courses. A majority was seeking to increase faculty from "under-represented populations." Half had multicultural-advising programs and more than a third had multicultural centers or institutes. The study was headed by Arthur Levine, then at Harvard's Institute for Educational Management. (No more-recent figures are available from any private or public agency.)

Even the most modest-sounding, required multicultural courses have sometimes generated bloody battles. At the University of Texas (UT) in Austin, for example, the liberal-arts dean approved revisions based on issues of "difference" for the required first-year writing class, English 306. They seemed a small step in the right direction for a university that had 5,000 Latina/o students, not to mention many others of color. Revisions included adding readings from U.S. court decisions on various civil rights cases (among them, a case that led to the admission of UT's first African-American student).

But some faculty began redbaiting advocates of the new syllabus as "neo-Marxists" who were taking over the university and establishing "thought control." The battle raged on in 1990–91 until six faculty members—the entire committee that had approved the changes—resigned. Finally the faculty voted 759-434 to reject having a required multiculturalism course.

At the University of California in Berkeley, students and progressive faculty had to fight long and hard to have a multicultural requirement for graduation. As of 1987, the campus had a majority students of color (52 percent) for the first time, but with a faculty that was 90-plus percent white (and 86 percent male). Students proposed a multicultural requirement; the faculty rejected it; students began to demonstrate. When they occupied the elegant faculty club at lunchtime, filling the corridor between professors and their sandwiches, it was like war. "You can take your multicultural proposal and shove it up your — ," one faculty member hollered, according to Professor Ron Takaki. Finally, the Academic Senate voted 227-194 in 1989 to adopt an "American Cultural Breadth" requirement.

Today that requirement is institutionalized. Cal's 20,000 students can choose from courses in 43 disciplines to meet the requirement. More than 265 new courses were approved and 105 actually offered in 1996–97. The courses have to address issues relevant to understanding race, culture and ethnicity in U.S. history and society. Each course must draw on the experience of at least three population groups of color and Euro-Americans. Areas of study range from architecture to music to public health and more.

On the other hand, even when concessions are made, the result has sometimes been rendered toothless and gutless. At liberal Antioch College in Ohio, for example, the 1992 multiculturalism requirement was so feeble that it could be met by taking French. There's a concession for you.

One of the most serious obstacles to genuine diversification is that on most campuses the faculty remains lily-white and male. This has sparked demands by students from California to New York for more faculty of color. To make an old problem even worse, faculties that took on a slight color after the 1960s will soon revert to their previous whiteness, as many professors of color retire and few replacements become available. Tony Platt of California State University, Sacramento, wrote in a 1996–97 study of Latino/a faculty, "Unless emergency action is taken … it is quite possible that a decade from now, when most of the first wave of Latino/a faculty will have retired, it will be a very rare event to see a Latino/a professor teaching [there]," although Latinos represent the fastest-growing ethnic population in California.

In another arena of the diversity struggle, we find Ethnic Studies programs at some high schools—thanks to the persistent efforts of student organizers. Too often, however, we find multicultural tourism instead—quick jaunts to the worlds of various colored folk. Some call this the cafeteria approach, whereby students take a small bowl of soul food here, a little Latino spice there, some inscrutable-Oriental salad over yonder and a Native American ceremony for dessert. The cafeteria does not, however, serve differently flavored worldviews, different collective memories, different perceptions of history.

<<< >>>

In all our schools, all our institutions, the issue is still power. It's not just a struggle to get a course added here or there. Any challenge to the existing educational system eventually means challenging the kind of faculty on hand at a given institution; the criteria for recognition and scholarship; the administrative structure—the entire package of power relations on a given campus. In the end it means challenging the ruling class's position on whose interests education should serve.

So don't expect a national education policy that challenges the idea of "Western values" as the basis for our educational norms. Don't expect curricula that recognize racism as a pillar of U.S. society. The concessions made thus far represent recognition by the corporate elite that its interests are best served by adding a measure of non-white cultures to the mainstream. (The essay "Whose Chicano History Did You Learn?" on page 31 describes the role of right-wing think tanks in this process.) Similarly, the academic elite may recognize that campus turmoil is undesirable. The issue continues to be power.

In that light, many people of color distrust the concept of multiculturalism. Many see it as an attempt to co-opt our demand for decentralizing whiteness, and that may indeed be its goal. Many say, "We want an end to racism, and access to the corridors of power—not another brand of corporate cosmetics." Others feel the concept liquidates the particularities of each community of color.

But the ferocious attempt to block any non-Eurocentric, non-traditional educational effort has shown the need to expose the attack on multiculturalism, *while insisting that it be defined as anti-racism.* Interpreted that way, and not simply as additive, it is truly subversive, for it defies the centrality of a Euro-dominated nationhood. Let us define multiculturalism, then, as a united front against White Supremacy.

Anglo teachers, students and activists should recognize that today's reactionary opposition to a genuine multiculturalism signifies a chilling repression of independent thinking in general. It signifies a readiness to curb any systemic critique of U.S. society. Yet even those apparently concerned about social justice seem indifferent to such threats as compared to the perceived threat of diminished race-power. One wants to holler: "Yo, *gringitos*—wake up! They'll be coming for you in the morning, if you don't stand with the rest of us tonight."

chapter fifteen

CAMPUS RACISM
Tip of an Iceberg

Tracking the Hatred

The poster announcing my talk on multiculturalism at the University of Vermont in Burlington had been defaced. A white man had been drawn on top of the original sketch of a woman, whom he was raping. Long, dark, tangled hair had been drawn over the woman's face and head to make her look uncivilized. With the man's penis erect and his bloodied right arm raised in victory, the ugly scene hardly needed any caption. But there it was anyway, neatly lettered: CONQUISTADOR.

I had gone to speak at the university, knowing a struggle against racism had raged on that campus for years. Back in 1969, students of color at this 95 percent white institution in an almost all-white state had managed to end "Kakewalk," a campus-wide dance performed in blackface. Later they won from the Board of Trustees a commitment to "cultural diversity." The administration ignored that promise and, in protest, a group of students of color took over the president's office in 1988. Again promises were made, called the Waterman Agreements, and again they were broken.

Students occupied the president's office in April and May 1991 to press their demands once more. The three-week occupation ended with a massive show of police in riot gear at dawn. Not only were the sit-in students arrested, but the administration moved to prevent further protests with internal hearings, expulsions, fines and placing students on disciplinary probation for the duration.

Two days before the occupation ended, supporters had put up a shantytown on the university green that became a strong, ongoing symbol of their cause. It provided a space for the anti-racist, "liberatory education" they wanted and a base for radical political action. Diversity University (DU), as it was called, offered courses such as "Native American History" (Indians make up a significant portion of Vermont's population), "Racism in the Women's Movement," "Revolution and Spirituality," "Radical Sexuality" and "Visionary Art."

The DU group became a collective that included some of the most creative and committed student activists I have ever met. Their backgrounds combined different cultures and nationalities—African-American, Chinese, Jamaican, Japanese, Latino, Sikh and Syrian. Recognizing that DU (like all of UVM) was located on land of the Abenaki Nation, whose self-determination movement had also been under attack, they requested and were given authorization by Abenaki chief Homer St. Francis to locate DU there so long as the students respected "Mother Nature and observe the laws of the Nation."

Physical attacks on DU and legal harassment by city authorities became an almost daily occurrence. Elsewhere on campus an Asian-American woman, a Latina woman and a gay man all suffered physical or verbal assault. (Homophobic attacks increased in general, with slogans such as "The only good fag is a dead fag.") When DU's buildings were leveled one night, students rebuilt a one-room cabin that still stood when I visited. The word "revolution," in huge red letters, covered one side.

Apparently this symbol of defiance on the main campus quad maddened numerous people, including an ex-Marine student. Gus Laskaris ('93) vandalized DU every Monday morning with spray-painted slogans such as "Resist the politically correct" and "Columbus is okay." He could not tolerate the "weirdo culture" housed at DU, according to his letter published in a campus newspaper. On November 4, 1992, he called the media to come and watch him crowbar a wall; when they came, others tried to talk Laskaris into less violent forms of protest. The media then turned the whole incident into "a fight." The administration fined Laskaris for trying to damage DU: a little slap on the wrist, at best.

When I was speaking at UVM some two weeks later, a young African-American woman suddenly marched up onto the stage and placed the defaced announcement of my talk on the podium—my first sight of it. Some kind of apprehension could be felt in the auditorium, but no incidents occurred that evening. The next night, at about 11:30 p.m., DU was fire-bombed and totally destroyed. As the flames rose, a group of men nearby could be heard singing "God Bless America."

Three days later the assistant director of the Office of Multicultural Affairs, Anthony Chávez, began to receive a series of death threats shortly before midnight: "We know who you are and you're dead," all in the same slow, muffled voice. His car, and the cars of neighbors, were forced open and the glove compartments searched—

but nothing was taken, which led Chávez, a transplanted Chicano from California, to suspect it was FBI work.

The police and fire commissioner were unable to find a single person responsible for the assaults. No one, including Chávez, believed that Gus Laskaris was the culprit; he remained on campus, continuing to write his letters, but "you can talk to him," people said. The fire-bombing investigation was minimal and failed to pursue a lead provided when janitors found the makings of fire-bombs in a fraternity-house basement.

UVM's president, Thomas Salmon, made some toothless statement deploring violence. On Martin Luther King Jr. Day, a forum on hate crimes took place, attended by Salmon and top Vermont politicians—the first gesture of recognition of student demands. "But," as Christiana Keith of the DU collective and the Alianza Latina, observed, "Salmon reduced the whole struggle to a problem of hate words and then said maybe hate words couldn't be banned because that would violate First Amendment rights. While he and other administrators debate that issue, we're walking around hoping nobody kills us." Karl Jagbandhansingh, another DU leader, became the favorite target of the UVM administration, which hit him with charges at every opportunity throughout 1992. If one was dropped, they found others equally far-fetched.

In the state of socialist Rep. Bernie Sanders, we might have expected stronger support for the students, stronger pressure on the UVM administration. The mayor of Burlington did denounce "racial animosity" at the King Day event, but nothing more. Even progressive whites in Vermont seemed to find UVM a touchy issue; they could not deal with the students' militant tactics; they couldn't deal with racism beyond therapy-like discussions of race relations. "It takes a lot to make them listen," Chávez said, "and then they listen only after putting what you've said into *their* language."

Perhaps, as some have commented, the students should have done more outreach to explain their struggle to the Burlington community. But the fact remains: without strong support from whites in power they could not uproot a deeply ingrained Eurocentricity that simply doesn't understand *or doesn't want to understand* "all the fuss" about diversity.

As Chávez insisted: "The University needs to recognize the need for a basic civil rights policy that outlines affirmative action and other policies to ensure equality. That's the necessary basis for a diversity program. Until we have that, talking diversity will get us no-

where.... Right now the university is a plantation." (Apparently
Massa later had a slight change of heart. After an early version of this
essay was published in *Z* magazine in April 1992, the administration
agreed for the first time to sit down with students and discuss their
demands. No doubt it also helped that the students had held a 21-day
hunger strike and testified at a hearing before the U.S. Civil Rights
Commission.)

Three days before going to Burlington, I was at the State University of New York (SUNY) in Oswego, invited by the Latino Student Union. Lilliana Almendares told me of recent incidents on
campus. Someone had shoved "a very ugly letter" under the door of a
white student's room asking, "Why is a nice girl like you hanging out
with those spics?" During rush week, Latinos being considered for
membership ("They admit Latinos, but only the most white-looking")
were not allowed to speak Spanish. "None of that *'¡Mira, mira!'*—
'Look, look!'*—stuff," the frats told them. Sad to say, the Latinos accepted this on the grounds, I was told, that "it's just for rush week."

Stereotypes abound in the racist acts against Latino students,
not to mention acts against Black students. On a trip to southern California, I found a protest scheduled against a student "humor" newspaper, *Koala*, at the University of California at San Diego. It had
published a list of five things students could do in Tijuana, across the
border in Mexico. These included "contract a disease from someone
named Juanita" and "call people fucking beaners." Another publication, *Vista*, at the University of San Diego, a Catholic school, carries a
"Crimewatch" section, apparently to alert students to possible sexual
harassment or similar problems. One item stated, "Two suspicious
Hispanic males were seen in the phase B parking lot. No crime was
reported, as of yet."

That was 1992. It was almost impossible to visit any campus in
the early 1990s and not hear reports of racist attacks, both verbal and
physical. It was the same story in 1995. When I spoke at the University of Minnesota in Duluth, Latino students told me how they had
asked the student government for funds to have a dinner for parents.
They were told okay, "but go to Taco Bell." In another incident, a
white fraternity member made death threats against the president of
the Latino student organization; he was found guilty of harassment

and put on probation, but this didn't stop other fraternity brothers from continuing such threats. The university president never took a stand against the threats at the time. The fraternity filed a lawsuit for "defamation" against the Latinos who had complained.

By 1997, little had changed. You could still hear lots of "beaner" and "gangster" labeling of Latinos. Howard Ehrlich of the National Institute Against Prejudice and Violence in Baltimore, Maryland, an information clearinghouse, had told me in 1992 that partial surveys indicated 20 to 25 percent of all students of color are victimized by bigotry at least once in an academic year. (No complete nationwide survey has been carried out.) This means 800,000 to one million people. Three out of ten are victimized more than once during the year, which means the number of incidents is even higher. The bigotry takes on still more chilling proportions when we remember that, as Ehrlich pointed out, "those victimized by racial prejudice are more traumatized and suffer greater stress than assaults unrelated to a person's race."

Five years later, on the telephone from the Prejudice Institute, as it is now named, Ehrlich said that overall those figures had changed little. There was much variation from one campus to the next, according to its particular ethnic mix; in general, as a racial or ethnic group increased in number, it was more likely to be victimized. Gays and lesbians were now the most targeted group, especially if they were also of color.

Tactics have varied from up-front racist assaults to the more sophisticated Klan-style harassment typified by David Duke; the latter can be seen in the manipulation of free-speech rights to justify verbal racist attacks and confuse the public. This doesn't mean that uninhibited fascism had been abandoned. Opposition to multiculturalism can still be heard in attacks on "the mud people," and we can still read campus newspaper letters like the one from tenured economics professor Ernest Bucholz (now retired) at Santa Monica College opposing multiculturalism because it promotes the "Turd-World." Right-wing forces also build on popular distrust of the mass media and textbooks to challenge *all* recorded history— including the Holocaust. They don't necessarily despair at some defeat, since the goal is often a long-range recruitment effort to get people accustomed to hatred.

When you go from campus to campus and hear one story after another of repressive and racist incidents, you have to ask: is there a national right-wing organization behind all this? If not, are there local organizations on individual campuses?

No one I met on the campuses pointed to a coordinated national campaign as the force behind campus racism in the early 1990s. In interviews, journalist Sara Diamond said she saw no such level of organization, nor did Dan Levitas at the Center for Democratic Renewal (formerly the National Anti-Klan Network, founded in 1979) in Atlanta. Levitas did not even think most racist acts on campus were the work of local organizations or their members. He saw campus assaults as one of three kinds of hate violence: campus, neighborhood, and skinhead, all of them carried out by whites. According to arrest records, Levitas said, the perpetrators were usually white males ages 15 to 21 who share other characteristics, including financial insecurity, a lack of moral leadership and being influenced by the reactionary climate around them that has been fostered by campus publications such as the *Dartmouth Review.*

At several schools, neo-Nazi youths have been organizing White Student Union groups that openly advocate racist violence; some, mostly in the South, have had Ku Klux Klan support. During the campaign of David Duke and his National Association for the Advancement of White People, numerous White Student Unions reportedly existed across Louisiana. At the University of Minnesota, Tom David wrote for the local WSU that "America is quickly becoming a Third World Slum. The non-white flood of immigrants must be stopped; instead of the Border Patrol, the southern border should be defended by National Guardsmen following a single order: 'If it ain't White, waste it!'" (Robin Templeton, "White Supremacist Attacks Progressive Students at the University of Minnesota," New Liberation News Service Packet 2.3.)

The University of Florida at Gainesville had a White Student Union, organized in January 1990 by Mark Wright. A former Klan activist, Wright often ranted about "rampant reverse racism" that victimized whites through affirmative action. (*Iguana* [University of Florida student paper], January 1991.) Apparently the WSUs come and go, with questionable impact on policy; in 1997 Howard Ehrlich thought they had never really caught on. "But right-wing groups do have a new weapon now: a Web site," he added.

To understand the racist assaults on campuses, we need to remember that today's youth are children of the Reagan-Bush years. Their political consciousness has been formed in a climate of reaction; if anything, it is amazing that they are divided at all—which they are—on issues like affirmative action and women's rights. As Ehrlich pointed out, given our segregated society and White Supremacist institutions, most students come to college with little if any multicultural experience. Almost no value has usually been attached to such experience.

Add to this the brutal cutbacks in higher education, which mean that graduating from college will now take many students five years instead of four, because increased fees mean working more hours to pay tuition, courses aren't available, library hours are shorter and so on. A generalized anxiety therefore runs high—which, among white students, increases in the many parts of the country with new demographics. White students then scapegoat the growing populations of color. Ehrlich also points to the authoritarian culture of the fraternities and the aggressive, super-"masculine" sports tradition. The dormitory is where students' cultural isolation and lack of multicultural experience gets played out in racist attacks. Liquor often becomes the catalyst for assault in all these settings—fraternities, sports and the dorm.

What do we do, what can be done, to stop the relentless wave of overt, often violent racism on campus? The abolition of affirmative action in California made it clear in 1996 that those assaults, though ugly, are only the tip of a monstrous iceberg. But that doesn't mean efforts on campus are not worthwhile.

What Can Be Done?

Everything points to the grave need for a much stronger counter-strategy than we have seen to date. Let's look at the anti-racist programs at two state universities, one on the West Coast and one on the East Coast.

No single anti-bigotry program can do the job: that's the general approach at California State University, Sacramento (CSUS). The total student body of almost 25,000 in spring 1992 was 9.94 percent Asian/Pacific Island American; 8.7 percent Latino; and 5 percent African-American (five years later, there were still about 25,000 students, now roughly one-third students of color). In a conversation with Tony Platt, an Anglo professor in the School of Social Work and a longtime radical analyst of social justice issues, he spelled out five key arenas of effort to make the university an institution that will help create new social relations of respect.

First, the administration must make a commitment to equality and diversity. Those that do are in the minority; at CSUS the president has taken a pro-diversity position publicly. "In the absence of student activism, such a stand makes a significant difference: it sends a message down the bureaucratic ladder," Platt pointed out. "The administration must also create a campus culture in which racist assaults are an unmistakable no-no." We should recall that during the serious protests by Black students against white racist conduct at Olivet College in Michigan in 1992, one of the most angering moments for Black students came when the whites were not even reprimanded for their racial threats and name-calling. Not much to ask—an official reprimand.

Second, physical space has to be available, with a staff whose job is diversification. Such a space provides a base for student groups to carry out multicultural activities and a place for students to go with grievances. CSUS has such a center.

The third arena where the administration must make an effort to counter campus racism is the hiring and recruitment of students and faculty. Improvement on this campus has come more for women (most of them white) than for people of color. Since 1992, Black and Latino/a faculty have declined, Latinos the most. Out of 781 full-time faculty in 1992, Latinos numbered 48; five years later they were down to 37. Black and Latina women are especially underrepresented; in 1997 there were only 14 Black and 12 Latina faculty. CSUS also saw three Black administrators leave, so there is only one senior administrator of color left.

The future looks even more grim; Platt predicted a steady decline in faculty of color as those hired in the 1970s near retirement. Replacements will be blocked by budget cuts, the end of affirmative action, and a bad image that will discourage some of the best applicants of color. As on other campuses, fear of losing funds if the school doesn't abandon race-based recruitment—as legally required by Proposition 209—has helped create a climate of great caution. These problems exist statewide.

The fourth arena is curriculum. CSUS has one required course in Ethnic Studies and racial issues. More promising than a single course is its Beyond the Canon Project. When that project started, faculty members met regularly with a view to transforming *how* they teach various courses—not just *what* they teach. For example, the instructor of a course on European economic history would not merely add works by women and people of color. Students would look at

Europe as part of a world economy, unlimited by traditional geographic boundaries. Thus her course would include studying the effects of the slave trade, including the Arab slave trade. In a music course, students would listen to music with characteristics unfamiliar to their ears, not as a study of some exotic form but with the goal of understanding that music expresses a worldview.

Changing the dominant worldview in the curriculum, more than just adding material—which is what the Beyond the Canon Project has tried to do—really raises hackles. Otis Scott, an African-American who heads the Ethnic Studies Department at CSUS, told me that "with this project we should not only make students familiar with new perspectives or new literature but also make them realize that there are ways people of color perceive and interpret the world that are different and valid. We're trying to make race or gender or sexuality part of the basic analysis, not another tacked-on thing." In other words, it's not like a recipe that says, "Add Latinos (or Black folks or women, etc.) and stir well." What has been unusual about CSUS is the collective way in which faculty work together regularly: those who have made changes help others who want to do so.

"Although most students have been happy about our approach, some have resisted it," Scott observed. "Those embarked on career preparation like teacher training have ideas about what is legitimate, what knowledge will make them competitive." Not focusing on the canon could hurt their careers, they think. Other students cling stubbornly to Eurocentric perspectives. For example, when an English literature teacher added some slave narratives and works by writers like Frederick Douglass, a few students complained: "That's not really literature."

Today the Beyond the Canon Project has declined, said Tony Platt, because the administration withdrew financial support as a result of cutbacks. Faculty members are trying to revive it with fewer funds—which is hard. There is a new effort, Educational Excellence through Diversity, a CSUS organization dedicated to increasing the diversity of students, staff, faculty and knowledge. Any and all efforts seem much needed. In Scott's words, "the campus culture is racist, sexist and classist, and the white students need to deal with diversity." When I asked him about the white-robed Ku Klux Klan posters on campus that I had seen two or three years earlier, he answered: "I'm more worried about the Klan in doctoral robes."

Scott is very active in the larger community—on issues such as police abuse and independent politics—as are most of the Ethnic

Studies faculty. They also assign students to do work in the community. Here we come to that fifth necessary arena of change: student activism. On almost any campus it takes a student movement pushing for multiculturalism and against racist assaults to make reluctant administrations take a stand.

<<< >>>

Such a movement is strongest when multiracial; also, white students need to take the initiative in protesting racist acts. When a Black student at a midwestern university I visited put a Black History Month poster on the door to his room and someone set it on fire, only Black students protested. A different example comes from Pitzer College in southern California. There, Asian students wrote "Asian American Studies" on a campus wall as a demand, since no such program exists there. Someone had altered the lettering to read "Asian Americans Die." Students of all colors, not just the Asian Americans, protested strongly.

At the State University of New York in Stony Brook, Frederick Preston, vice-president for student affairs and an African American, speaks with pride about efforts to combat racism, reduce racial tension and celebrate campus diversity. These efforts help explain the high retention rate of students of color, Preston said, when I spoke with him in 1992 and again in 1997. Of roughly 18,000 students over the last five years, about 28 percent have consistently been of color, with Asians and Asian-Americans being the largest group today. As for racist assault, "there has not been much intra-student conflict—a little graffiti but nothing as sensational as elsewhere." Physical violence, he told me in 1997, occurs perhaps once every other year on the average, usually when someone comes from off campus and a fight starts.

These successes, said Preston, can be attributed to the many campus organizations that serve communities of color: African-American, Latino, Caribbean, Iranian, Filipino, Muslim and Korean, along with two clubs for Chinese students, a Club India and a Gospel Choir. The campus has published a Diversity Calendar for over five years, with each month having a different theme or combination of themes; co-sponsored activities receive grants. Developing a "culturally literate campus environment" is the declared goal.

SUNY Stony Brook also has a first-year-student-orientation course that covers racism and diversity; most students take it. Also, advisers in the dorms have held workshops. For example, a Haitian student and the president of Hillel organized a panel on a conflict in Brooklyn between a Haitian and a Hasidic Jew, with people from both communities coming to participate. The administration has taken a strong position that any harassment is not freedom of speech and won't be tolerated.

What about interaction between students from different clubs or other groups? It's not always easy. A study done of racial intolerance revealed that the Blacks and Latinos thought there was a low degree of interaction while whites thought there was a high degree. Why? As Preston told me in 1997, the groups differed in how they defined interaction. The whites felt that passively attending events of other students was interaction, whereas the students of color meant real engagement.

In 1992 and again five years later, Preston said the Asian students were still "not on board" in terms of cultural involvement, but a $25 million grant had just been made for an Asian cultural center on campus and this should have a major effect. For Latinos, Preston saw ups and downs. At one time the Latin American Student Organization was active, but in recent times there has been a lack of Latino student leaders, leaving a vacuum in which stress can be more common. Latinos may feel like they are an afterthought. On the other hand, Preston said in 1997, "Latino culture has blossomed on campus and Hispanic Heritage Month is the best of the Diversity Calendar—mainly because of work done by female students and staff who include outstanding artists and scholars, with one of them a provost."

The Interfaith Center takes on such issues as a disrespectful article in the campus newspaper about the death of rapper Tupac Shakur, which provoked Black student anger. The center also works in the larger community, creating a model for the campus. This linkage probably gives Stony Brook much of its strength in dealing with racial issues.

In early 1998, Amiri Baraka, poet and faculty member at Stony Brook (now retired), told me that he felt the cutting edge of resistance on that campus to the anti-democratic and racist trend sweeping the nation had been the formation of a United Front of Student Organizations including white ones. When swastikas had been scrawled on the walls, a common call for opposition went out from the Afro-American Studies department and a rabbi from Hillel. Thus, Baraka said, "an informal, objective united front was put in place that 'short-stopped' such actions."

As on other campuses, "there is a lack of sufficient staff." When Preston first came to Stony Brook in 1981, it had an all-white staff; today it is mixed. But the faculty is still heavily white and male; as of 1996, Asian/Pacific Island Americans provided the highest percentage of color, 9.7 percent.

<<< >>>

Evaluating anti-racist and "diversification" programs could become moot in the near future, as public university funding is slashed and thousands of part-time faculty are laid off (many if not most of them are faculty of color). Fees are being raised, which means fewer students of color can attend. All the cutbacks breed student anxiety—and this in turn aggravates racist actions by white students. As Tony Platt said, "the more fearful they become, the more they act out." In California, Proposition 209, abolishing affirmative action, has already meant a huge drop in the enrollment of Blacks and Latinos in law, medical and other professional schools. For example, the 1997 entering class at UC Berkeley's law school plunged 66 percent from what it had been the year before; Blacks went from 75 to 14.

Where will the anti-racist struggle in education be in the year 2000? It is easy to make gloomy projections. We need to stop the reactionary attacks on what exists, and struggle for more. Also, work should begin much earlier than college—in kindergarten, for instance. Along with ideological measures, systemic reforms are needed, such as more financial aid and an end to escalating fee increases.

Again we need to say: student organizing is key to all this work. The history of campus struggles, such as the 1996 sit-in for Ethnic Studies at Columbia University or the 1997 student movement at the University of Massachusetts in Amherst, carry a strong message. The message is that reforms begin when youth mobilize, build continuity into their strategy and generally make it impossible for the university bureaucrats to continue business as usual. In doing this, students must build anti-racist unity among themselves. Bigotry directed at one color is bigotry against all: let everyone see this and act on that knowledge.

chapter sixteen

BROWN DAVID v. WHITE GOLIATH

Racism at the University of California

"You have a chance in a hundred of winning," people told Chicano historian Rudy Acuña when he filed suit in 1992 against the University of California regents for discrimination based on his political work, race and age. No person of color had ever managed to bring rich, powerful UC to trial. "But how can I not try?" Acuña would answer. "How can I tell one of my students to fight injustice, or report a rape, or whatever, and not do it myself?"

Three long years later, on October 30, 1995, Acuña walked out of a Los Angeles federal courtroom the victor against UC. A radical, activist professor of Chicano Studies, with a crew of unpaid, mostly Chicano/a lawyers, had defeated a group of powerful administrators defended by million-dollar attorneys. As some observers commented, it was a brown David triumphing over a white Goliath.

Many also saw Acuña's victory as a win for all progressive people in today's battle against reactionary control of education and ideology. The regents he defeated were the same ones who had voted a few months previously to abolish affirmative action. Acuña's victory represented a strong challenge from below to the upper-class view of "scholarship" in general and of history in particular. It affirmed Chicano Studies. It was a ringing call to desegregate the University of California—its administrators, faculty, staff, workers. The Acuña case also brought to light an astounding record of abused power, in which UC has used lies, dishonest procedures, character assassination, retaliation against dissidents and tons of taxpayer dollars to maintain classist, racist and sexist practices.

How did the extraordinary confrontation of *Acuña v. UC Regents* come about? The story began quietly enough, in 1990, when students at the University of California, Santa Barbara (UCSB), asked Acuña to apply for a position in the Chicano Studies department there. He did, and the chair of that department, Yolanda Broyles-González, recommended him for the post after the whole department reviewed 33 applicants and voted to name Acuña. One of the goals was for him to help develop the first program in the United States that would grant a PhD in Chicano Studies.

Broyles-González and others had little doubt about Acuña's being the best applicant. During the movimiento years of the 1960s, he had founded Chicano Studies to meet student demands. At California State University, Northridge, where he has taught since 1969, he built what became the largest Chicano Studies department in this country. It is one of the few in the United States with a master's degree program. For years, one of his historical works, *Occupied America*, has served as the basic book on Chicano history at colleges and universities everywhere. Acuña played a crucial role in winning recognition for the Chicano/a experience as a signifcant part of U.S. history and the present society. He even wrote two children's books about Mexican Americans, because there were almost none at the time.

Acuña was also a noted activist. He had often supported demonstrations on issues of social justice, to the point of being arrested several times for his participation. Over the years he had published many op-ed articles on Latino issues, local politics and other events in the *Los Angeles Times* and, before its demise, the *Herald Examiner* of Los Angeles. Acuña would bring not only scholarship to UC Santa Barbara but also a deep commitment to his community's well-being.

Act I: Acuña Vetoed

In a one-sentence memo dated June 19, 1991, Yolanda Broyles-González was told the nomination of Acuña had been vetoed. What happened? And what did it mean when she herself was later removed?

All appointments recommended by a department head at UCSB are reviewed for approval by several other bodies. In Acuña's case, an "ad hoc committee" did the hatchet job, with its membership and its report to Chancellor Barbara Uehling kept secret. Acuña could obtain only a summary of the secret committee's report, with names removed. It explained that the refusal to appoint him was due to inadequate scholarship and the fact that the committee did not find his "fiery brand of advocacy" appropriate for a professorship. It discredited his many letters of recommendation from outstanding scholars, while suggesting his high public profile would enable him to be "dictatorial" in the Chicano Studies department. (Memo of June 19, 1991,

"Proposed Appointment for Rodolfo Acuña. Recommendation of Jeffrey B. Russell, Chair CAP. Denial of appointment.")

Acuña believed UCSB had moved against him from fear of what could happen if his radical political perspective came onto that campus, backed by his national reputation and senior stature. "Their motive is to censor me politically under the guise of what is or what is not scholarly," he said at the time. In a larger context, he added, the secret committee's action expressed a political climate that sees "token reforms like multiculturalism as a threat to their Euro-American hegemony and [they] are raising the barricades to defend [it]."

Charges of discrimination could be brought against UC for its action, Acuña believed. At first he tried to negotiate, offering not to file suit if UC would write a public letter of apology. During a later mediation he proposed other conditions, such as UCSB's establishing a permanent Chicano cultural center, tripling the Latino faculty by 1997 and developing long-range plans for Chicano Studies.

Those conditions spoke to a stark reality at UCSB and UC in general, a reality that has been repeatedly protested by students with hunger strikes and by workers through union action. Acuña documented one case after another in which the hiring of qualified Chicanos had been blocked by the violation or manipulation of procedures—an old tradition. The result: out of 583 tenured faculty at UCSB in 1990–91, only 5 percent (27) were Latino and only one of the 27 was a woman. Such was the situation in a state officially 26 percent Latino, according to the 1991 census. The numbers did not improve for the non-tenured, or for other people of color. An official 1991 study had shown systematic employment discrimination by UC against people of color and women.

Acuña estimated that out of the 5 percent of the faculty who were Latino, fewer than 1 percent were of Mexican extraction (Chicano/a); most were Cuban, South American, etc. At the same time, the UC system usually treated Chicano Studies as an illegitimate discipline. How it could develop in the absence of scholars and experts remained a mystery.

Designed to improve that entire situation, Acuña's conditions for not suing were refused by UCSB. He then told the *Santa Barbara News Press* that he would sue. With typical Acuña in-your-face aplomb, he asked: "What do you want me to do, act like a good Mexican boy, say 'Sí, señor,' and go away? Those days are gone forever." Acuña felt he had no choice but to go to the court of law and of public opinion.

The wheels of litigation then began to turn, as Acuña's lawyers filed suit in September 1992. Originally the grounds were discrimination based on race, national origin, political orientation and age (Acuña was 59 at the time). Judge Audrey Collins, whose sympathies would become clear to everyone at the trial, threw out the first two grounds. Political discrimination was dropped through an attorney's procedural error. Only ageism remained, but the team decided to go ahead—"You work with what you've got"—and there was direct evidence of age discrimination. To have a court find UC guilty of discrimination in any form would be historic.

Act II: The Secret Report Revealed

Utilizing a U.S. Supreme Court decision in a Pennsylvania case concerning access to documents, Acuña's lawyers were able in 1993 to obtain the full secret committee's report and identify its members, three white men. One, Wallace Chafe, had worked for the Central Intelligence Agency for five years and was considered an expert on Native Americans. Asked in his deposition for his opinion about various scholars, he said that Noam Chomsky was a charlatan. A second committee member, Giles Gunn, was a professor of English literature who claimed to know the history of culture but had no knowledge of Chicano Studies and had never heard of Acuña before.

Robert Kelley, the ad hoc committee's chair, was an unabashedly Eurocentric historian who stated in his deposition that Acuña had lied in saying the United States started the war on Mexico of 1846–48. In the 1986 edition of one of his history textbooks, Kelley still refers to undocumented Mexican workers as "wetbacks." The person originally nominated to be chair of the ad hoc committee (but replaced by Kelley) was Otis Graham, one of the founders of a notorious anti-immigrant organization, the Federation of American Immigration Reform (FAIR).

Such was the team assigned to evaluate an appointment that would have a major effect on UCSB's policies toward students and faculty of color as well as Ethnic Studies as a discipline. This trio received full support in their decision against Acuña from the chair of UCSB's Committee on Academic Personnel (CAP), Jeffrey B. Russell. A historian, Russell has stated that Acuña's work was Marxist because he used terms like "hegemony" and "subjugated peoples." In his deposition of November 17, 1995, Russell said the role of the scholar is to search for truth; however, "absolute truth is whatever would exist in the mind of God, to which we have no access.... [W]e cannot even hope to get close to it [absolute truth]." In a March 7, 1991, lecture "Pluralism, Truth and University Goals" and confirmed in his deposition, Russell stated, "The purpose of the University is to proclaim the intricate mystery and glory of God." (Citations are from documents made available to the author or quoted in court.)

Who selected those three men on the ad hoc committee? The answer: Associate Vice Chancellor Julius Zelmanowitz, who puts together all such committees. Zelmanowitz has enormous power and is known for organizing a committee that will be sure to usher in a candidate smoothly—or guarantee the candidate's being rejected. Before the trial, Zelmanowitz publicly insisted on the "integrity" of the process with Acuña and that no campus procedures had been breached. But in the trial itself, witnesses testified to improper phone calls, meetings outside review channels and other violations.

The ad hoc committee's report reads like postmodern McCarthyism. It begins by noting that Acuña is "an extraordinarily visible historian," then goes on to term him "a cult professor." In the Chicano world, "he is thought of as 'a master spirit' who can achieve remarkable things." Images of hypnotic priests and satanic rituals dance in the reader's head as the committee goes on to comment that Acuña has "an aura and prestige which far overshadows that of anyone else currently on [UCSB's] faculty." They feared Acuña's influence would be decisive in future hiring, merit increases, promotions, research and writing. It would determine the evolution of Chicano Studies.

This dictatorial potential, they said, would be enhanced by Acuña's being the first professor to hold his appointment entirely in Chicano Studies—not as a dual appointment, when a professor is hired for Chicano Studies and another department as well. That system has served, many believe, as a safeguard against Chicano Studies' having independent control over its own faculty and growth.

The report then tried to go for "weak scholarship." After reading Acuña's work, as they claimed to have done, committee members felt "he is an inveterate polemicist and pamphleteer who ... shapes his analyses and narrative to serve a political purpose." *Occupied America* is a "moralizing work" and not objective; Acuña is "on a soap-box, ranting." His book is "counter-hegemonic"; it cannot qualify as "solid history." The committee dismissed it as "a cult book." Even committee member Giles Gunn later said in court, when I attended, that he didn't agree with some of the language of its report.

Also in court, committee members admitted they had each read, at most, only one Acuña book. But that did not prevent them from concluding that "placing an historian with Professor Acuña's definition of what constitutes scholarship in a predominant position" would be an error. His mind was not the kind needed "in a field as yet so inchoate and lacking in firm intellectual identity as Chicano Studies." With those words the committee laid bare the heart of the matter: ideological control, particularly over Chicano Studies (which, by its very content, leads to an anti-imperialist, anti-racist historical perspective).

What about Acuña's ten supportive "extra-mural" letters from scholars, some of them nationally known experts and some high-level UC professors? CAP's chair, Jeffrey Russell, dismissed the letters by saying "with few exceptions they are solicited from people favoring politically 'activist' over objective scholarly approaches." Russell then quotes from every letter—but only four could possibly be described as praising Acuña's activism or polemical views.

Even before the secret committee's report became public, strong support for Acuña had been built. Students noted that UCSB's chancellor had waited to announce Acuña's rejection until summer—when it would be harder to mount protests. On October 17, 1991, about 600 to 800 students and others demonstrated. A march and rally in Santa Barbara on February 1, 1992, drew some 2,500 people from California, Texas and Colorado. Meanwhile, Acuña continued teaching at Northridge and writing.

The lawsuit moved along slowly. "I've never been in a case that was so hotly litigated," lead attorney Moisés Vázquez told me. The University of California tried to kill its adversary with paper: filing a river of motions, sending an avalanche of letters and faxes to be answered. When Acuña's lawyers asked for UC personnel records, they received nearly 50 boxes—probably 200,000 sheets of paper—to sort through (on unpaid time). The university's witch-hunting tactics included researching and reviewing every word Acuña had ever written (on well-paid time) for supposedly subversive or radical content, anything that might hurt his case.

A high point came when UC sent a team of five men with three photocopiers to Acuña's home to copy all his papers. Acuña says UC also contacted people all over the United States in a hunt for damaging information about his personal life. After filing suit, which again suggests a desperate search for dirt, he was audited by the IRS three times.

Acuña is also certain that UC had agents monitor speeches he gave at public events. Two were exposed, identified as campus police by students when he went to speak at a UCSB class. The university also had informants among the students.

To finance all this, UC spent an estimated $4 million even before the October trial. At the other end, Acuña's lawyers worked thousands of hours *pro bono* and sometimes even paid for expenses out of their own pockets. Small community-based fund-raisers, often with artists and performers donating their services, kept the lawsuit afloat thanks to people like Mary Pardo, who also teaches at Northridge.

Act III: The Trial

The saga of David *v.* Goliath continued in the courtroom, beginning October 10, 1995. You could see it when you arrived: the Gucci/Armani look of UC's Anglo attorneys, with their expensive display-equipment for evidence, and Judge Audrey Collins with her body language clearly indicating sympathy for UC. Observers commented on her scornful eyeball-rolling at Acuña's attorneys' arguments and her deferential attentiveness when UC's team spoke.

Judge Collins had limited the grounds for the Acuña suit before the trial, throwing out race and national origin. Thus she accepted as truth UC's claim that racism had not been an issue. She also limited the time allowed for Acuña to prove his case; his lawyers requested six weeks, she granted 20 hours. She severely limited the number of experts his lawyers could call. She limited the number of scholars who could testify in court about their letters supporting Acuña to just one out of a possible ten. Again and again Judge Collins put chains on Acuña's grievance.

What does it mean that Collins owed her appointment as a judge in part to a letter of recommendation written by the man serving as UC's lead attorney on the case she was presiding over? Even non-experts would call this a potential conflict of interest. If Acuña's attorneys chose not to challenge her presence, they must have had doubts about getting anyone better in federal court.

In the trial, the evidence for Acuña included numerous references in UC reports to his age as a liability—references that were gratuitous or inappropriate. For example, the ad hoc committee noted that Acuña "would be arriving at UCSB at age 59, and would necessarily have to spend much of his remaining time on the active faculty learning how to carry out this most difficult and demanding of instructional tasks, the teaching of students at the PhD level." CAP's report describes as a drawback the fact that "Acuña, at age 59, has never trained doctoral students." The secret committee's report said that "many younger scholars would think him obsolete." That would be because his anti-imperialist, anti-capitalist views are not as "thoughtful" as those of today's scholars, they implied.

In court, UC's witnesses made statements that contradicted their earlier depositions. For instance, Giles Gunn of the secret committee testified repeatedly that members never discussed Acuña's age in their meetings. But when reminded of his deposition about Acuña's age, he agreed "we did think that over." Gunn denied the need to correct any contradiction between the statements; it was, he said, simply that "age was not the central factor." The judge sustained UC's objection that Acuña's lawyer was being "argumentative" in identifying the contradiction.

The only Raza witnesses for UC were two Latinas and one Latino from the UCSB Chicano Studies department: Rosalinda Fregosa, Francisco Lomeli and Denise Segura. Back in 1991, the three had abstained in the vote called by chair Yolanda Broyles-González to recommend Acuña for a UCSB post. The secret committee made much of the divided vote (three in favor, zero against, and three abstentions).

However, at the trial none of the three who had abstained stated that Acuña was unqualified for the position. Denise Segura testified that Broyles-González had "intimidated" her into abstaining. As usual, campus politics played its role in the saga of *Acuña v. UC Regents*, and the opposition was not all white. But the main game didn't play at this level of small-time academic antics; it was upstairs with the big power brokers.

After two working days, the jury came back with its unequivocal, 8-0 verdict for Acuña, ruling that UC had discriminated on the basis of age. Dozens of supporters had been in the courtroom all month—students, elected officials, teachers, workers, parents. Now everyone celebrated the verdict.

No Rest for the Weary

The saga did not end immediately after the verdict. Just two weeks after the Acuña victory, UC's lawyers moved that the judge either throw out the jury's unanimous verdict for Acuña and rule instead for UC—or order a new trial. They maintained that the jury had "a complete lack of substantive evidence to support" its verdict. The eight-person jury (customary for a civil suit in federal court) consisted of four Latinos, one African American, one Filipino, one Asian/Anglo, and one Anglo. In a report to the UC Regents after the trial, UC attornies stated that none of the jurors had a college education and most barely had a high school education, so they could not understand the abstract, technical issues of the case. That jury was just too diverse and working class for their taste.

Failing in their effort to have the verdict thrown out, UC attorneys prepared "Information Bulletins" loaded with attacks on Acuña's character, which were distributed on the Santa Barbara campus. Their goal was to prevent him from being granted an appointment at UCSB. Given Acuña's victory, Judge Collins had to decide whether to compel UC to grant him the appointment (in which case he would receive $90,000 compensation) or not (in which case he would receive $325,000). To nobody's surprise, she decided against ordering the appointment.

In late November 1995 the Faculty Legislature of UCSB voted to "thank" UC for going to court and "defending" its procedures. This unprecedented move signified a closing of ranks against any and all challengers. Even before the trial, UC had shown its intention to wage all-out war on dissidents when it removed Broyles-González as chair of the Chicano Studies department. Yet she had just received an evaluation of "superior performance." The excuse given, in veiled language, was her support for UCSB students who had waged an 11-day hunger strike to win more Chicano Studies faculty and other demands. She told me that the reason was "retaliation for my support of Rudy Acuña, absolutely. So much for academic freedom." Broyles-González also said that the secret-committee report distorted her statements at one of its meetings, which she had been allowed to attend for one hour. It quoted her as agreeing on a criticism of how Acuña's work would be considered dated by younger scholars. "I never said that, they twisted a different comment," she said.

At times the whole case echoes with conspiracy. Acuña points to a strange coincidence. Before filing suit, he published dozens of articles in the *Los Angeles Times*. After filing, he submitted five to ten pieces on different issues but none were accepted. Later he learned that a vice-president of the *Times*, Marilyn Lee, is a past president of the UCSB Alumni Association and a close friend of former UCSB chancellor Barbara Uehling. Lee's husband is associated with the University of California, Los Angeles. The *Los Angeles Times* also terminated Broyles-González as its theater critic after the Acuña suit began.

Throughout the five-year struggle, Acuña's politics have not been simply race-based. As he says repeatedly, "We're not fighting white people, we're fighting capitalism. There is a great danger in associating whiteness with capitalism. You might forget stands taken by people like Eleanor Roosevelt, or Woody Guthrie with his song 'Jesús and María' about Mexican immigrants. We also have to look at our own errors, like sexism and homophobia. And it's true that we have to decide what kind of Chicano Studies we want. It has to be progressive."

The case of *Acuña v. University of California Regents* is about the mind's struggle for air in these suffocating times. We can ask if it really matters whether there is freedom of thought at the university level when so many youth are too poor to get past sixth grade. Acuña's case says it does. When we talked on one of the last days in court, the issue was again: why fight this endless suit? You cannot win. Acuña said: "No. I can't lose. You empower people by giving them historical memory. Even if we lose this case, knowledge is gained. Memory is established. You can show why we lost, if we do. You can expose what happened. As Malcolm X said, 'If you don't know your history, you're no better than a lower animal.'"

The struggle has gone on and on in small ways: Goliaths are bad losers. When Acuña filed for his team's legal expenses to be paid by UC, as ordered, the judge reduced the amount requested by 80 percent. This had to be appealed. In 1997, he was denied the right to file a political-discrimination suit in federal court. Meanwhile, with his $200,000 in damages he set up a foundation to support people who want to bring charges against UC for employee discrimination. An important case is that of Alfred Arteaga at UC Berkeley, denied tenure despite outstanding qualifications. Predictably, the Internal Revenue Service has hassled Acuña about the tax status of the new foundation.

Yet he did win against the one of the biggest, richest universities in the world. Professor Yolanda Broyles-González, the other main UC target, had a major victory too. In 1997, she won the first suit in history against UC for unequal pay to women. She also obtained an unprecedented permanent injunction issued in Santa Barbara Superior Court that, when finalized, will guarantee protection against gender, race and political discrimination, as well as against retaliation, by UC.

Goliath has not fallen as a result of the two Raza victories, but light is shining on his illegal and deceptive ways as never before.

chapter seventeen

ON TIME IN MISSISSIPPI

In a book of essays about Latinas and Latinos, does it seem odd to see a title that says something about Mississippi? Does it seem odd to be looking back at the Black civil and human rights movement of the 1960s rather than the Chicano movement? Who do I think I am, anyway?

When I worked for the Student Nonviolent Coordinating Committee (SNCC) from 1961 to 1968, first as a volunteer and then as full-time staff, it seemed perfectly natural. If a person wanted to spend her life tearing down the prison called White Supremacy, what better place to go than the Black movement? And proudly, too. It took a few years to wonder, how does a person who isn't white—but not Black either—fit into the color scheme of this color-obsessed society?

After a while, some unexplored Mexican spirit inside, and the changing times outside, drew me to the Southwest, where I had never been. It had its own prison of White Supremacy. But the two prisons were really one, and the fight was really one, and a perfectly natural voice said: Let us tear down all prisons together. Amen.

<<< >>>

Outside the red-brick county courthouse in Philadelphia, Mississippi, a middle-aged Black man named Ben Chaney stood facing some 75 people gathered for a rally on June 25, 1994. About ten miles away, his brother James had been murdered, along with two young whites from the North—Andrew Goodman and Mickey Schwerner. All three were civil rights workers. Their killers, local Klansmen, included the deputy sheriff based in that courthouse at the time.

Thirty years had passed since the murder. Now Ben Chaney began his brief speech by asking the crowd, "How many of you are from Philadelphia?" A janitor and a policeman; nobody else. "That shows," said Chaney slowly, "how far we have to go." His words hung in the afternoon stillness.

The courthouse rally, part of a weekend reunion of civil rights workers, ended after four other people spoke. I walked through the courthouse, moving quickly past the door marked "Sheriff." Outside, the main street looked as though it had changed little in three decades: a few blocks of small shops, the Bible Book Store (and no other), large well-built churches and not a single café. A sullen kind of silence muffled the street, as if whites in this small, notorious town resented being once again the center of national attention.

It was time to drive out to the site of Mount Zion Methodist Church, the Black community church whose destruction by arson had led Chaney, Goodman and Schwerner to come and investigate. They had been arrested by Sheriff Lawrence Rainey of Neshoba County (known for boasting to people about having killed two Black men "in the line of duty"). Released from jail late at night, they suddenly found themselves being chased by a police car, stopped and taken from their station wagon, driven down a remote dirt lane and shot to death. Mount Zion marked the beginning of that horror. It was also one of 35 Black churches set on fire by racists during the summer of 1964.

Our group needed directions to the church, and someone asked a state trooper standing by. He said it was hard to find, so he would escort us. A police escort? Too many old images came rushing by. Then I saw the trooper he was tall, thin ... and Black. In that moment the world around seemed much safer.

The rebuilt Mount Zion church lies on a narrow road with little sign of life except an occasional trailer or rundown shack. In front of its entrance stand three towering, hand-hewn wooden crosses and, nearby, the original church's bell on display. A metal plaque tells the story of Chaney, Goodman and Schwerner. The truth of that brutality and sacrifice is here, but hidden away in a remote corner of Neshoba County where few whites will have to look at it.

Still, the trooper was—yes, he was—Black.

<<< >>>

Mississippi Homecoming 1994, the Jackson-based reunion and conference of June 23–26, marked the anniversary of the 1964 Mississippi Summer Project when more than 1,000 volunteer civil rights workers—most of them white, college-age youth from the North—had come to the state. The project's goal was to break the racist grip of fear and isolation on Mississippi by bringing the outside world there, including federal protection. Voter registration, then a life-threatening action for Mississippi's Black people, played a central role in that strategy. Volunteers also worked at Freedom Schools in 47 towns and community centers. The summer project involved four major civil rights groups under the umbrella of the Council of Federated Organizations (COFO). But its roots and inspiration lay primarily in work done by the Student Nonviolent Coordinating Committee and project director Robert Moses.

Thirty years later, some 400 to 500 former volunteers, SNCC staff members and other activists gathered in a reunion that seemed to be joyous for most, and wondrous for all. A 1964 volunteer not given to superlatives was heard to say after one day at the reunion, "This is about as perfect as anything can get." I realized one morning that I had been smiling steadily for two straight days. The media would make sure to report that people had grown grayer, fatter, balder or whatever, and it was true enough; but they could not see what we saw in each other's faces: the remembered trust, courage, commitment and oneness in a cause.

Politically, most people seemed to be in a progressive place. Many were active for social justice, from organizing against homelessness to producing anti-racist educational material like the television series "Eyes on the Prize." New projects spontaneously emerged during the reunion, such as some native Mississippians who had moved away long ago deciding to organize support for reforms in their old hometown. The nonprofit Mississippi Community Foundation, which sponsored the reunion as part of its work to review and document the history of the movement, had various plans. They included working with Universal Studios on a feature film to counter the distorted movie *Mississippi Burning* that made FBI agents into anti-racist heroes.

Willie (now Wazir) Peacock, a SNCC field secretary from Greenwood, Mississippi, had two words—perhaps the best—for the weekend. "It was," he said, "on time." People came from all over the country who had not come to any previous SNCC reunions. Local leaders attended, along with former volunteers and SNCC staff ranging from our hardy band of photographers to celebrities like Julian Bond, Mary King, U.S. Representative John Lewis and Bernice Reagon. People embraced across the Black-white line, the staff/volunteer line, and the North/South line with an ease often absent during the summer project or the last difficult years of SNCC. Volunteers were praised by SNCC staff members for their historic contribution. On the plane going to Jackson, Bob Moses had said the reunion might be an occasion for healing, and so it seemed in various ways.

On Saturday, former volunteers traveled back to towns where they had been stationed in 1964: Greenwood, McComb, Ruleville, Vicksburg and others. One group found the local Black barber, still there after 30 years, who gave them all free haircuts. Another knocked on the door of an elderly Black woman who peered out the window at a person unseen for 30 years and without hesitation asked: "Kathy?"

<<< >>>

That weekend found some people saying that nothing had really changed for Black people in Mississippi, and others pointing to changes like the Black state trooper. To debate this issue would keep us trapped between two absolutes, two abstractions, without a sense of history or process. Instead, we need to look at precisely what has changed for the better and what hasn't and why; what has happened to some of the changes; and who is doing what about it. A host of revelations then appear.

At the reunion, the sense of positive change began at the airport, where a large official banner proclaimed "Welcome Homecoming 1964–94" to my disbelieving eyes. It grew with the big roadside sign at the Holiday Inn announcing "Welcome Freedom Summer Reunion." It mushroomed when former staff and volunteers returning to visit towns where they had once worked, whose white residents had often wished them dead, were given keys to the city. Not quite the Mississippi most of us remembered: a world of White Supremacist hate, jailings and bombings; a world where we kept a sharp eye out for Dixie flags on pickups with gun racks.

Again and again we heard about Black Mississippians now in political positions unimaginable three decades ago. The summer project laid the foundation for such victories by exposing Black people's near-total exclusion from the electoral process. That in turn led to the 1965 Voting Rights Act. As a result Mississippi, where only 6.7 percent of African Americans had been able to register by 1964, has more Black elected officials today than any other state.

Many examples of these and other gains linked to the summer project emerged that weekend. In Greenwood, SNCC staff members found a progressive Black woman elected to the city council whom they remembered as a high school student in 1964: "She came by the office after school every day, every day." When former volunteers went to Hattiesburg, they were met by a group of Freedom School "alumni" who are now MAs and PhDs, and who said they never would have gone on to college without that 1964 inspiration. Long time freedom fighter Aaron Henry, who was once refused television time for a campaign ("No, nigger," he was told), is now chair of the TV station's board.

All these advances could be described as simply bringing Mississippi up to the level of other states. But no one should take that lightly, as today's nationwide war on redistricting tells us. Based on the 1965 Voting Rights Act and the 1990 census, a number of voting districts in various states were redrawn so that Blacks or Latinos could win office (almost none were ever elected from majority-white districts). But the new districts have been under sharp reactionary attack ever since. In a panel at the reunion, law professor Frank Parker of Washington, D.C., grimly concluded that if this tendency persisted, "it means the end of the Second Reconstruction" as the 1960s Civil Rights Movement has been called. Two years later, in 1996, the U.S. Supreme Court ruled that four of the new districts were unconstitutional because they were race-based; three previous Supreme Court decisions had said the same about other new districts. The tendency did persist.

Mississippi has one problem area that showed few signs of positive change: the economy. The African-American unemployment rate can run as high as 50 percent, one speaker reported. Another pointed out that middle- and even upper-middle-class Blacks could now be found, but improved status has not reached the lower echelons. Dorie Ladner, former SNCC staffer, bluntly stated that the Black people elected to political office had no economic power.

It would have been good to have had more discussion of these problems and related class issues in the reunion panels and workshops. Along with the focus on electoral politics, politicians and upward mobility, it would have helped to include a strong dose of SNCC's historic commitment to help organize plantation workers, sharecroppers, janitors, hotel maids and all manner of poor folk. The voice of the grassroots, of people like Mississippi's Fannie Lou

Hamer, must always be heard if we are to understand the past and move effectively toward the future.

Nothing spoke more energetically to those questions of "what has changed for the better and what has not" than the youth at the reunion. Almost all were African-American students, with many from Tougaloo College or Jackson State University, where reunion events took place. More than 20 came from junior and senior high schools in Washington, D.C., sponsored by Frank Smith, a SNCC worker who became a D.C. City Council member. A significant number had movement parents. Altogether they created the most dynamic moments of the weekend.

It began Friday during the "Workshop for Children: Telling the Story of the Civil Rights Movement," whose title was turned upside down before the afternoon ended. During the discussion, only one youth spoke at first. Then, as the elders continued, three young African Americans standing in a row raised their hands high and kept them there a long time, waiting with silent persistence to speak.

Finally all three were called on, beginning with Derrick Johnson, who was about to be a law student and proved a powerful speaker. First he countered a statement by one older workshop participant that there was no movement today. Then Johnson laid out the *Ayers v. Mississippi* case, which began with a 1975 lawsuit to win for the state's historically Black colleges and universities (referred to as HBCUs) resources equal to those of white schools. A 1992 U.S. Supreme Court ruling avoided the issue by ordering Mississippi to "disestablish" segregation. In response the state proposed to merge one of its three HBCUs with a white school—and make another one part of the prison system. Calling that proposal educational genocide, thousands of students all over the South marched, rallied and circulated petitions (25,000 signatures on one) in a "Save Our Schools" (SOS) campaign.

The Ayers case, as it came to be known, speaks bitterly to what has and hasn't changed in Mississippi. It reveals the same old racism against Blacks: a refusal to upgrade plantation-style education, typified by run-down schools, tattered textbooks and ill-paid teachers. (Later, the Ayers suit succeeded and the HBCUs were maintained.) The SOS campaign shows how the intensified racism of the past 25 years has left African-American youth today pressing much less for acceptance by the white world, and much more for upgrading Black institutions. The Ayers case is controversial for some progressives. What does not seem controversial is that many African-American youths today must find it hard to imagine the moral climate of the 1960s, resonating as it did with "Black and white together, we shall overcome."

At the reunion's "Workshop for Children," it soon became clear that the youth and the elders wanted to hear from each other. So Bob Moses did not speak as scheduled but instead asked everyone born after 1964 to move to the center of the group. Those over 30 moved to the fringes. For people who knew Moses in SNCC, or his current Algebra Project, with its goal of empowering young Blacks, the request was in keeping with his liberatory style of leadership. It guaranteed that youth—who had already begun finding their voices in the workshop—would dominate the discussion for the rest of the afternoon.

One person, the son of a former SNCC field secretary, launched a dialogue with his comment that activists are too often conscious people talking to other conscious people. How could we reach the grassroots, he asked, "the people at the bottom of the totem pole?" Another asked, how can we overcome all our differences? They found no neat answers, but they did ask crucial questions.

Many of the youths who spoke were women. This made a happy contrast to most reunion panels. Although the panels were generally excellent, with presenters who spoke strongly and relevantly, all but two of them had a 3-1, 4-1, 5-1 or even 6-1 ratio of male to female participants. And one of those two exceptions addressed parenting skills, a concern traditonally viewed as belonging to women. The 1994 youth workshop pointed in a different direction.

Another sign of positive change: one young African-American woman, daughter of two SNCC veterans, announced without hesitation: "I'm a lesbian. That doesn't mean I'm not a Black woman." Rejecting the frequent demand for a single identity, she explained, "I want to deal with sexism and homophobia, not just racism." Perhaps a quarter or a third of the room clapped for her comments, but it is impossible to imagine any such openness 30 years ago. We can also be cheered by the fact that Rep. John Lewis, from Georgia, former SNCC chair, spoke against homophobia—strongly and unasked.

Sitting among the students, a daughter of Pakistani immigrants told how her mother had been fired from her job because, she was told, "You smell." This came, the daughter explained, from the spices used in traditional Pakistani cooking. You could feel a sympathetic response rising in the room. "And people told my mother to try harder to understand English. But why don't they try harder to understand *us?*" Young Blacks and others clapped loudly for her angry rejection of cultural racism. They seemed to have room for people who did not look like them, including immigrants, but with whom they shared being despised.

That afternoon, and during the evening program, youth made it clear they wanted to be heard and heard seriously. "Listen to us," said one, "we know everything you know and more!" Did they need to be so adamant with this reunion crowd, who seemed quite ready to pass that torch? Probably not. But their intensity signaled political energy and the promise of a new youth movement. The Civil Rights Movement was not an event; it is a process and it goes on. Process says one should learn the language of youth, respect them without glorifying them, take a long look at what we could have done better and pass the lessons along.

At the roundtable on "The Civil Rights Movement in Retrospect," movement veterans spoke chillingly about what we are up against today. Bill Strickland, now teaching at the University of Massachusetts, Amherst, observed how the political climate had worsened with the Reagan-Bush years. "The Civil Rights Movement smashed American mythology, which isn't easy today because the opposition is more sneaky... Every issue today is a coded racial issue ... and when you tell the truth about racism it gets called discrimination."

In the present era of devalued dreams and mocked hopes, we need to confront immoral power with moral power. That was the message of SNCC founder Ella Baker and the essence of the 1960s movements. The Jackson reunion often echoed the importance of linking the past and the present, and demonstrated the need for a new Civil Rights Movement. Call it human rights if you prefer; we still live in a time when the denial of civil rights becomes the denial of humanity. Look at the beating of Rodney King, the repeated lynchings of Blacks in Mississippi jails, the church burnings, the forces that would deny health care and schooling to immigrant children because they lack the right piece of paper. We need to fight all such barbarity with a movement that calls on all colors to fight on all fronts.

<<< >>>

That rally at the Philadelphia courthouse on June 25 ended, as you might expect, with people singing "We Shall Overcome." For years I have half-dreaded this moment at an event because the song makes me cry and holding hands as people do with "We Shall Overcome," how to wipe away the tears? But on this day, for the first time in thirty years, the song did not make me cry.

Don't ask why it didn't, but one answer might go like this: "We Shall Overcome" gave us a vision of community in an era of collective defiance whose courage brought prideful tears. In later years we could also weep for the elusive beauty of that vision. But the reunion transcended the past and pointed to the need for a new movement with many hard questions to answer. No time for tears. It's just harder—more complicated—to make that freedom train come now. So get on board, as the movement song says, and help make it come. Wherever you are, get on board!

part five

WOMAN TALK:
No Taco Belles Here

Queremos conocer sus luchas
y platicarles como luchamos nosotras
y como nos organizamos. Queremos que nos oigan
pero más queremos oírlas.

We want to know about your struggles
and talk with you about how we women struggle
and how we organize ourselves.
We want you to listen to us
but even more, we want to listen to you, sisters.

—*palabras zapatistas/EZLN*
—from the Zapatista movement

chapter eighteen

IN PURSUIT OF LATINA LIBERATION

The story of feminist Latinas spreads across centuries and is rich in heroines who demolish the stereotype of the "passive Latin woman." The landmarks are numerous in Mexico, from the openly feminist seventeenth-century intellectual Sor Juana Inés de La Cruz, a nun, to the first feminist congress of 1911 and the suffrage movement of the 1930s. Aside from the self-defined feminists, we know that América, the hemisphere, is rich in indigenous traditions that often put women at the center of society. Powerful pre-Columbian queens and goddesses ruled alongside male dieties. In daily life cultural mainstays like the timeless *curandera*, or "healer," demonstrate the power of women's historical presence.

Many Latinas might not have defined themselves with a term like "feminist," but their lives expressed great strength and defiance of male restriction. Micaela Bastides, an Inca who led the revolt against Spain's rule in the eighteenth century alongside her husband, Tupac Amaru, continues to be a haunting figure for those lucky enough to learn her story. In Mexico, many women helped to launch and later participated in the Mexican war of independence from Spain (1810–21) and the Mexican Revolution. Their collective image resonates with power. In the Dominican Republic, the beloved Mirabal sisters, known as *las mariposas* ("the butterflies"), gave their lives to end the long Trujillo dictatorship. The day in 1960 when they were assassinated by Trujillo forces, November 25, is commemorated all over Latin America as the Day Against Violence Toward Women. Today Rigoberta Menchú, a Maya of Guatemala and an activist who became the first indigenous person to win the Nobel Prize for peace, lives on as a symbol of defiant survival.

The list goes on and begs for an encyclopedia of Latina feminism. Here we want to look at Chicanas and Latinas in recent times, including some of the advances and failures by Mexican women and Chicanas confronting male supremacy during the past 25 years.

During the Chicano liberation movement of 1965–75, open challenges to sexism began to be heard from Chicana participants. As sociologist Alma García tells us in her 1989 essay "The Development of Chicana Feminist Discourse 1970–1980," and confirmed by my personal experience, the contradiction of encountering male-supremacist practices within a movement supposedly fighting for social justice spurred many Chicanas to new consciousness. In the process they made minimal feminist demands. (Women in the African-American and Asian-American movements of the 1960s and early 1970s were similarly pushed in a feminist direction by experiencing sexism inside their movements.)

In response, male supremacy hurled two weapons at such Chicanas. The first was the accusation that "you're acting like a white woman"—*agringada* ("gringoized"). In other words, you're a traitor to your people, your culture. This could be devastating to Chicana activists, given that a central goal of the movimiento was liberation for brown people from Anglo-imposed domination. That charge sometimes resonated with Chicanas, based on their accurate perception that the women's liberation movement was then dominated by Anglo women. The second counter-insurgent weapon was the accusation that "you're being divisive." It, too, could be devastating, because unity and the sense of Raza as family were so important to the movement. What could be worse, in a hostile society, than to be divisive among your own, oppressed people?

As a participant in New York Radical Women in 1968 (the only Latina member at the time), I shared the powerful sense of feminist discovery that illuminated those years. Yet I also came to understand why so many Chicanas in the Southwest saw the women's movement of that era as irrelevant or alienating because it was overwhelmingly Anglo and middle-class. Again, like many African-American and Native American women, Chicana activists believed the women's movement saw men as the enemy. That was a view they could not accept, because Raza were fighting racism and oppression as a people; men suffered from those same forces. To focus on women's oppression alone and to discount racial and class oppression, as the national women's movement often did, contradicted our perception. This sense of clashing worldviews, which resulted from having such different historical experiences, became a major reason why only a few Chicanas looked for alliances that could be forged with Euro-American feminists.

In the next 20 years, a self-defined Chicana feminism flowered, mainly in academia and most visibly among young faculty and graduate students. Under pressure, the National Association for Chicano Studies (NACS) established a women's caucus at its 1985 meeting in Sacramento, California, and later changed its name to the National Association of Chicana and Chicano Studies (NACCS) to assert inclusion. Another organization, Mujeres Activas en Letras y Cambio Social

(MALCS), emerged in the 1980s as the locus of Latina feminist academics' work for social change that prioritizes mentoring young Chicana scholars. Its initial leadership came from Adaljiza Sosa Riddell at the University of California, Davis, and the University of California at Berkeley's Mujeres en Marcha, a graduate-student women's group.

The most striking change during the past 20 years can be seen in attitudes toward homophobia. In the late 1960s and early 1970s, an almost total silence hung over gay and lesbian advocacy. No openly gay person could be a movement leader. Today homophobia persists; most progressive, straight Chicanos as well as Chicanas still fail to see gay and lesbian rights as another struggle of other oppressed people. Too many still fail to see homophobia as a sometimes murderous force of discrimination. But the situation has improved, especially in some major cities, in academia and among youth. A lesbian caucus of NACCS was formalized at its 1992 national conference in Albuquerque, thus establishing an official rejection of homophobia toward lesbians. Gay and lesbian Raza groups and individuals are out there now, as they never could be before. The work of Chicana lesbian artists and intellectuals such as Gloria Anzaldúa and Cherríe Moraga has been crucial to this liberation, with benefits going beyond *las lesbianas*. Wherever one finds strong voices for women among Chicanas, they often come from lesbians.

When the announcement came in my mail about a two-day conference to be held at UC Berkeley in April 1997 sponsored by La Familia de UC Berkeley, there could be no doubt that the sexism and homophobia of the 1960s movimiento had been dealt serious blows. For "La Familia" was no traditional Mexican collectivity of blood relatives; it is a "gay, lesbian, bisexual and transgender student organization" of Latinos and Latinas. Times have changed, *gracias a dios.*

At the undergraduate level, signs of growing feminism exist alongside visible hesitation about being labeled feminist. As elsewhere, symbols and terminology often define the debate. Changing the name "Chicano Studies" to "Chicano and Chicana Studies" (as NACCS had done, Spanish being a gendered language) became common on California campuses in the 1990s. At the same time, when I speak about feminism as such to Latina and Latino undergraduate students in the same room, a combination of reactions often occurs. Few Chicanas support my ideas publicly or declare themselves feminist; few if any men are sympathetic, and many air sexist attitudes or make such statements as "I believe in equal rights for women but not feminism"; and several Chicanas express agreement but only after the event, in private. As might be expected, feminist expression intensifies in any all-women's gathering, where Chicana students will analyze and grapple with issues of patriarchy and sexist practice.

These developments suggest two realities. First, the women's movement of the 1960s has had positive effects, despite its racial and class biases. The idea of women organizing separately, once anathema to Raza activists and energetically opposed by the men, has become widely accepted. Latina lesbians would have stayed in the closet longer without the national women's movement to encourage them to come out. The articulation of concerns common to almost all women, such as health, child care, domestic violence, rape and reproductive rights, is much more frequent than it was two decades ago.

Our second reality is that Latina feminism, like other forms of feminism, has been sabotaged by backlash forces that rage everywhere. We can thank those forces for making the term "feminist" so unpopular, for making so many Chicanas and Chicanos accept today's bra-burning, man-hating labels. In the case of Chicanas, another political trend sometimes strengthens the general assault on feminism: a nationalism that has intensified in direct relation to the racist backlash of the past 20 years and especially since President Reagan's election in 1980.

Looking over the past two decades, we see close ties between gender-related attitudes and political ideology. A law seems to exist that sexism and heterosexism almost always travel alongside reactionary types of nationalism. Chicano liberation is then seen as an expression of manhood, and manhood is defined as domination. Thus Corky Gonzáles' epic poem "I Am Joaquín" was a powerful cry of proud identity in its time and still is, but today we realize how it echoes the tendency to reduce women to a handful of roles like the beloved, all-suffering mother. It reminds us painfully of how, within the movement, Juana usually stayed home with the kids or typed the minutes or nursed a domestic black eye while her *mero cabrón* played Aztec chieftain. "Chicanismo" was supposed to mean pride in our peoplehood; too often, it was "for machos only." By the 1970s a serious number of Chicana activists were asking our male counterparts, simplistically but truthfully, "Why does your need to be more in this racist society mean I have to be less?"

That question remains. The anti-sexist struggle today thus seems almost surreal in its contradictions. One can observe young Chicanas who will unequivocally distance themselves from the word "feminist" but act in ways that are so very feminist, objectively. Still, the future promises more advances than setbacks. For example, the California division of the Chicano student organization Movimiento Estudiantil Chicano de Aztlan (MEChA) declined a few years ago to establish a

Chicana caucus, despite urging from a women's workshop I attended. It now has such a caucus. More than a few MEChA chapters in California are formally headed by women, which rarely happened 10 or 15 years ago (despite the fact that women were often the real leaders in practice). In the 1993 hunger strike for a Chicana/o Studies department at the University of California, Los Angeles, half of the strikers were women students. In 1994, women also formed a major part of the hunger strikes for similar causes at the University of California, Santa Barbara, and the University of Colorado in Boulder. In the May 1994 Stanford University hunger strike, the fasters were four Chicanas. Through such experience, women have often developed new attitudes toward themselves—perhaps the most subversive change of all. This has taken concrete form in networking; the fasters and supporters from Boulder, for example, came to Santa Barbara to express solidarity with the hunger strikers there.

As for the reactions of Latino men on California campuses, contradiction is often written across their faces. The same Chicano student who articulates extremely backward ideas about women may also recognize that change is blowing in the wind and he can't oppose it in obvious ways. A day or week devoted to "La Chicana" or Latinas in general is institutionalized on many campuses. Unfortunately, this is less true with respect to gays and lesbians; among Latino college students, homophobia still runs more freely than sexism toward women.

At the level of junior high (middle school) and high school in California, one can find an even stronger current of self-conscious feminism (without the word being used) than at the college level. In 1995 I spoke before 600 Latino high school seniors who had come for "Raza Day" at UC Berkeley, an annual event that draws students to that campus as a university they might want to attend. My talk was about Latina history. I began by describing how, at marches and other demonstrations, you could hear cheers for this man or that—"¡Viva Zapata! ¡Viva César Chávez!"—by name. "And then," I said, "we hear '¡Viva la mujer!'—'Long live women!'" I intended to make the point that a specific woman's name is rarely cheered and then ask the students why women, unlike men, were celebrated so anonymously. But this audience upstaged me, shaking the auditorium with thunderous applause and cheers: "¡Viva la mujer!" Dozens of young women were jumping in their seats.

More examples have accumulated since then, during various encounters with junior high and high school girls. Feminism supposedly doesn't appeal to young women, but the opposite often seems true for activist Chicanas in the San Francisco Bay Area, so long as the word itself is not used. In 1994, Latino and other students from 38 schools in 11 Bay Area towns held walkouts—called blowouts—to demand educational reforms: more bilingual counselors, more retention programs, no more cutbacks, a relevant multicultural curriculum. At the staging-area rally, during the march downtown and at the main rally facing City Hall, a good half of the speakers were female. That would have been unthinkable during the 1960s movement years. Women also handle security for marches and other major events.

During the San Francisco walkouts, it was the women who called loudest and most clearly for unity and peace among their peers rather than gang warfare over "colors." One moment that vividly demonstrated this concern came when the marching crowd was chanting a denunciation of Gov. Pete Wilson's educational cutbacks: "Wilson, Wilson *a la chingada* ['To hell with Wilson']/ *Viva, viva* Che Guevara!" I overheard one young woman say to another, "We have to change that chant—the kids from Wilson High will think it's about them." So they started shouting, "Pete Wilson/ *a la chingada*" to make sure listeners knew they were trashing the governor and not their peers.

The mostly Latina/o student organizations formed since 1993 and continuing today have been organized by various groups. Several have a 50-50 rule for male-female participation in leadership, handling the press, subcommittee membership, etc. Given the high rate of student turnover, this principle has to be reaffirmed constantly, especially now that high school students are taking more initiative on their own, with less mentoring from college students. The April 1998 walkout by more than 2,000 middle and high school students, sparked by longtime Latina/o organizers but strikingly multi-racial, showed the fruit of anti-sexist work by youth over the years.

We can also wonder just how deep the teenage women's feminism runs. For example, does it operate at home when mother tells daughter (as has happened for many years), "Make your brother's bed"? More and more daughters are protesting that demand today, I think. Two Latinas, ages 13 and 14, who had participated in the "blowouts," told me that "in this protest we do not feel put down.... Boys have not put down girls for being leaders." On the personal-relations level, however, "we get called 'ho' if we have sex, but for a boy, it makes him a man." Despite these and other contradictions, the evidence of a Latina feminist consciousness evolving among young women has been persistent. New feminist groups formed by other young women of color, especially Asian Americans in California, are setting a strong example. Welcome to the Dragon Ladies!

In the provocation and shaping of that consciousness, Chicana artists and writers have had great influence. We would not be as far along as we are today without the heretical work of painters Yolanda López and Ester Hernández, whose militant transformations of the Virgin of Guadalupe offer a liberation never before available. We would not be this far along without painter Juana Alicia's images of Latina women as strong survivors. We would not be this far along without some biting poems from Sandra Cisneros, the multifaceted work of feminist writer Ana Castillo, the beautifully bold writing of lesbian authors Cherríe Moraga and Gloria Anzaldúa mentioned above. Not to mention the performance art of lesbian comedians like Marga Gómez and Monica Palacios. So many more names could be set down; all have nurtured the feminist impulse of young Chicanas, especially those in their upper teens and early twenties.

Working Women Who Speak Feminist Tongues

Chicana workers and other community women who do not define themselves as feminists but lead objectively feminist lives have been among us since the United States took half of Mexico by war in 1848. Often this resulted from their becoming involved in labor organizing and other forms of collective struggle. They have provided the backbone of male-dominated groups but also formed all-women's groups. Today various Latina labor organizations offer shining examples of such activism.

Look at Fuerza Unida ("United Force," or "Strength"), formed in San Antonio, Texas, when Levi Strauss laid off 1,100 garment workers there in 1990 and moved to Costa Rica for cheaper labor (see the essay "Levi's, Button Your Fly...," chapter ten). Angered by their experience of lies, broken promises, inadequate compensation, pathetic retraining and no special aid to workers with carpal tunnel syndrome, the Fuerza Unida women have steadily developed as leaders. Mujer Obrera ("Working Woman") has also been an inspiration. Founded in El Paso by garment workers, these Latinas demanded thousands of dollars in back pay and won some of it with such bold tactics as chaining themselves to their sewing machines.

The garment industry is one arena where Latinas are super-exploited; another is the *maquiladoras*, plants in the U.S.-Mexico border zone where workers assemble everything from bikinis to transistors. The corporate strategy: hire them young, suck out the best of their energy, exploit their inexperience as workers and their fear of angering the boss—then toss them aside like so many rag dolls when they become pregnant, injured or "trouble-makers." But these women are fighting back, often with a clear sense of being a class unto themselves as *maquila* women.

We can also look at the Farmworker Women's Leadership Development Institute, founded in August 1993 in Fresno, California, where a hundred women came together from all over the state. They discussed not only labor issues such as wages, pesticide poisoning and contracts but also sexual harassment, domestic violence and sexual discrimination. In workshops at that founding conference you could sense the women's desire to talk, to tell their stories, along with their feelings of awkwardness and perhaps fear.

At the beginning I was concerned that only the workshop facilitators and other prepared participants would feel able to talk. But as one spoke, another gathered strength to open up on painful subjects, and then another. Very few outsiders like myself had been allowed in the room, and we were wisely assigned to sit on the outer edges. Subsequent statewide gatherings have seen the farmworker women continue to discuss strategies to win social justice, including those thorny issues once called "personal." Líderes Campesinas ("Women Agricultural Worker Leaders") continues today, a serious and established force.

Among Latina workers, no group demands attention more than immigrant women who face a range of abuses, including rape and murder. There is no more exploited, vulnerable person in the United States today than the undocumented woman worker of color. Her lack of papers means she can almost never fight back, no matter how vilely she is abused.

At the border, women have been raped and then murdered by Border Patrol agents. Once in this country, recruited to come as housekeepers or other kinds of servants for professional families, they endure absolute exploitation. They tell of being raped on their first day at work; of being kept on duty around the clock as housekeeper, nursemaid, cook, laundress, cleaning-woman, baby-sitter and personal maid; of not being paid for months at a time; of being locked up in their employers' homes; and of being kept ignorant about how to seek help in a strange land, or being too terrorized to try.

Yet even these Latinas are no longer silent, no longer invisible. In San Francisco, in March 1993, one woman after another described brutal experiences in a full day of testimony to the United Nations. Other immigrant women of San Francisco formed an organization, Mujeres Unidas y Activas, that has grown steadily and is widely respected today for its services, progressive politics and democratic structure. Here, in the ranks of the poorest and most vulnerable, we find women who give us all hope.

They are living examples of *Xicanisma* ("Chicanisma"), a Chicana womanism that bridges anti-racist and anti-sexist struggle. *Xicanisma* allows us to begin imagining a liberation without boundaries or hierarchies. It encourages Raza to confront our contradictions as a people more openly than we did in the past. Too often incidents of sexism or homophobia remain *chisme*, "gossip"; too often social crimes are reduced to private griping; too often we are intimidated out of criticism. Let us confront the contradictions *con valor*, courageously, and remember that feminism is no alien creature but a deep-rooted tradition for Latinas. Let the moon rise on a new century for new women. The opposition mounts new attacks to halt our liberation, but it's not a time for despair—just a time for sharp eyes and open minds.

chapter nineteen

CHINGÓN POLITICS
DIE HARD

"The old Chicano Dinosaurs and their High-Spanic off-spring will once again engage in organized revelry, militancy and joy with other consenting adults and their offspring," announced the call for the 20th anniversary Chicano Activists Reunion held in San Antonio, Texas, on December 27–30, 1989. The call kept its promise to a considerable extent. "Once again" also applied, unfortunately, to some things that we could do without. Among them: what some of of us call "*chingón* politics," roughly translatable as "tough-guy politics" (*chingar* means "to screw")—an affliction hardly limited to La Raza.

This was the first big, interstate reunion ever of Chicano activists from the 1960s. According to registration records, 130 people attended, but the actual number was higher. Officially 111 came from Texas, with sprinklings from California, Arizona, New Mexico, Colorado, Indiana, Wisconsin and Washington. Most participants seemed to be academics or public-school teachers, bilingual educators, social workers, union staff members or employees of government-funded programs and sometimes private industry. Among the nationally known leaders from the 1960s who came were José Angel Gutiérrez, co-founder of La Raza Unida (LRU) Party in Texas; Rodolfo Acuña of Northridge, California, noted Chicano historian (see "Brown David v. White Goliath," chapter 16); Mario Compeán, LRU Party leader and now university professor; Reies López Tijerina, former leader of the New Mexico land struggle; and Antonio Rodríguez, a Los Angeles–based activist-lawyer formerly in the workers' organization CASA. The fact that they were all men set the stage for the event.

The reunion call had been issued by Gutiérrez and event chair Irma Mireles. Now a Dallas attorney and investment-banking director for a securities firm, Gutiérrez was a student-protest leader in the 1960s and early 1970s. He had gone on to found the LRU Party with María Hernández as an alternative to the Democrats and Republicans. The party won stunning electoral victories in areas like Crystal City,

Texas. Cristal (its name in Spanish) is the spinach capital of the world, its big statue of Popeye standing prominently downtown while the Mexicans who grow the spinach for Del Monte stay out of sight. In Cristal, LRU took over the city council and school board. Today a chapter or two of LRU claim to exist, but barely; numerous former Texas LRU activists now work in the Democratic Party, while others have moved on to new struggles. Most of the volunteer cadre for reunion operations came from the LRU network.

Gutiérrez emphasized that the event was a reunion rather than a conference and, as he said, "not intended to decide things but to make it possible for people to confer and make agendas." The list of participants and the discussion sessions were open to any additions. Nonsectarianism would be the order of the day and, in public at least, this held true—for which, *mil gracias.*

The program offered a rich diet of activities, including a Labor Lunch, a walking tour of the Alamo, a "Chicano Power" rally, an evening of "Chistes Calientes y Cerveza" ("Hot Jokes with Beer"), a champagne and tamales breakfast, political discussions and panels, a banquet and dance, and a memorial mass for activists who had died, as well as films and book-signing parties. Headquarters was St. Anthony's Hotel downtown, but most gatherings took place at a community center or in restaurants.

When the reunion had ended and the lobby of St. Anthony's returned to being blond instead of brown, what could one say about it?

Super-Machismo Lives

Most striking to this writer were the issues still not dealt with after 20 years—for one, sexism. Discussion chairs, event hosts and speakers (except those on the topic of women) were overwhelmingly male. In "The Chicano Movement in Hind-Sight," the only panel that aimed to analyze the past, every presenter was male. Sexist jokes and asides could be heard at times even within the formal program, including one "joke" about Chicana lesbians. The reunion offered no child care. One of the new books touted at the reunion was *United We Win*, a history of La Raza Unida Party that fails to discuss the crucial role played by women in LRU; they are present only incidentally. The author, Ignacio García, acknowledges the omission in his preface, but adds that overall he's convinced the book includes "the most essential" material.

Reunion organizers had made efforts to recognize women's accomplishments. The featured speaker at the Labor Lunch and guest of
honor at the banquet was Emma Tenayucca, the young leftist heroine
of the huge Mexican pecan shellers' strike in San Antonio in the
1930s, called "La Pasionaria" by local people, and now in her 80s.
Male speakers at the Labor Lunch extolled women organizers. The
big reunion banquet was dedicated to honoring Chicana activists,
with a major speech by activist Rosie Castro of San Antonio in which
she criticized the way that the role of women has been obliterated in
books.

Such efforts would probably not have been made 20 years ago;
we can see real progress, and it would be wrong to characterize the
whole reunion as flagrantly sexist. But too often the merit of those efforts was subverted by other realities and the recognition of women
thus rendered pro forma or patronizing. When the subject of women
was not on the official agenda, old-style practices and attitudes reas-
serted themselves. At the end of the banquet dedicated to La Chicana,
a brief on-the-sidelines display of juvenile machismo sent us reeling
backward. The banquet itself was billed as a "tribute," and it is not
just sour grapes to say: tributes are nice, but how about something
more substantive?

The "Chicano Power" rally was a full-scale celebration of
"*chingón* politics," dominated by male speakers in numbers and time
consumed, with a special man-to-man show we would like to forget,
performed by two movement "heavies." During one hourlong address, the (male) speaker turned from the lectern every few minutes to
gesture and smile at another male speaker sitting on the stage, and totally ignored everyone else up there, including two women. The
seated man would smile back, and on went the spectacle of mutual
stroking to the tune of militant rhetoric. Was that trip really necessary, *compas*?

At the meeting to discuss agenda items for a future conference,
a mild proposal was made that the ongoing problem of sexism, as
seen at this reunion, be included. Numerous women clapped for this
idea. The men said nothing immediately, except for one, who may
have had too much champagne at the tamales breakfast and now protested angrily but not very clearly. Gloria Romero of Los Angeles,
one of those strong women who stand up against both sexism and racism, objected to his use of the word "chink" in his outburst (as she
said later, "We were the chinks of the 1960s"). The man, very upset,
let himself be led from the room by another man, to stand outdoors on

a large terrace. It felt like 20 years ago, and I could hear brothers in
New Mexico calling women who took feminist positions *agringada,*
"gringoized" (or more recently, when this writer was chairing a meeting of Mexicans and Chicanos in the Bay Area, the voice of a man
who arrived late saying, "Oh, so women run things here").

Then I saw through the big glass wall overlooking the terrace
that the man who had left was weeping. *Ay mi Raza,* and what do we
make of all this? I think we make of it something that African-American author bell hooks has critiqued eloquently: the effects of equating
freedom with manhood, of sexualizing liberation. *Chingón* politics
does the same, as we can see if we look at it closely.

Aztlan for Whom?

We can begin by understanding the narrow nationalism that
usually characterizes *chingón* politics. From the 1960s until now,
Chicanos have talked about Aztlan, that semi-mythical place north of
Mexico from which the Aztecs migrated hundreds of miles south to
build what became Tenochtitlan, today's Mexico City. As a dream of
homeland, a sort of Brown Nation thesis, Aztlan symbolizes the righteous rejection of racist oppression and the colonized mentality that
facilitates that oppression. It echoes a very genuine longing not to feel
like a stranger in one's own land, not to feel like some kind of misfit,
to taste self-respect. On the other hand, the concept of Aztlan can be
used oppressively; we need to remember that the Aztecs maintained
an empire and took deadly tribute from the other indigenous peoples
whom they conquered.

The concept of Aztlan has always been set forth in super-macho
imagery. The Chicano activist today rarely sees retaking Aztlan as a
concrete goal but might like to imagine himself garbed in an Aztec
warrior outfit, looking ferociously brave next to some red-lipped prin-
cess with naked breasts. If you note the whiff of sexual possession
there, it's no accident. As often applied, the concept of Aztlan encourages the association of machismo with domination.

Another reactionary aspect of *chingón* politics has been to advocate for "the culture" uncritically. In the 1960s many of us glorified
the family in its supposedly "traditional" form without examining the
patriarchal values and practices that prevailed. The family has indeed
served as a genuine bastion of Raza self-defense and survival in a
hostile society. But we don't need to defend blindly all deeds com-

mitted in its name. Research has turned up questions about just what "tradition," was, and fortunately the Chicano family itself—especially wife-husband relations—has changed over recent generations, with patriarchy yielding significant ground. These and other cultural issues call for new thinking. But too few Chicano activists or grassroots organizers take them on, except some youth.

"*Chingón* politics" also defines concepts and styles of leadership in a patriarchal way. In her fine banquet speech, Rosie Castro speculated that one reason histories of the movement have consistently neglected women's contributions "is that we have practiced a different kind of leadership, a leadership that empowers *others*, not a hierarchical leadership." We should extend her perception to say: the leadership that empowers others is the leadership we need.

Alas, too often we have had the old-style kind of leadership because *chingón* politics expresses a culture of domination—which means that not only women but also men are its victims. The rooster lords it over the hens and also fights other roosters for barnyard primacy. That drive to be top cock in almost any situation can seem compulsive, leaving no room for giving or receiving constructive criticism. Incidentally, these frantic roosters do not come merely in shades of brown; they could or can today be found in every color as well as white.

For years progressive Chicanos have talked about fighting the "colonized mentality" that makes Raza identify with the oppressor and denigrate ourselves. But we have thought too little about how the colonized mentality promotes the idea that penetration proves the man. Our history as a people of Mexican origin began with a hemispheric rape, and we carry in us, consciously or not, the idea that to be conquered is to be *chingado* ("screwed"); that to become unconquered requires dominating—even screwing—others. We have thought too little about how racism and sexism are interrelated, reinforcing structures in a system that identifies domination with castration, that quite literally casts politics in sexual metaphor.

And so the *carnal* who wept out on the terrace at the reunion must have thought he didn't know who he was anymore. Feeling threatened by criticism from a woman, without a new way to envision masculinity, he was cast into some kind of despair.

Internalized Sexism and More

Among women at the reunion, internalized sexism emerged when the women present minimized their own activism and importance. The problem has deep roots. Many working-class Chicanas, understanding the freedom-manhood equation, consciously choose to take a back seat to men and achieve their goals by manipulation rather than confrontation. Too often their hearts have been broken when a husband or brother or father cannot find work, cannot find respect and cannot tolerate life except at the bottom of a bottle. As much or more than men, Chicanas will insist that the term "machismo" actually embraces the best of manhood: dignity, a sense of reponsibility to one's family, courage in the face of adversity. In 1969, at the first Chicano Youth Conference in Denver, the women's workshop reported back, "We don't want to be liberated." At the reunion in San Antonio, one Chicana told another, "This is Texas, we don't talk that feminism stuff." In both cases, the Chicanas involved were probably thinking of feminism strictly in terms of the primarily white and middle-class women's liberation movement of the 1960s that pitted women against men as opposed to seeing them linked in a joint struggle against oppression.

But sometimes this thinking becomes an unconscious excuse for not examining sexism, both external and internalized. Chicanas need to find ways to affirm the strengths, needs and crucial work of women. Chicanos must find the road to self-respect without oppressing women. Both men and women need to reject a manhood that rests on demeaning womanhood, a sense of identity for one that requires annihilating the other. Some of us said those words in the 1960s; the San Antonio reunion showed how much they need to be said again.

Time Out

Early evening in San Antonio, warming again after a bittercold spell. In the hours before the reunion banquet, an activist friend from the 1960s takes a few of us to a magical place known as Burro Land. It's a sort of Chicano beer garden run by a pleasant couple named Rendon; people like to call it Rendon State Park. Lots of space under trees, some picnic tables, a big 1960s-style Chicano mural on the far wall, and a small building in the center where you can buy beer. Another small building stands discreetly at the back; you may enter there only if you do not *have papers, says the friend. Probably a joke but ... reserved for the undocumented? Hey!*

It's a chilly night and a big wooden pallet burns nearby, with more pallets waiting in a giant stack. About a dozen Chicanos have gathered around one of the picnic tables. Suddenly two men stand there in full-scale U.S. Air Force camouflage uniforms, Spanish names on their tags. One of them has a guitar and begins to play it, singing, while somebody whispers in my ear, "They're going to Panama. Do you know that 25 percent of the troops Bush sent there are Chicano?"

The Chicano with the guitar sings a song popular in the 1960s whose chorus melodiously repeats "Che, Che, Che" (as in Guevara), and people join in. The song echoes across Burro Land; so much for the Air Force. Then Manuel from Phoenix asks for the guitar with immaculate Mexican courtesy, and it is handed over. He and his buddy sing a corrido *("ballad") that they wrote about a young Chicano killed by police. The passing-around of the guitar has begun.*

One of the Air Force guys produces an electronic keyboard from somewhere, and starts harmonizing on the weathered picnic table. The fire crackles, the multi-colored Christmas lights strung on tree branches overhead sparkle. No man seems to need to put down another, and no fights start despite the growing mountain of empty beer cans on the picnic table. The night is big and mellow.

They are all men, the players, it is a man's show, and the heroes in too many of the songs are male. Still, on this particular night, the men share, they respect, they cooperate. They make beauty, in the best Mexican style. Maybe there's hope for the machos after all.

Meanwhile, in Struggle

On the afternoon of December 29, about 40 reunion participants—mostly women—met to talk about past activism, which often turned out to be present activism as well. None of the national movement "heavies" attended, which may have helped people talk about themselves and struggles they had waged. Their comments confirmed that indeed no Chicano movement exists today in the mass, national form it once took, but hundreds of individuals and small groups are working at the community level on mostly local issues. Women in particular—Severita Lara, Carmen Zapata and others—gave sometimes amazing accounts of dogged efforts over long years. Goals ranged from basics like a bathroom to replace the outhouse at an elementary school in a Mexican barrio to becoming the first Chicana county judge after a long struggle involving an election, a recount, new elections and new recounts.

As the women talked, *chingón* politics vanished from the scene. These were just ordinary folks fighting for their rights and their communities, full of pride and determination: the reunion at its best.

That same afternoon, people spelled out the many issues confronting Chicanos and Chicanas. They included such concerns as racism in the welfare system and how a woman with one child could possibly live on the Texas stipend of $137 a month; drug problems and "a phony drug war which doesn't try to offer youth any alternative," as María Jiménez, director of the American Friends Service Committee's Immigration Law Monitoring Project, commented. Other issues: alcoholism (stressed as much, if not more than, drugs), the school drop-out rate, youth, AIDS, U.S. policy on El Salvador, worker struggles, media accountability and the need for multi-culturalism (not just biculturalism).

Some participants thought the reunion might prove to be the launching pad for a revived La Raza Unida Party, but this did not materialize. José Angel Gutiérrez himself stated in an interview that "Conditions now are different than 20 years ago. Then there was no alternative to the Democratic Party. Now the Democratic Party [in some parts of Texas] is run by Chicanos who were in La Raza Unida. In that regard there's no need for an alternative party." On the other hand, Gutiérrez added, the idea that Chicanos should have independent political force, leverage and clout will live on.

Issues of class and the role of middle-class Chicanos surfaced occasionally in discussion but were not examined in depth. Ruben Solís, a veteran activist from San Antonio and now a union organizer, made a memorable comment: "I know some rich Chicanos who would sooner pick up a little dog on the road than give me a ride. There's a lot of materialism. It's the Gold Card mentality." On the other hand, Rudy Gonzáles of San Antonio called for more recognition of accomplishments by middle-class organizations, more coalition-building. Professor Rudy Acuña thought that "the left of the Chicano movement should have gone into organizations like LULAC [the League of United Latin American Citizens, the assimilationist middle-class organization born in the 1920s] and fought for political space." The president of LULAC had supported Bush on the Panama invasion, Acuña said. He attributed this and other problems to the lack of moral authority in Chicano politics. "I would support a Ron Dellums [the African-American representative from Oakland, California] before I would support any Chicano candidates on the scene now. We failed to build a political culture."

From Liberal to Left

The politics of reunion participants ran the gamut from liberal to left. In broad strokes they reflected the historical range from accommodation to resistance, but the "Hispanic" view that sees movement activists as too confrontational and out-of-step today did not dominate. No one insisted on electoral politics as the panacea. Some noted that Latinos now held 3,360 local- and state-government elected positions, well over triple the number in the 1960s, "but we have yet to grasp what has thus been gained for ordinary *gente*," not just individual political careers. One Los Angeles activist considered electoral politics hopeless in that city because "the Democrats and Republicans can out-fund any independent candidate."

María Jiménez saw the Chicano movement as having been both reactionary and progressive. In particular, she noted, "our nationalism stayed within the context of the existing structure of society. But actually we were part of a global struggle for national liberation." Mario Compeán pointed out that "as a result of our work—and people were killed in the struggle—institutions are now opening." Rudy Acuña agreed but added: "We haven't changed very much. We have in the White House a man who is the moral equivalent of a Colombian drug dealer.... We have to get more belligerent.... We have to come up with a vision that goes beyond brown capitalism."

The reunion offered a moment of unforgettable confrontation, thanks to the city of San Antonio itself. In one extra-curricular event, Acuña led a group on a "Mexicans Won at the Alamo Walking Tour." The Alamo was the fortress besieged and finally taken by Mexican troops in 1836, when Anglos were seeking to grab Texas from Mexico. Aflame with bad-loser spirit, Anglos raised the vengeful cry of "Remember the Alamo!" They rewrote history to turn a long, difficult battle into a massacre, and to make martyred heroes out of the defeated Anglos—a pack of filibusters, whose leaders included a slave trader and an escaped murderer. Now, with Professor Acuña, we would hear the true story.

About 30 of us gathered in front of the Alamo, where a sign commands, "Gentlemen Remove Hats" (out of respect) and a plaque on the wall exhorts, "Be silent friend/ Here heroes died/ to blaze a trail/ for other men." Acuña began talking when a stocky, uniformed "Alamo Ranger" bustled up to proclaim that he had to stop; he was not authorized to conduct a tour. After we all insisted on the right of free speech, the ranger finally departed, grimly. Then another ranger came, repeated the order, and was also defied. Acuña continued. A few minutes later, the ranger returned, accompanied by a solemn-looking civilian whose tag said "Curator." This man asked Acuña what he was doing there. "Talking," the professor answered with dignity. "About what?" asked the curator. For five seconds it felt like *High Noon*; were we all going to be arrested for trespassing on gringo history?

Firmly and with only a slight trace of irony, Rudy glanced at the building behind him and answered, "The Alamo." The curator nodded faintly and left. We Mexicans won the Little Battle of the Alamo that day.

But we didn't win that other, even older battle. No men at the reunion spoke about the need to combat male supremacy. As Gloria Romero observed, "When I look back at the reunion, I see that the women moved things, just as they did in the 1960s. And women raised the issue of sexism; the men were not going to. *Chingón* politics is everywhere, in academia or whatever, and we have to deal with it."

Very shortly after the reunion, a Levi Strauss plant in San Antonio laid off a huge number of workers, many of them Chicanas or Mexican women, and it was back to the street with picket signs, hunger strikes and learning how to talk to bosses. Another long fight by women was born, and it brought an unspoken message: the men can go on being *chingón* dinosaurs, if they must—but let us hope that instead you *carnales* find new ways to be strong.

chapter twenty

LISTEN UP, ANGLO SISTERS

Relations between women of color and Anglo women have histori-cally been complex and sometimes filled with conflict. The first part of this chapter, "Colonized Women: La Chicana," was written in 1970, under the name Elizabeth Sutherland, at the height of both the Chicano movement and the women's liberation movement. Its mes-sage still holds true today. The second part, "Caramba, Our Anglo Sisters Just Didn't Get It," published some 20 years later, exemplifies the problem and again calls for more understanding, more solidarity.

Colonized Women: La Chicana (1970)

For the women of a colonized group, even the most politi-cized, their oppression as women is usually overshadowed by the common oppression of both male and female. Black and brown people in this country often see themselves as fighting for sheer survival against the physical genocide of racism, war, police brutality, hunger and deprivation, and against the cultural genocide of Anglo institutions and values. As a result, most colonized women will feel an impulse toward unity with, rather than enmity toward, their brothers. When the colonized group is in the minority, as in the United States, this becomes even more true.

The woman from a colonized people also recognizes that many times it has been easier for her economically than for the men of her group. Often she can get a job where a man cannot. She can see the damage done to the man as a result, and feels reluctant to risk threat-ening his self-respect ever further. This may be a short-range view-point, involving false definitions of manhood, but it is created by immediate realities whose force cannot merely be wished away. It is also a fact that in many Chicano families, the woman makes many of the important decisions—not just consumer decisions—though the importance of her role will be recognized only privately. This may seem hypocritical or demeaning, but the knowledge of having real in-fluence affects how the Chicana feels.

The family is also seen differently by women from the colonial experience. It often serves as a fortress, a defense against the inimical forces of the dominant society, a source of strength for a people whose identity is constantly under attack. Within that fortress, the woman as mother remains central. She is the principle of life, of survival and endurance. The children survive through her willpower. So the family is a fortress in the face of genocidal forces, a major source of strength for a people whose identity is constantly being whittled away. For young, alienated Anglo women, on the other hand, the family—especially when nuclear—is often seen as an oppressive, patriarchical institution that limits women to the roles of housewife and mother. Her attitude is almost the opposite of the Chicana's.

The family is but one example of how the culture or lifestyle of a colonized people becomes a weapon of self-defense in a hostile world—even when that culture or lifestyle might be oppressive to half of the people. To challenge such a lifestyle often means to risk being seen as adopting the enemy's position. "We don't want to become like the dominating Anglo women," you could hear Chicanas say in the 1960s and 1970s—and in later years as well. The comment shows a lack of understanding of the Anglo woman's struggle, but it also reveals how, for a colonized people, cultural integrity is deeply interwoven with survival. The middle-class Anglo woman must therefore beware of telling her sisters of color to throw off their chains without at least first understanding the origins and reasons for those "chains." She should also first ask herself: are there perhaps some aspects of these other lifestyles from which white women might still learn?

At the same time, we can hope that women from the colonized populations will listen with open minds to their Anglo sisters' ideas about women's liberation and then take another look at their own values. There is, for example, nothing worth preserving about the tradition of two young Chicano males fighting at a dance over some girl whom both hardly know, to prove their manhood. There is also much to be gained by considering the idea that male authoritarianism does not oppress women only, but also the masses—many being people of color. In other words, feminism must be anti-racist (since vast numbers of women suffer racism) and anti-racism must be feminist (since half of those suffering racism are women).

Such an open-minded exchange of ideas will often be difficult. But for those who seek to affirm a revolutionary vision and change the basic system under which we live, does any other real choice exist? How else can we create a society based on interdependency and balance instead of hierarchy?

Plagued by Western habits of either-or, dualistic thinking, we all may fail to understand that race, class and gender interconnect to sustain a corporate ruling class. In the language of African-American essayist bell hooks, they are interlocking systems of oppression. Neither Latina nor Anglo women should yield to the temptation of making a hierarchy of oppressions where battles are fought over whether racism is "worse" than sexism, or class oppression is "deeper" than racism, etc. Instead of hierarchies we need bridges—which, after all, exist to make two ends meet.

Caramba, Our Anglo Sisters Just Didn't Get It

Today, when a strong defense of reproductive rights by women of all racial and ethnic origins is urgently needed, what do we find? Too often pro-choice Anglo women just don't ... "get it." The historic April 5, 1992, march in Washington, D.C., to defend reproductive rights became another occasion when women of color saw their demands for a front seat denied and their protests against such treatment drowned in a deluge of defensiveness. Once again they heard those familiar claims of good intentions. Once again they heard that patronizing line about how African-American and Latina women are just too busy fighting racism or too constrained by their religion to be concerned with choice.

One begins to wonder: maybe it's wrong to say they just don't get it. Maybe they do "get it" but don't want to yield any degree of control. In any case, the story needs to be told and lessons drawn.

A few days before the Washington march, an ad hoc coalition embracing six organizations of Asian/Pacific Island, Black, Latina and Native American women, together with the International Coalition of Women Physicians, spoke out about the National Organization for Women (NOW). In its public statement the ad hoc coalition—called the Women of Color Reproductive Rights Groups—listed criticisms of NOW actions related to the march. These included failing to contact organizations of women of color in time for them to participate in planning and strategizing for the march; failing to acknowledge the suggestion that a women-of-color delegation be prominently located in the march lineup; and failing to seek their input about rally speakers. Those criticisms reflected long experience of being invited to join an action after plans had been made (by Anglo women), of being relegated to the back of a march and of being scheduled to speak late in the program when people would already be leaving.

The coalition's statement spelled out the heart of the matter:

> Historically, the relationship between women of color and the broader reproductive rights community has suffered due to the uneven power relationship between the long-established repro- ductive rights organizations and the newly-established women of color reproductive rights organizations. In spite of our limited resources, [our activities] have been responsible for the in- creased awareness and for the educating, organizing, and mobi- lizing of our communities.... If NOW's leadership is serious about strengthening their relationship with women of color not only our right to reproductive freedom must be respected, but our right to decide who our representatives will be—the right to self-determination—must be respected.

One of the main organizers of this protest was Luz Alvarez Martínez, director of the Organización Nacional de La Salud de La Mujer Latina (National Latina Health Organization) in Oakland, Cali- fornia. According to Alvarez Martínez, NOW president Patricia Ire- land originally said she wanted women-of-color organizations to feel included in the march—then failed to implement this beyond contact- ing three African-American groups in Washington, D.C. (but no other Black groups and not any Latinas at first). In the days that followed, Alvarez Martínez said, national NOW leaders responded with inac- tion and excuses to women-of-color demands for a key role in plan- ning, marching and speaking.

The ad hoc coalition then urged women going to the march to wear green armbands as a sign of protest, to march together and to write letters of protest to NOW's board. NOW had asked Alvarez Martínez to be a speaker at the Washington rally but, she said, "after getting no input whatsoever, we were not about to be used as window dressing by speaking at the rally." As it turned out, five other Latinas did speak that day—all of them before the march, and none during the official rally program.

Throughout this struggle, the ad hoc coalition stressed that their protest aimed to strengthen the reproductive-rights movement. Coali- tion groups were committed to fight for the right "of all women—es- pecially poor women and women of color—to safe, affordable, and quality reproductive services." The National Latina Health Organization and others urged members to march on April 5. But, as Alvarez Martínez told me, "NOW and others like them must change. That's our goal—to achieve real unity so we will be stronger."

"Some in the group would like to meet with NOW," Julia Scott of the National Black Women's Health Project in Washington, D.C., commented to me at the time, "but mostly the top priority is to develop and organize ourselves so that this problem never happens again. So that we come to the table as equal partners. They have to learn to operate differently with us." That is the heart of the matter, Scott said. "It's about doing things differently. Realizing that maybe your way isn't the best way. Right now, when faced with diversity, they resist changing." An urgent need to fight some appalling new piece of anti-choice legislation becomes the justification for not taking the time to resolve this issue. Scott saw a particular need to challenge NOW's rhetoric of inclusion.

The conduct of national NOW in the April 5 series of events was typical of the mainstream feminist movement. As Scott pointed out, "White feminism's biggest mistake was not working with poor, working-class women. The problem isn't just racism on their part, it's also a middle-class perspective. It includes a failure to study the lessons of history about white feminism's mistakes in relating to women of color."

The Conference on Population Control held in Cairo in 1994 showed that those lessons of history still needed to be learned, above all the lesson that issues of class and race can still divide the pro-choice movement if not recognized. According to Alvarez Martínez, the Cairo conference focused heavily on abortion rights, and the document coming out of it did not take seriously the needs of marginalized women and women in poor countries. Still, it was the first time women of color were included in an international conference on those reproductive-rights issues. By the time the United Nations Fourth World Conference on Women and the accompanying conference of Non-Governmental Organizations took place in Beijing in 1995, the old ad hoc grouping had become the Coalition for Reproductive Health Rights. The voices of women of color could no longer be denied.

Back in Oakland, Alvarez Martínez not only criticizes Anglo sisters whose attitudes need to change; she also points to those who *have* grown, including NOW leaders. In San Francisco, women of color for reproductive rights experienced a local struggle similar to the one around the Washington, D.C., march. Out of the resulting dia-

logue came a good working relationship with NOW leader Elizabeth
Toledo, Planned Parenthood and other predominantly white groups.
"They don't always see what they do wrong, but when you tell them,
they get it," Alvarez Martínez said after the dialogue. This experience
suggests a model for joint pro-choice efforts around the country.

The problem has often been rooted in a racist arrogance un-
derlying the attitude of many Anglo women toward Latina views
on reproductive rights. In the guise of understanding our culture,
or sympathizing with our daily survival needs, they have charac-
terized Latina feminism as inherently more conservative than the
Anglo variety. Much ignorance of Latina views and experience
feeds that stereotype.

If we look more closely at Latina views, we find that reproductive freedom is a major concern of Latinas and not some taboo subject or minor matter. In 1977, when Congress ended federal funding
of abortions, the first victim was a 27-year-old Chicana—Rosie
Jiménez from McAllen, Texas, daughter of migrant workers—who
died at the hands of an illegal abortionist after six days of suffering.

The Rosie Jiménez case was one reason for the formation in
1990 of an ad hoc coalition, Latinas pro Derechos Reproductivos
(Latinas for Reproductive Choice), by Luz Alvarez Martínez and five
other women. The appointment of David Souter to the U.S. Supreme
Court, and the increasing likelihood of the court overthrowing *Roe v.
Wade,* also spurred this action. It is a myth, the group maintains, that
Latinas do not have abortions; they just don't talk about them. In fact,
the Latina abortion rate in 1994 was 26.1 per thousand, compared
with 26.6 per thousand for non-Latinas. ("Unintended Pregnancy in
the U.S.," *Family Planning Perspectives,* January 1998, Alan
Guttmacher Institute, Washington, D.C.)

Today, Latina abortions constitute about 13 percent of the total
in the United States, which is disproportionate to the Latina percentage of the population. According to a poll of women of color on re-
productive-health issues that was conducted by the National Council
of Negro Women and the Communications Consortium Media Center
(both in Washington, D.C.), only 25 percent of Latinas are opposed to
abortion in all circumstances.

It has never been easy for Latinas to advance abortion rights. A
Latina in Corpus Christi, Texas, is believed to be the first U.S. Catholic excommunicated for pro-choice activism. In the face of such experiences, one of the goals of Latinas pro Derechos Reproductivos was
to break the silence on reproductive-rights issues. At the same time,

they considered abortion too narrow a focus. "We are redefining choice," Alvarez Martínez said; choice has to include having all the health-care services and information that enable a woman to make her own decision freely.

Choice also has to include freedom from sterilization abuse—another form of reproductive oppression. For women of color this is a major concern. While a Medicaid-funded abortion may be hard or impossible to get in some states (it is still legal in California), sterilization services are provided by states under Medicaid, and the federal government reimburses states for 90 percent of those expenses. Some public hospitals have two films they show to women seeking contraceptive information: the English-language film emphasizes conventional contraceptive methods, and the Spanish-language film stresses sterilization. Sometimes a woman must agree to sterilization to get an abortion. Sterilization rates run up to 65 percent for Latinas in some parts of the United States; in New York, for example, the Latina rate is seven times higher than that of white women. Yet too often prochoice Anglo women ignore or downplay sterilization abuse. Even though there are now laws against it, such abuse continues. Choice also has to mean freedom from the abuse of birth-control methods like Norplant.

The word "choice" has no meaning if women don't first have access to quality health care. That means a national health plan, information and education on sexuality that is culturally relevant and in the necessary languages, and affordable birth control. It means adequate prenatal care so healthy babies can be born. It means access to fertility services, which are never considered an issue for poor women. All these needs point to the fact that class differences cut across the choice issue again and again.

In short, Latinas' views on reproductive rights are often more radical than Anglo women's views and not "conservative," as some say, because their definition of choice requires more profound social change than just abortion rights or preventing pregnancy. As Alvarez Martínez told me in early 1998:

> We are for social change. Our focus is on Latinas and health, not just reproductive rights. We are trying to change the way funding is done. It shouldn't just be focused, for example, on preventing teenage pregnancy by preaching abstinence. It has to look at the entire social situation of the women.

The need continues, she added, to push for more understanding in Anglo women concerned with reproductive rights. "Many are still not aware of Latina women as active in this field." Yet today we have not only the National Latina Health Organization but also the National Latina Institute for Reproductive Health, which in the 1990s came out of Catholics for Free Choice, based in the Washington, D.C., area and does regional organizing; the more grassroots Latina Roundtable on Health and Reproductive Rights, in New York (also founded in the 1990s); and the Mujeres Project in San Antonio, Texas, which focuses on reproductive health.

Differences with Anglo women in the struggle for reproductive rights reflect inter-feminist relations in many arenas. Problems explode periodically and demand constant discussion. Latina, Black, Asian/Pacific Island American and Native American women are unlikely to unite with the war cry of "Abortion is liberation!" but they can and will work with Anglo women when respect and space are given.

Among women of color, increased communication and coordination are future goals. The coalition that opposed NOW policies in 1992 did not become permanent, as once hoped, for lack of funding, Alvarez Martínez said. Funders forced them to choose between support for their individual projects and for collaborative work; most had to choose the former. But the groups are still in touch and collaborate informally. They can all take the stand that as women of color in the reproductive-freedom movement, "We will no longer be silent or invisible!"

chapter twenty-one

THE THIRD EYE OF CHERRÍE MORAGA

Cherríe Moraga's first book, co-edited with Gloria Anzaldúa, was *This Bridge Called My Back: Writings by Radical Women of Color*, and it made history when published by Kitchen Table Press in 1981. The two pioneering lesbian authors passionately celebrated relationships between women, and their dream, as they said in their foreword to the second edition, was of "a unified Third World feminist movement in this country." Up until then you heard little, if anything, spoken publicly in Chicana/o circles about feminism, much less lesbianism. Such taboos weakened as Chicana feminism evolved in its varying forms and different camps.

During the 1980s, Moraga continued breaking ground with a bold collection of her own prose and poetry, *Loving in the War Years*, two new theater works and other writing. Her play *Heroes and Saints* laid her politics on the line in a story of resistance by farmworkers and their supporters to deadly pesticide spraying.

In *The Last Generation*, a collection of essays and poems (South End Press), Moraga elaborates on themes she has explored over the years. They include feminism in general and lesbianism in particular; her mixed parentage (Chicana/Anglo), nationalism, internationalism and the search for a revolutionary social vision. Moraga notes the lack of distinction "between my art and activism," then illuminates it with the essay "Art in American con Acento," which affirms that "An art that subscribes to integration into mainstream Amerika is not Chicano art."

That manifesto flows from her vision of past and prophecy. In these ahistorical United States it cannot be said too often: what happened thousands of years ago is, for many of La Raza, and for all indigenous peoples, not so distant. Chicanos are children of violence, a people who literally did not exist before Columbus and the subsequent rape of indigenous America and its women. Shall such a people now melt away?

Moraga fears that today's is that "last generation," as the world of "individualism, profit and consumerism" engulfs us. The 500-year process of colonization is culminating today, as she sees it, in the dis-

appearance of Chicanos as a people, a culture, under the forces of assimilation. "We risk being swallowed up in the 'Decade of the Hispanic' that never happened."

Whether one accepts that we are seeing the end of the Chicano line (and there is reason for doubt unless migration from
Mexico ceases), the push to embrace capitalist and Anglo culture
is relentless. This includes Chicana/o authors: Moraga is concerned that our young writers will look solely to the northeastern
United States for recognition, that they will find themseles writing
more and more in translation, through an Anglo-American filter of
self-censorship. "I still believe in a Chicano literature that is hungry for change, that has the courage to name the sources of our dis-
content both from within our raza and without, that challenges us
to envision a world where poverty, crack, and pesticide poisoning
are not endemic to people with dark skin and Spanish surnames,"
Moraga writes in *The Last Generation.*

In this spirit she remains "passionately committed to an art
of resistance to domination by Anglo-America." And what is her
vision for the future? She says the words few people utter aloud:
"If the Soviet Union could dissolve, why not the United States?"
Why not, indeed? And why not a new confederacy of equal, mutually respectful cultures and peoples? "The road to our future is the
road from our past."

Moraga did not come simplistically to such a view. She was
born of a Mexican mother and Anglo father, symbolized in a touch
of magic realism by her one brown eye and one blue eye: "those
pitiful/ lonesome/ product of mutation/ eyes." In time she came to
choose the side of Raza to work on, but has ceased to despise her
white side (noting that her father's family was even poorer than
her mother's). This peace-making journey includes recognition
that her light-skinned face "has often secured my safe passage
throughout the minefields of American racism." More than peace-
making, she attains what is almost a celebration of the mongrel.
"My lovers have always been the environment that defined my
color," and her lovers have come in all colors.

Lesbianism is the other main way that she is "queer," we could
say: another, connected hall of identity to explore. "My real politicization began, not through the Chicano Movement but through the
bold recognition of my lesbianism." She passed years of pain, described in other books, when she was considered a traitor for refusing
to choose the traditional family, considered central to Raza survival in

an unfriendly world. Today Moraga's love poems, her commemorations of love between women, include silver laughter, tear-stained despair and homegirl entanglements. Through these and other writings she presents us her vision of a Queer Aztlan: a Chicano homeland that can embrace all its people, including its gays and lesbians.

Moraga's commitment to lesbianism and to Raza both find root in a monumental pre-Columbian feminism. Think "essentialism," if you like, when she writes of god being woman, woman being Earth, all the power of life in female hands; but you cannot catch her so easily. She knows that the road to the female god is filled with hatred, humiliation and heartbreak.

If I had to pick a single image to represent this book, it would be the third eye. Moraga quotes an unidentified Latino writer: "Your cosmic or third eye is a synthesis of your two eyes. Neither left nor right views, just vision." And later: the third eye "seeking both sides to everything/ keeping each eye, right and left/ from wandering off/ too far." It "never cries/ it knows."

Though Moraga doesn't say so, that third eye could surely echo the belief found in various indigenous cultures that gay and lesbian persons have an extra eye. In any case, she is ready to face painful contradictions within a framework of progressive thinking and values. Moraga tells of going to an anti-Bush demonstration in San Francisco shortly after the Sandinistas were defeated in the Nicaraguan elections. To her dismay, she found a group of Latinos shouting "¡Viva Bush!" while those opposing Bush were young, middle-class and white. One cannot view the world only with a left (eye) or right (eye).

She also observes the opportunists: "a tiny Latino elite who often turn to their racial/cultural identities not as a source of political empowerment, but of personal employment as tokens in an Anglo-dominated business world." She rejects what could be called people-of-colorism (a glorification of all that's not white) and essentialist feminism. "I have at times seen Black women as cold as any white woman in their 'gringa' chauvinism, and I have seen Latinas as spineless as any man in their disloyalty to women." When she articulates her choice to identify with Raza, she ponders the influence on this decision of her being mixed. "Had I been born a full-blooded Mexican, I sometimes wonder whether I would have struggled so hard to stay a part of la raza." So much for knee-jerk nationalism; it's not Moraga's cup of *menudo*.

Devoid of moralism or superior airs, her third eye nails some thorny contradictions of our movement—the "isms" nobody wants to talk about. In the past 20 years, she writes, "I experienced the racism of the Women's Movement, the elitism of the Gay and Lesbian Movement, the homophobia and sexism of the Chicano Movement, and the benign cultural imperialism of the Latin American Solidarity Movement."

Moraga is both nationalist and globalist, so enabled by that same third eye. With an echo of Frantz Fanon, her book ends at a dawn for the next 500 years:

And we ... remove the white mask
We wait and watch the horizon
Our Olmeca third eye
begins to glisten
in the slowly
rising light.

When this book was written, "last generation" had a personal meaning: Moraga was childless and so "my line of family stops with me." Since then she has had a son, Rafael Angel. And so life changes, meanings are altered, and of one thing we can be sure: this writer also changes, growing as she goes.

Afterword

Those words preceded the publication of Cherríe Moraga's 1997 book *Waiting in the Wings: Portrait of a Queer Motherhood* (Firebrand Books). This new book hums not only with a new subject but a newly grown voice to speak about it. The subject is not a joyous, one-dimensional hymn to motherhood; Rafael Angel's dangerously premature birth was hardly simple and he could have died many times. What makes this book magical (among various sources of magic) is the way the author discovers a relationship of life to death that leaves us understanding both sadness and joy, yet dominated by neither. She gives us a sense of balance amid fearless exploration of new emotions.

chapter twenty-two

OF PASSION AND POLITICS

In the worlds of film and television, cultural gringoism is almost pathetic. Mainsteam recognition of Chicano and Chicana homegrown authors did not begin until the discovery that the Raza world could be colorful, amusing, exotic, magical. Rarely was that world projected as full of anger at racism, struggles for justice or revolutions of the body and spirit by women as well as men.

Now come the new books of Julia Alvarez and Demetria Martínez, both with radical political themes. They have garnered flattering reviews, but profound political or social questions raised in both books have gone ignored; most critics seem happier with the romancing.

Julia Alvarez' book *In the Time of the Butterflies* (Algonquin Books) is a fictionalized biography of *las mariposas* ("the butterflies"), which served as the underground code name for the Mirabal sisters, beloved national heroines of the Dominican Republic. Born to semi-rural comfort, servants and a convent education, they seemed unlikely candidates for the underground movement against Dominican dictator Rafael Leonidas Trujillo. But they joined it, one by one, each in accordance with her own character and within her world of parents, lovers, husbands and children. The transformation of Minerva, Patría, and María Teresa shows how a person can become a traitor to her or his class. How concessions that seem trivial may lead down one road and a refusal to make such compromises can lead down its opposite. How rebels are not always born but certainly can be made.

You suspect Minerva will be the first when, at a large social gathering of the nation's elite, she slaps dictator Trujillo for sexual harassment in front of everyone. Then she leaves the party before Trujillo does, which is literally against the law. It's not such a big step from there to running guns.

The highly religious Patría seems least likely to join the movement, but she does, after witnessing a hideous government massacre of peasants. Her long journey from traditional Catholicism to revolution is a major theme in this book.

María Teresa, the youngest and least political or even spiritual sister, first declares that love of a man goes deeper for her than some higher ideal, but she too eventually changes. Only Dede, following her conservative husband's wishes, does not join the others in their new life in the revolution, in prison and finally in death, when they are ambushed on a winding mountain road along the north coast of the Dominican Republic. That day, November 25, 1960, is commemorated all over Latin America as International Day Against Violence Toward Women.

Within a year of assassinating the butterflies, Trujillo was overthrown, but this did not lead to a society of the sisters' dreams. Instead, there were hapless new rulers, more killing and the rise of a young privileged class living in luxury where guerrillas had once fought. "Was it for this, the sacrifice of the butterflies?" asks Dede, grappling with grief and guilt. But she also tells an old friend, "I'm not stuck in the past, I've just brought it with me into the present. And the problem is not enough of us have done that."

Julia Alvarez, now a professor at Middlebury College, was brought to the United States at age ten by her family to escape Trujillo's repression. After her first successful and lighter book, *How the Garcia Girls Lost Their Accents*, Alvarez took up the challenging task of telling the story of the butterflies. Some Dominicans have berated the author for supposed errors. The book isn't perfect reading; it tells almost nothing about issues of class and color or the Afro-Dominican experience, for example. But the book remains a treasure, for Alvarez has told a story unknown to most people in this country and told it unforgettably. In her last message about the butterflies, the author says: "by making them myth, we lost the Mirabals once more, dismissing the challenge of their courage as impossible for us, ordinary men and women." This she seeks to correct by making them real people, whose courage is thus made real, too.

<<< >>>

Demetria Martínez' first novel, *MotherTongue* (Bilingual Press), begins with a sentence widely quoted by reviewers, for good reason. Speaking of a Salvadoran refugee as he arrives in the United States, her character Mary/María writes: "His nation chewed him up and spit him out like a piñon shell, and when he emerged from an airplane one late afternoon, I knew I would one day make love with him."

At that point you know you are in the hands of a poet as well as a writer of strong political conscience. Demetria Martínez became known as a reporter/activist from Albuquerque, New Mexico, who went on trial along with a minister for helping two refugee Salvadoran women enter this country. Their acquittal in 1989 signaled a major victory for the sanctuary movement. Martínez made poems from those years and others, published in *Three Times a Woman*.

MotherTongue is about the Salvadoran people's long struggle against a U.S.-supported dictatorship. It is about a young Chicana who seeks to define herself through loving a man from that struggle. It is about a feminist theology in the making, as the author puts it.

In the beginning María declares herself not political and makes clear that her attraction to José Luis rises more out of the hope he will save her from an ordinary life than out of insurgent solidarity. Yet the two forces slowly begin to meld and expand. She discovers that the many strange marks on his body are from cigarettes stubbed out by torturers, and then begins to see that the scars inside him are even worse. No wonder his face "was boarded up like a house whose owner knows what strangers can do when they get inside."

A sort of dance begins in which the bodies of María and José Luis make love but their realities do not quite connect. María longs to "take the war out of him"; José Luis thinks she loves the idea of him, the dissident, not the real person—flaws and all. Too often he sees María as alien: "Even church bells mean something different to us. She hears them and sets her watch. I hear them and remember the endless funerals." But to the reader, María seems less cause than effect; a symbol of why "there is a bomb ticking inside" José Luis. Finally he leaves without notice.

Twenty years later, María and her son by José Luis go to El Salvador to find out what happened to him. He was not killed, they learn. But María has changed. She has begun to participate in low-key political activism. She accepts the separate reality of her son and of José Luis. She does not become an insurgent like José Luis, but she does defy the prison of patriarchy that told her to become a person through loving another: "I am just beginning to become me."

MotherTongue is a short work of strength and complexity that challenges borders between Latinos, between men and women, between life experiences. Its author has a magical way with words that can be addictive. Just try to put her book down. Go on, try.

part six

LA LUCHA CONTINUA: Youth In The Lead

Nosotros, los huérfanos de oportunidades
nos hemos atrevido a traspasar la puerta abierta
por los zapatistas y entrar al otro lado del espejo
donde tod@s podemos ser iguales
porque somos diferentes,
donde no tiene que haber sólo una manera de vivir;
donde se conjuga el rechazo al sistema actual
con el deseo de construir un mundo
donde quepan muchos mundos.

We the orphans of opportunity
have dared to pass through the door opened by the Zapatistas
and cross to the other side of the mirror
where everyone can be the same
because we are different,
where there can be more than one way of living
where rejection of the present system
exists together with the desire to build a new world
in which many worlds will fit.

—*palabras zapatistas/EZLN*
—from the Zapatista movement

chapter twenty-three

WHATEVER HAPPENED TO THE CHICANO MOVEMENT?

In the late 1980s the CBS drama lineup included an evening soap opera called "Falcon Crest" with a lot of rich folks sparring over a big chunk of land. "Falcon Crest" was new and different in one way: it had a Mexican American in a major role, and a woman at that. No pouting airhead, either, but a calculating businesswoman appropriately named Pilar (which means "spear" in Spanish) who manipulated her way upward as fast as she could go. This Pilar was no spic, she was clearly a 'spanic.

Those were the years when the first wave of mass media attention to "Hispanics" crested with movies such as *La Bamba*, *Born in East L.A.*, *The Milagro Beanfield War* and *Stand and Deliver*, along with singers such as Ruben Blades and Linda Ronstadt. Edward James Olmos made the cover of *Time* with the headline "Hispanic Culture Breaks Out of the Barrio." Madonna recorded lyrics in Spanish. One could grumble, and some Latinos did: so we're good as entertainers, didn't they used to say "Negroes" really could sing and dance?

A glance at the financial news suggested that the "discovery" was not primarily of a people and their culture but of a burgeoning market. Since 1980, Latinos had increased nationwide at almost five times the rate of the general population. Also, Latinos were and still are the youngest population group in the country. At the thought of all those potential yuppie consumers, marketing directors licked their chops and started cleaning up corporate images. Coors Beer, for example, which had been sporadically boycotted since the 1960s because of its discrimination against Mexican Americans, put down its name as a sponsor of the national touring art exhibit "Expresiones Hispanas."

Yet all the hoopla about "Hispanics" has not brought serious national attention to the grinding problems of poverty and racism that face most Latinos every day, nor the 1990s attacks on immigrant rights, affirmative action and bilingual education. Does this silence exist because the Chicano movement of the 1960s and early 1970s, which compelled public awareness of Raza struggles, is dead? What are the possibilities of rebirth, or does the future belong to the Pilars of this society? We can begin trying to answer these questions, for they threaten to be with us into the next century.

<<< >>>

Chicanos and Chicanas in the United States—let us say "Raza" for the sake of brevity—have a long tradition of rebellion and resistance. After the United States took over half of Mexico by war, what we now call the Southwest saw an almost classic colonization imposed on people of Mexican origin. Within a few decades the violent repression of armed rebels (labeled "bandits") gave way to Anglo control through domination over institutions and ideology. Violent repression has been revived whenever serious resistance appears.

By the twentieth century "Mexican Americans," as we called ourselves then, were responding to the colonization process in ways that included organizing mutual aid associations, cultural institutions such as Spanish-language newspapers, middle-class organizations seeking first-class citizenship primarily through assimilation, and massive strikes by agricultural workers and miners.

The 1960s saw a multifaceted explosion of protest. The new Chicana/o movement included thousands of students demanding changes in racist school systems; a struggle to recover lost land grants in New Mexico; the formation of a Chicano electoral party, La Raza Unida; community organizing around such issues as police abuse and health-care needs; and opposition to the war in Vietnam. Although César Chávez saw himself primarily as a labor organizer rather than a Chicano movement leader, the farmworkers' struggle that he headed was embraced by many Chicanos as part of that movement. Art, poetry, plays, songs and more than 60 Chicano magazines or newspapers flowered.

In response to all this, Chicano activists were beaten, jailed and killed. In one Los Angeles demonstration, up to 30,000 people marched against the war in Vietnam; three Chicanos were killed by police that day, including noted journalist Rubén Salazar. In Albuquerque, New Mexico, police set up and killed two Black Beret activists—Antonio Córdova, a grassroots journalist, and Rito Canales—on January 29, 1970.

At the heart of the movimiento lay the issue of identity, often expressed in Raza nationalism—cultural, political or both. For years the term "Chicano" had implied being lower-class and non-white. For years Chicanos aspiring to middle-class status had affirmed with dogged patriotism, "We are Americans first." Convinced that overcoming second-

class citizenship required accommodation and integration, they preferred to call themselves "Mexican-American" or even "Spanish-
American," or in some areas "Hispano."

But young activists of the 1960s movement replaced "Mexican-
American" with "Chicano," much as "Negro" was replaced with
"Black" in those same years. Calling oneself Chicano served as a proud
response to the confusion and racist feelings of inferiority that could
flow from being a people whose cultural wealth and uniqueness had
been brutally negated. Identified with both Mexico and the United
States, and with neither, Chicanos felt they should have a new name
that expressed their very particular reality. Thus identity served as a major, anti-racist motor of the movimiento and led to the establishment of
Chicano Studies, bilingual education and affirmative action in the
1960s.

The spirit of those times came across in a familiar song that said:

You soy Chicano, tengo color
Americano, pero con honor

"I am Chicano, I am of color,
American, but with honor."

By the 1980s that sense of identity and *chicanismo*, that militant
clarity, was hard to find. "Young people don't want to be called Chicano today," more than one professor of Chicano Studies commented to
me. "It isn't really that they don't want to be called Chicano, it's more
that the term has no special meaning to them, they don't know about the
movement," said a former Chicana activist. At many schools, Chicanos
and Chicanas were more likely to be taking courses in business administration than Chicano Studies. Ah, some of us sighed, where is Che
Guevara now that we really need him? The right-wing blitz, which had
been launched in the late 1970s, was in full gear. Reagan's election in
1980 confirmed the reactionary turn, but the most alarming aspect was
how rapidly Raza internalized it.

English-only laws passed in 23 states, often with Latino support.
California passed such a law in 1980 with 41 percent of the Latino voters favoring it. In the same election 39 percent of Latino voters also
failed to support the reconfirmation of Cruz Reynoso, a distinguished,
liberal state supreme court justice of Mexican descent, and 46 percent
voted to re-elect the Republican governor who had axed state-funded
bilingual programs. Since 1980 an approximately 40 percent conservative vote by Latinos on national and state issues has been fairly predict-

able. By the early 1990s we would see more and more Latinos registering Republican.

One reason Raza has internalized the rightward turn is relentless conditioning by the mass media to reinforce the colonized mentality that makes so many Raza accept the dominant ideology. Thus the Right has been able to exploit Raza traditions with rhetoric about "family values." Or it has manipulated the strong Raza belief that education is the key to advancement into the idea that learning English requires forgetting one's original culture. The Right has also exploited the growth of a Chicano middle class during the 1980s and the intensified class divisions that resulted, leading more established Chicanos to join Anglo reactionaries in denying human rights to newly arrived immigrants.

But even as the "Me Generation" went into full swing in the 1970s and 1980s, grassroots activism never died. Chicano and other Latino organizations from Austin to Seattle worked on issues ranging from toxic wastes to AIDS-education programs. Some community institutions dating from the movement years not only survived but grew, one example being the Centro de La Raza in Seattle. It started with the 1972 takeover of an abandoned school building and had 70 staff members 20 years later. The Clínica del Pueblo (People's Clinic) in Tierra Amarilla, New Mexico, has tripled in size since its start more than 25 years ago. Militant labor organizing also continued, as shown by the two-year strike against the Farah pants company in Texas and the Watsonville, California, strike of cannery workers, both dominated by Mexican and Chicana women. The exploitation and abuse of undocumented workers, Border Patrol atrocities and new anti-immigrant legislation were all becoming galvanizing issues.

Throughout the 1970s and 1980s, solidarity with people in Central America and Mexico was strong, though not widespread at the grassroots level. Many students and other activist Raza traveled to Nicaragua and El Salvador to support insurgent struggles. Then-governor Toney Anaya declared New Mexico an official sanctuary state for Central American war refugees. More than 70 percent of the Latino voters in Chicago favored a referendum urging Illinois' governor to stop the training of the Illinois National Guard in Honduras. We also saw Chicano activism stimulated by the stunning rise of progressive forces in Mexico, centered around opposition to the party that had been in power for more than 60 years.

Despite the conservative trend at the national level we saw many local struggles to combat the systematic dilution of Chicano voting power. Redistricting victories sometimes enabled Chicano candidates to win office, as happened in Santa Cruz, California, long a Mexican-dominated town, which finally put its first Chicano on the city council in 1985. By 1990 the enormous proportion of youth in the Chicano population suggested an upcoming renaissance of mass activism. The identity issue promised to revive in the wake of intensifying racism and nativism.

Movement, But Not a Movement

This quick survey tells us that there has been movement in Raza communities over the past 25 years but not yet *a movement,* in the sense of a force with sufficient mass involvement to compel widespread social change. Activism and organizing have continued stubbornly at all levels, despite constant assault from the Right. What, then, is needed today to build a more massive offensive?

A few thoughts about this—hardly a whole strategy—begin with recognizing that survival is the main goal for most Raza today. The mode and the mentality tend to be defensive, and it is difficult to nurture a revolutionary perspective. Grassroots organizing, labor and student struggles and other major projects have been essentially reformist and not radical, rarely aiming to transform power relations at the base of society.

But Latinos are a skyrocketing population, estimated to number almost a quarter of the nation by 2050. Will this translate into greater political power, and can it be translated into revolutionary change? Also, most Latinos once represented three national backgrounds (Mexican, Puerto Rican, Cuban); we now find many more. If building unity was always complicated by national and class differences, it is even more of a challenge today. What strategy can we devise for a population in such constant, intense transition?

Contradictions are everywhere. The same demographic changes that complicate unity are also being used by conservatives to scapegoat immigrants and pass anti-immigrant proposals. On the other hand, the conservative attacks have had backlash effects in the late 1990s. They have activated Latino organizing and protest across class lines, increased Latino participation in electoral politics and stemmed the tide of growing support from Latinos for the Republican Party. The number of Latino voters in California increased by 45 percent between 1994 and 1998. (*San Francisco Examiner,* Feb. 2, 1998).

The sum total of these contradictory developments is likely to be greater politicization—a stronger consciousness of racism and exploitation and the need to unite against those forces. That growing consciousness can be most clearly seen among Raza youth, who have been carrying the movimiento torch in various parts of the country. But we have to do more. The pockets of Raza resistance need coordination. It surely won't happen overnight, but if we define our goal as replacing fragmentation with a cohesive program, illuminated by a positive vision of the society we want, it will be a big step forward.

An urgent piece of that strategy is forming alliances across color lines. The success of divide-and-conquer, divide-and-control tactics haunts us. Raza need to set aside any narrow nationalisms so that we can see our commonalities with African Americans, Asian/Pacific Island Americans and Native Americans. Of course alliances are also needed with progressive Anglos, but at this stage we see new strains of the division virus spreading so rapidly among people of color that they call for special attention.

Then we come to that basic question: where is our Chicano left? Where are those committed to a worldview that serves *los de abajo,* the underdogs of our planet, and cannot tolerate the denial of their needs? For some, "left" refers to socialism (but a socialism from the bottom up) or even communism (with a small "c"). For others it may simply mean a vision that goes beyond "brown capitalism." If you prefer the word "revolutionary," *¡ándale!* However defined, "left" is not a dirty word to describe narrow, dogmatic, sectarian, rude, divisive, competitive political behavior—although leftists can be all those things. "Left" refers to a real politics, an encompassing view of society. It demands recognition of worker-community struggles as the most consistent force all through Raza history and crucial again today. We must grow a new, Raza left to expose divisive forces, perceive linkages, and work on that larger vision.

We also need to ask, where are the organic intellectuals—those whose political intelligence grows out of their life experience rather than being imposed by formal education? They are needed to provide analysis and help to define our vision along with the strategy and tactics for achieving it. Organic intellectuals are hard to find today, and again the ideological climate of our era discourages their emergence. But they are vital to defining the revolutionary strategy needed.

So let the Pilars of our society make it up the ladder, if they wish—and they will do so. But what about the rest of La Raza? We have no guarantee that our collective determination to end racism, injustice, age-old exploitation and dehumanization will triumph. It is also true that our goal cannot be denied forever. A great anger can often be seen, flashing signals of a new movement in the making. That movement will be born when we forge our various struggles into one great human adventure, and draw a new map for the journey.

chapter twenty-four

TO NEW MEXICO WITH LOVE

New Mexico harbors an exceptionally high number of dinosaur remains, I've been told. Running across a dinosaur when you're out deer hunting is no big deal here (one man who did so couldn't even get the state to come pick it up, for the Museum of Natural History). Such indifference isn't really surprising, given that indigenous peoples in this land speak of prehistory with easy familiarity, and those of Mexican or Spanish descent may refer to events 300 years ago as though they happened the day before yesterday.

So it is normal, then, that things move slowly, especially in the rural villages of northern New Mexico. A slower sense of time can have its drawbacks; hard feelings, for example, may linger for generations. But a sense of having deep roots helps to keep people grounded and moving, despite ups and downs. Those roots lie in the earth, whose reality is impossible to escape in this area. If you listen to the earth, you and your *causa* will continue. Here's one reason why an impressive number of people who were highly committed and respected organizers in the 1960s are still around today, still committed, still respected, still active. Some of their stories are told here.

Twenty years ago, New Mexico ranked forty-ninth in per-capita income, with only Mississippi below it. In 1996, New Mexico had the highest poverty level in the United States, according to a U.S. Census estimate. In some largely Raza counties the unemployment rate has remained between 20 and 30 percent. Among Native Americans it can be even worse. Imagine a southwestern Appalachia, where the welfare rolls are long and the outhouse is a creature of the not-so-distant past.

Before the 1848 U.S. takeover, much of New Mexico comprised land grants issued by Spain or Mexico to encourage colonial settlement, especially as a line of defense against Native Americans. Most of the land in the grants was communally used by small farmers to graze their animals, cut firewood and collect fruit. Small plots within the grant were privately owned by the family who had received it.

Under U.S. control, four-fifths of the former grants were ripped off by mechanisms ranging from the fixed land tax to straight-up violence. The National Forest Service took millions of acres of communal lands from villages without compensation, slowly but relentlessly squeezing out the local owners, who resisted in ways that included fence-cutting, burning Anglo barns and other acts. Secret organizations like the Mano Negra ("Black Hand") and the Gorras Blancas ("White Caps") flourished. The village people speak a Spanish of 300 years ago, and more than a few believe in what others would call witchcraft. This is a magical place where time has stopped, so resistance hasn't.

In the 1960s poverty fueled an intense renewal of the long-standing struggle for land and water rights. The Alianza Federal de Mercedes, an organization of land-grant heirs led by Reies López Tijerina, worked to force federal action on their claims. Citing the Treaty of Guadalupe Hidalgo, which ended the U.S. war on Mexico of 1846–48 and promised respect for Mexican property, Alianzistas occupied federally owned lands, mostly in the national parks. The struggle centered on the Tierra Amarilla land grant comprising 600,000 acres in the heart of the mountainous north.

On June 5, 1967, a group of armed Alianza members took over the courthouse in the village of Tierra Amarilla in response to suppression of their right to organize. One policeman was injured, the judge hid in the bathroom, the jailer jumped out a back window—and ten angry Chicanos shook up the Anglo power structure across the state. The word went out that Cuban-trained guerrillas were on the move toward Los Alamos, headquarters for development of the nation's nuclear-energy resources. National Guardsmen and tanks rolled into Tierra Amarilla to repress the protest.

Alianzistas were arrested. In the first trial, Reies López Tijerina acted as his own lawyer and won acquittal. Later he was imprisoned for a year on another charge. The Alianza headquarters was bombed. Still, some of the "courthouse raiders," as they came to be called, continued to work for land and justice. Moisés Morales probably has the longest record of community activism and is now a county commissioner. This was the New Mexico I came to in 1968, straight from New York City, for a two-week visit that turned into eight years. Trials, bombings, the National Guard and police abuse all spoke of familiar 1960s repression—but the land was something else. An abiding sense of its beauty and the respect it demands began on one of my first days when driving through flat land toward the north. Rain began coming down heavily all around the entire, wide-open, 360-degree horizon. *"Mangas de lluvia"*—"sleeves of rain"—said one of the courthouse raiders, José Madril, as he pointed to huge sheets of grayness that stretched from the clouds to the ground. That and so many other wonders testified to the fact that New Mexico would be like no other place in this vast country.

My work was to support the Raza land struggle—an unending struggle because land is so fundamental to human existence. The same holds true for water rights, without which the land dies. While I was living in northern New Mexico, Tierra Amarilla became the home of another struggle: to establish a clinic in this isolated area. The Clínica del Pueblo de Tierra Amarilla was finally born, grew and survived for the next 25 years. The Che Guevara posters of the 1970s are gone from the clinic waiting room today, but some of the original founders and supporters are still around, still active.

In 1989, TA (as everyone called it) was again the scene of Chicano struggle for the land. Developers had become the new enemy, calling to mind the stream of Anglo merchants along the Santa Fe Trail who paved the way for the nineteenth-century military takeover. But today's Fifth Column came bearing ski lifts and river rafts. One of the developers, an Arizona-based investment partnership named Vista de Brazos, claimed title to 1,900 acres near TA. The company wanted to build vacation homes and condominiums there. They ran into trouble with Amador Flores, who had formally claimed 500 acres of the same land two decades earlier. A 16-month struggle followed. Ordered off the land in April 1988, Flores burned the injunction and subsequently spent 62 days in jail for contempt. On his wooded hillside, supporters set up armed bunkers and barricades behind *"Tierra o Muerte"* ("Land or Death") posters bearing the image of Mexican revolutionary Emiliano Zapata—the same image we saw in the 1960s and would never stop seeing among Chicano youth everywhere. A year went by and no law-enforcement agency was willing to move on the encampment. An out-of-court settlement finally gave Flores 200 acres and more than $100,000.

The best-known voice of this struggle, Pedro Arechuleta of TA, had been active in the Alianza 20 years earlier. He had gone to the 1968 Poor People's Campaign in Washington, D.C., and became known as a strong believer in militant direct action. Pedro also spent time in prison for refusing to testify before a grand jury investigating criminal charges against Puerto Rican nationalists. As his life suggests, it would be a mistake to see the New Mexico land struggle as an isolated, strictly rural issue.

This is also the lesson from the life of another longtime organizer, Valentina Valdez. As a young woman she worked with the Alianza and then on the movement newspaper *El Grito del Norte*, where she learned to write about issues ranging from New Mexican cultural traditions to the Vietnam War. She became a key figure in establishing and developing the Clínica del Pueblo de Tierra Amarilla and finally settled in TA, where she is active working on community issues.

Another struggle for land in the TA area developed in the 1980s, but this one centered on sheep. A cooperative of sheep owners called Ganados del Valle had begun in 1981 as an economic project based on a traditional use of the land—raising sheep. Ganados was to be a self-help model for a highly depressed area of families long dependent on food stamps and welfare. During the next few years a weaving project emerged, using the cooperative's wool in traditional designs, and then Tierra Wools began to market its products. Again an activist from the 1960s was involved—María Varela, out of Students for a Democratic Society, the Student Nonviolent Coordinating Committee, the Tierra Amarilla clinic and other projects.

Ganados tried for years to get grazing rights on wildlife land. Then came an immediate crisis: a temporary lease on Jicarilla Apache land expired, and the sheep had nowhere to go.

In 1989 the state Department of Game and Fish again denied the co-op's request for land in wildlife areas. Among other arguments, they claimed the sheep would ruin the wilderness for hunters, who pay fees to the department and who want elk—not sheep. After many fruitless hearings, one night Ganados owners secretly drove their 2,000 sheep onto state wildlife land without permission. The next day, banner headlines filled the press and a whiff of *High Noon* rose in the air. Fortunately, the game and fish director said, "I'm not going to saddle up the guys and send them up there with Winchesters." After New Mexico's governor promised to help find a long-term solution for land-poor ranchers, the co-op agreed to move its sheep elsewhere.

What about the original inhabitants of these lands, the various nations and tribes? They rarely made common cause with Chicanos, who were, after all, descendants of the same people who had once invaded, robbed and enslaved them. But Chicanos and Native Americans did come together in the Tonantzin Land Institute to combat threats from developers, and the state and federal government. Founded in 1982, it became a network involving more than 50 organizations of traditional land and water users throughout the Southwest. Again we can find activists from the 1960s. They included John Redhouse, a Native American who edited *Tribal Peoples Survival*, the institute's excellent quarterly newspaper. Very-longtime activist and writer Enriqueta Vásquez was one of Tonantzin's founders. Director David Lujan was a Chicano youth organizer during the 1960s in the southern town of Roswell.

Lujan has said that the key to developing a measure of unity was convincing Native Americans that Chicanos respect the sacredness of Indian lands and that Chicanos understand the spiritual importance of such practices as the sweat. Creating trust is a long, slow process, carried out in a low-key, quiet way, and it's still far from over. "Sometimes," Lujan told me with a little smile, "you have to let people duke it out."

The foundation for unity is the idea that the land does not "belong" to anyone; it is not a question of ownership but of how you care for the land. This concept of stewardship forms the basis for Indian-mestizo relations, and work gets done on this level. Stewardship requires embracing the indigenous view that the land is not real estate or property, to be bought and sold. It is our mother. But sometimes, in the outside world, property rights must be affirmed. Tonantzin negotiated the first agreement in history with the U.S. Forest Service on its management plan, an agreement that incorporated such changes as the cancellation of a planned ski resort.

In the cities, veterans of the 1960s and early 1970s were still active 20 or 30 years later, often leading new organizations and new struggles. Richard Moore, who had been a founder of the Black Berets (which existed at about the same time as the Brown Berets), moved on to help build a movement for environmental justice with the SouthWest Network for Environmental and Economic Justice. Mimi López, another veteran, moved on to the current fight for immigrant rights.

By the 1990s the right-wing backlash had struck in the school system. Taos' superintendent of schools issued a formal statement that the top priority was respect for the flag and next came discipline. Bilingual programs essentially served to teach English to the Spanish-speaking, with little intent to preserve or develop Spanish-speaking culture. Worse, there was little interest among Chicanos in learning Spanish; mostly Anglos were demanding it. Schools now frowned upon the word "racism"; one must speak of the need for "cross-cultural communication." In Albuquerque on Martin Luther King Jr.'s birthday, a Chicana elementary school teacher wanted to use the anniversary, which was generally observed in a tokenistic way, to introduce some important words and concepts. In this spirit, she wrote *"racismo"* on the blackboard and also used some relevant English terms. The school principal entered, sat down and after a minute told her that she was supposed to be giving a Spanish class. Later she received a transfer notice.

The "English Only" campaign never had a chance in New Mexico; the governor announced his personal opposition. But the basic Eurocentric attitude persists. You can find the same kind of Anglo crusade here against "reverse discrimination" that has been found in other states. In Santa Fe and Albuquerque, for example, Anglos filed suit charging that it was discriminatory to allow only Indians to sell jewelry on the plaza.

But the culture wars seemed to have little impact in rural areas, which have such a long-standing culture of their own. The pulse of resistance remains steady, even though young people often leave for opportunities elsewhere and those who stay have their conflicts. It's still true that 20 or 40 or 60 years is not so long in a land where the earth provides your sense of time. No surprise, then, that effective organizing and some nationally significant victories (by the environmental justice movement, for example) have come out of New Mexico, home of long-term warriors.

Now, what finally happened to that dinosaur the man found while deer hunting? It's still there, I was told. This happened at the time of the struggle of the Sandinistas to build a new society in Nicaragua, and many activist Raza in the United States supported that struggle. So one Chicano said he might call the relevant state authorities and tell them that if they didn't want to remove the dinosaur, he would do so—and send the bones to Nicaragua. The Sandinistas probably didn't have much of a dinosaur collection, he would explain. I don't think he ever did it, though.

If you don't believe my story, too bad. Things like that happen in New Mexico. "Land of Enchantment," it says on the state's license plate, and so it is. The land makes people very special.

chapter twenty-five

BE DOWN WITH THE BROWN!

For ten days that shook Los Angeles, in March 1968, Chicano and Chicana high school students walked out of class to protest a racist educational system. The "blowouts," as they were called, began with several thousand students from six barrio schools, then increased every day for a week until more than 10,000 had struck. Shouting "Chicano Power!" and *"¡Viva la revolución!"* they brought the city's school system—the largest in the United States—to a total halt.

As scholar-activist Carlos Muñoz Jr. later wrote in his book *Youth, Identity, Power,* the strike was "the first time Chicano students had marched en masse in their own demonstration against racism and for educational change." Not only that; it was the first mass protest specifically focused on racism by any Chicanas or Chicanos in U.S. history. (This is not to deny the many huge strikes of Raza workers with labor demands that often had their roots in racist conditions on the job.) With the 1968 protests, students moved beyond the prevailing politics of accommodation to a new cry for "Chicano Power!"

The blowouts sparked other protests, including the first action ever by Chicano university students, at San Jose State College, and then Chicano participation in the long, militant Third World student strikes at San Francisco State and the University of California, Berkeley. New Raza college-student organizations emerged, while existing ones grew rapidly. All this took place at a time of youth rebellion nationwide and worldwide—from Mexico to France to Japan. Here, Raza students stood out because the great majority came from the working class. Their main goal was affirmation of their own culture's values and history rather than a counter-culture, such as many Anglo youth were celebrating.

Almost 30 years later, Raza high school students from California to Colorado repeated that history with new blowouts demanding more Latino teachers and counselors; Ethnic Studies (not only Latino but also African-American, Native American and Asian/Pacific Islander); bilingual education sensitive to students' cultural needs; and Latino student-retention programs. Other issues were often added; in

California, these included combating repressive new anti-crime laws, preventing the re-election of right-wing Gov. Pete Wilson and fighting Proposition 187 with its inhumane call to deny educational and health services to anyone suspected of being undocumented.

California's blowouts focused on public schools in the northern part of the state at first, then spread south. The students, mostly of Mexican or Salvadoran background, came from high school, junior high and sometimes elementary school. Why a walkout during school hours rather than a march or rally on the weekend? Because, as they learned, California's public schools lose $17.20 or more for each unexcused absence per day. This pocketbook damage provided the economic centerpiece of the students' strategy. With it, they made history.

<<< >>>

The first wave seemed to burst out of nowhere. On April 1, 1993, more than 1,000 mostly Latino junior high and high school students walked out of a dozen Oakland schools. On September 16, celebrated as Mexican Independence Day, more than 4,000 blew out in San Francisco, Oakland, Berkeley, San Jose and the town of Gilroy. Arrests and violence were rare, although in Gilroy police did arrest teenager Rebecca Armendariz and harassed her for months with charges of contributing to the delinquency of a minor, apparently because she signed to rent a bus that students used. In right-wing-dominated Orange County, 300 students clashed with police while some were beaten and pepper-sprayed.

Another wave of student strikes unrolled in November and December in northern California. In Exeter, a small town in California's generally conservative Central Valley, 500 high school students boycotted classes when a teacher told an embarrassed youth who had declined to lead the Pledge of Allegiance in English: "If you don't want to do it, go back to Mexico." It was the kind of remark that had been heard too many times in this school where 40 percent of the 1,200 students—but only six of their teachers—are Latino.

At Mission High School in San Francisco, 200 Latino and other students demonstrated for the same anti-racist reasons as elsewhere, and also for being stereotyped as gangbangers if they wore certain kinds of clothing. The school board agreed to their main demand for Latino Studies, and then offered just one class—to be held before and after the regular school day. The basic message: this concession isn't for real.

On to February 2, 1994, which marked the anniversary of the 1848 Treaty of Guadalupe Hidalgo confirming the U.S. takeover of half of Mexico—today's Southwest. In Sacramento, the walkout movement spread like wildfire. Some 500 high school students and supporters from various districts shook up the state capital. "The governor wants more prisons, we want schools. He wants more cops, we want more teachers. We want an education that values and includes our culture. We want all cultures to know about themselves," they said, as reported by the local paper *Because People Matter*.

For César Chávez' birthday in March, nearly 150 Latino students from four city schools marched on district offices in Richmond. On April 18, half of the elementary school pupils in the town of Pittsburgh boycotted classes, with parental support, because a Spanish-speaking principal had been demoted. They had their tradition: 20 years before, Pittsburgh elementary school students had boycotted for lack of a Latino principal.

The spring wave climaxed on April 22 with a big, coordinated blowout involving more than 30 schools in northern California. It was unforgettable. Some 800 youths gathered in San Francisco under signs such as "Educate, Don't Incarcerate" and "Our Story Not History," and with beautiful banners of Zapata and armed women of the Mexican Revolution.

Calls for unity across racial and national lines and against gang warfare rang out all day. "Don't let the lies of the United Snakes divide us!" "Latin America doesn't stop with Mexico," said a Peruvian girl. Another shouted, "It's not just about Latinos or Blacks or Asians, this is about the whole world!" Some of the loudest cheers rang out from a 16-year-old woman who cried "We've got to forget these [gang] colors!"

In the town of Hayward that day, 1,500 high school and junior high students boycotted more than 20 schools. About 300 of them turned in their red or blue gang rags for brown bandannas—brown for Brown Power and unity. Later some of them set up a meeting to help stop the violence. "You wear the brown rag, be *down*. Be all the way down for every Raza," said Monica Manríquez, age 17.

Cinco de Mayo, May 5, brought more blowouts, followed by a June gathering in Los Angeles of 900 high school students. The youth themselves were startled by their own success. Sergio Arroyo, 16, of Daly City, spoke what others were thinking: "People didn't think it could happen, all that unity, but it did." Lucretia Móntez from Hayward High said, "We're making history. We're making history."

Why did this new round of blowouts explode in 1993–94? The current generation of Latino teenagers had seen little in their lifetime except the intensified reaction and racism established under Presidents Reagan and Bush, unchanged under Clinton. Attempts at multiculturalism, bilingualism, and affirmative action had been repeatedly attacked by staunch advocates of White Supremacy. A prolonged recession had further eroded young hopes for a decent life. At the same time, Raza were being fingered as the cause of those economic problems by the campaigns to scapegoat immigrants.

Racism in the school system stood at the top of the list of reasons for the blowouts. Nationwide, Latinos have the lowest high school graduation rate of any population group. For every 100 Latinos who enter kindergarten, only 55 graduate from high school. Of those 55, just 25 enter college. Of those 25, 7 finish. Of the shining seven, four go on to graduate school—and two finish. Those figures come from a 1985 study, but the count today is even worse. For example, in 1995, fewer than 60 percent of Latino 18-to-24-year-olds had completed high school or earned an equivalent degree, which was lower than the 77 percent rate for African-American students and the 82 percent rate for whites, according to the American Council on Education. (*New York Times,* May 19, 1997.)

Along with the poverty that makes so many quit school to find work, how can Raza feel encouraged to continue at schools like Jefferson High in Daly City, which had a 47 percent Latino student body but no Latino Studies and only two Latino teachers in 1994? Or Christian Brothers High in Sacramento, where a teacher called a student "dumb Mexican" to his face. As recently as 15 years ago, teachers would sometimes place a dunce cap on a Chicano student's head when he or she first showed up in class speaking Spanish, seat the student in a corner and explain that the cap would be removed when the student could speak adequate English.

Another reason why the blowouts occurred when they did was the general climate of angry alienation, if not despair, among young people in general. African-American youth influence other youth culturally and thereby politically, rapping a common anger. Thus Latino student activism has mushroomed in a nationwide climate of youthful frustration with society as they find it. In Los Angeles, racially mixed youth marched against the state's new "Three Strikes and You're Out" crime law. In May 1994, 55 multinational students were arrested at Soledad Prison in northern California for protesting the construction of another prison there. Youth of color have also come together in cultural projects, such as Education for Liberation in San Francisco, which was initiated by former members of Roots Against War, a highly creative and radical anti–Gulf War group.

Other regional and national developments also sparked the Latino blowouts. In 1992, the anti-Quincentennial celebrations of indigenous people encouraged a rapidly growing belief called indigenismo that tells Latinos: you too descend from the native folk of these Americas and share their cultures, their spirituality. This philosophy became a positive force for youth in the face of adversity, a source of pride and identity that accompanies righteous anger. The historic January 1, 1994, indigenous uprising led by the Zapatistas in Chiapas further strengthened the new sense of self. By April 22, 1994, it seemed that the spirit of Mexico's revolutionary hero Emiliano Zapata had marched straight from the mountains of Chiapas to Dolores Park, San Francisco.

The many tributes and events celebrating the life of César Chávez after he died in 1993 also helped to mobilize young Raza. Known to few teenagers until then, César and the farmworkers became an inspiration almost overnight. His birthday and the day of his death, both in April, have provided occasions for major protests. Activist Juanita Chávez of San Francisco, the niece of César Chávez and daughter of Dolores Huerta, has strongly influenced Latino teenagers.

Finally, to answer the question of "Why now?" the high school students had immediate examples to follow, set by their sisters and brothers in college. These included the April 1993 Latino occupation of the chancellor's office at UC Berkeley to protest a policy that would subvert Ethnic Studies; the May–June 1993 hunger strike by Latino students at the University of California, Los Angeles, to win departmental status for Chicano Studies (described in chapter 26, "They Really Were Willing to Die"); and the hunger strike held by four Chicanas at Stanford University in May to protest the outrageous, without-notice firing of Chicana associate dean Cecilia Burciaga after 20 years of service. Michigan State University, the University of Colorado at Boulder, Harvard, Cornell and the University of New Mexico also saw Latino student action on issues ranging from racist advertising by a campus radio station to the removal of racist murals glorifying the Great White Fathers and respect for murals celebrating Chicano/Mexicano history. On some campuses the struggle went back 25 years.

Little wonder, then, that the hour of Raza high school students had come.

How Did They Do It?

As usual, the media hounded the young activists with their favorite question: "Who organized all this?" One thing is clear: the blowout youth may have received information, ideas, contacts, resources, tips on security and other help from college students and experienced organizers, but, in the end, they did it themselves. Rebecca Armendariz from Gilroy told me, "We organized the rally so that no adults would run it. The kids just jumped on the stage."

No single group organized and coordinated all the blowouts. At some schools certain existing structures did help pave the way. The 25-year-old national Chicano student organization Movimiento Estudiantil Chicano de Aztlan (MEChA) played that role in the Sacramento area and elsewhere. At most schools, it would be the local Raza club. There were also special occasions that brought hundreds of high school students together from near and far, like Raza Day at UC Berkeley and UCLA, a day that is officially for recruitment but that students have often turned into an organizing event. Several youth I interviewed said that day woke them up in a flash to the need for Chicano Studies.

Members of a new group originally named Fund Our Youth, then Student Empowerment Project (StEP), and later Voices of Struggle (VOS) helped organize at many schools. It was initiated by Gabriel Hernández of Oakland, longtime coordinator of the Chicano Moratorium Coalition and a union organizer, with other young adults, including Adriana Móntes, a pharmacy technician and his wife, who has done much to help the young women involved to develop politically. Gabriel told me: "We would go into schools at the request of the local Raza club or other students and bring them together for workshops on issues like identity.... We would work with them, breaking down the problems at their particular school, then talk about what to do. The students are really looking for someone who will listen to them. Once they hear, see and feel this concern, their dignity and power are unleashed."

Then students would set up committees, such as outreach and publicity, and have 20 to 80 people coming to every general meeting. After their walkout, they would get together to decide what to do next and to develop an organization. Regional coordination came from a small number of hard-traveling UC Berkeley students like Benecio Silva; Gabriel Hernández also did much of this work.

For the vast majority of students the walkout would be their first demonstration ever. It wasn't easy to organize. A Sacramento student, Kahlil Jacobs-Fantauzzi—half Puerto Rican, half Jewish—spoke of tensions when the students first started to organize, such as some groups wanting to dominate or high school students distrusting the college students involved. Another problem was described to me by 17-year-old Monica Manríquez of San Leandro High: "The guys in my high school are really still in junior high, they don't take things seriously. They are wannabe gangsters. I've been called a sellout for organizing. If you're Mexican and not a gangster, you've sold out. At first I wondered what I was doing wrong, but I kind of understand. They are afraid to pick up a book, they'll let down their friends. Everybody wants to fit in."

A few important pockets of experience did exist. Ixtlixochitl Soto (her name means "Obsidian Flower" in the Nahuatl language of pre-Columbian Mexico) from Yuba City, age 18, was the daughter of a Chicano Studies instructor; she became president of MEChA and helped organize walkouts. Rebecca Armendariz' family goes back five generations in the Gilroy area; her father is a socialist who organized prison inmates. "He taught me how to organize," said Rebecca, who pulled together a small walkout against the Gulf War. At Christian Brothers High School in Sacramento, Kahlil Jacobs-Fantauzzi had been elected class president on a political platform and organized many multicultural activities with another student ("Not just food—history!"). His mother was a longtime activist and college professor.

Elsa Quiroga of Hayward dates her activism back to eighth grade, when all but one of the Latino counselors at her school were removed. She and three other students made a video about the need for counselors. "We showed it to the school board," Elsa told me, "and they said they would keep the counselors. The newspapers said 'Students Save Counselors.' But it wasn't done." By the age of 16, Elsa had attended various leadership conferences, worked on a summer youth program, served as a peer counselor and become president of the La Raza club at school. "That club used to be just social"—a common problem—"but it should be more about issues!" She even researched and taught a lesson on the Aztecs because her regular history course included nothing on the subject.

For the April 22 blowout, Elsa did two months of organizing, set up committees, made flyers and worked on outreach. "The principal called me in and asked if I knew anything about what was happening. I explained and he said, 'A walkout is stupid.' Other teachers said the same. When the day came, the police were ready for violence at first, but then they said, 'You're very organized.' We're just taking baby steps now, toward bigger steps later."

Another key to walkout success: students organizing a blowout never announced the actual date and time until the last minute, so nobody could do anything to stop it. As a result, they took school officials by surprise and avoided co-optive moves or possible threats or subversion by intimidation of students' parents. (For example, according to University of California, Davis, student Marlene Molina, one counselor told parents that they were likely to be deported if their children got involved with MEChA.)

Taking time to talk with parents about such worries also strengthened the walkouts, especially since so many protesters were young women. "We had a workshop for parents and explained that we aim to give back to the community," Marlene Molina told me. Gabriel Hernández described how he and others had gone to visit Elsa Quiroga's Mexican parents, whom she described as strict and concerned about her, their youngest child. Finally they agreed she could go on a two-day César Chávez march and later to a conference in Arizona. "Okay, but no slumber parties," they said.

It Ain't the Sixties

The Raza high school student activists of northern California broke the patriarchal 1960s movement mold in several important ways. At the April 22 rallies in San Francisco, the majority of the speakers were female, a sight never seen in the 1960s. Out of 15 people suggested as key organizers for me to interview, all but three were female. At the Sacramento protests, security—long a super-macho domain—was female. Some key groups that emerged from the walkouts observe a 50-50 rule: not only leadership but also committee membership should be half female, half male. So each committee in the East Bay area, for example, has two coordinators, one of each sex.

Leticia Bustos, age 14, felt that "boys have not put down girls for being leaders." Her friends had been inspired by talking with participants in Mission Girls, a San Francisco program noted for its progressive mentors and activities. Monica Manríquez thought the walk-outs had changed young male attitudes. "At first they said about me, 'What does she know—a girl?' They wouldn't help me bring in a speaker. But when they saw I was serious, they changed." As back-up, perhaps, Monica belongs to a young women's club in town, Latinas y Que?—"Latinas, and So?"

UC Davis student Marlene Molina brought good news: "We had very successful skits in MEChA on what to do about sexual harassment and abusive boyfriends. In Bakersfield the guys are creating their own caucus to talk about how the men are messing up. There are few men like that!" At a large StEP meeting, I sat in on the outreach committee; it was composed entirely of women that day. When the committee reported to the full body, they duly noted this as a failing that had to be corrected: why weren't men serving on the committee? Gabriel Hernández commented on such incidents: "I think these students think equality of men and women is how things are supposed to be—normal."

The problem of homophobia has hardly been eliminated, but at least it is addressed and sometimes publically criticized. Straight Latino students will tell you they have a responsibility to defend gay people against gay-bashing, with their lives if necessary, as they would any community under attack. MEChA was once openly anti-gay; today many chapters have moved away from such positions. At least one respected MEChA leader is openly bisexual ("no big deal"), which would have been impossible in the 1960s.

Among this new generation of Latino activists, gone are the days when the ideal was a *cacique* type of leader with a tough style, preferably charismatic, and overshadowing all others. These youth avoid projecting individual leaders and still have no officers beyond the local school organizations. Some groups have a rule that no one can speak a second time at a meeting until all others have spoken. What a joy to those of us who have been droned to sleep by someone in love with the sound of his (usually) own voice. "No work, no talk" is another guideline. Most groups usually make decisions by consensus, not by voting (MEChA does vote). And they don't go for what one student described as the chilling effect of "John's Rules of Order—or who? Robert's? Anyway, they told me I was out of order at that conference, so I fell asleep," he reported at one meeting.

Some of this suggests an idealism that may lead to problems as the numbers grow, with increasing political differences and the need for leadership training to guard against dependency on some experienced individual. There are already other contradictions to be faced and resolved. One is the Raza student relationship to African Americans and Asian/Pacific Islanders. Conflicts between Latinos and Blacks flare up at many schools, reflecting tensions in the larger society. "They try to punk us but we punk them back," commented 13-year-old Maribel Sainz. Then she went on to say, "But when we walked out, about 20 Black students walked out in support." They have come together politically—to demand Ethnic Studies and to oppose repressive new laws related to immigration and crime.

No matter how difficult, unity remains the dream of many Raza walkout youth. When I interviewed 14 of the activists, almost all said their great dream was unity. "I want to see everyone together, all of the colors and races," 14-year-old Leticia Bustos told me. "I want other races to run the government, like a Black president." Anglos are also included when the students talk about who has helped them and who should be supported in return.

During the summer of 1994 and into the fall, high school students from Los Angeles to Denver gathered regionally or locally to plan for the future. The Bay Area group VOS held a retreat, which they call an "advance," attended by 70 youth. They discussed what they had done and how, and made plans for the coming year, all the while living together peacefully in tents for four days. No small thing, I was told, given that they came from many different schools where gang and other divisions often generated tension.

VOS youth continued to meet regularly, with a structure incorporating five committees: outreach, campaigns and events, policy, education (external and internal) and barrio warfare. They worked on door-to-door campaigns and voter registration, especially with a view to combating the anti-immigrant Proposition 187 and anti-affirmative action Proposition 209. Using the bases created in that work, they launched a campaign to get high school Chicano Studies courses established, with college students teaching them. After chalking up several successes in the Bay Area, members moved on to the Los Angeles area, where they are continuing that effort. (See chapter 28, "Back in the Early 1990s ... ")

This work reminds us of the Plan de Santa Barbara, born from the 1968 "blowouts." It called for the institutionalization of Chicano Studies and student organizing. In this profoundly ahistorical society, young people can remember history when they want to—and make history, too.

chapter twenty-six

"THEY REALLY WERE WILLING TO DIE"

When Latino student activism began sweeping across northern California in the early 1990s, the question arose: is a new movement being born and, if so, how will it be different from 25 years ago?

It soon became clear that if a new movement were to emerge, it would need an agenda that would also be new, in certain important ways. Such an agenda had to move beyond narrow cultural nationalism and recognize the need for serious, nonsectarian coalitions with other progressive students of color and whites. It needed to be internationalist—which included grappling with class contradictions—while remembering the powerful need for a sense of positive group identity. It had to take on sexism and homophobia.

These issues—and more—were raised by the dramatic struggle at the University of California, Los Angeles, which began in May 1993. Its origins date back to the Plan de Santa Barbara of 1969, when Ethnic Studies was born in the tear gas of student strikes and protests across the state. The Movimiento Estudiantil Chicano de Aztlan (MEChA) was also established then. Five years later, a Chicano Studies program was created at UCLA. Then began two decades of attacks and subversion, recommendations that it be abolished and a yearly budget of only $1,500. In 1990, MEChA demanded that a Chicano Studies department be established, with its own faculty and autonomy. A proposal was drafted.

Chancellor Charles Young repeatedly failed to announce his decision on that proposal as promised. He finally did so—on the eve of César Chávez' funeral—and his decision was no. Young's announcement came in the wake of another: to cut resources at the Chicana/o Studies Library. Those two straws broke our burro's back. They epitomized the elitism of UCLA, which is located on the primarily middle-class West Side, far from East Los Angeles and other Latino neighborhoods, with Latinos numbering only 1.4 percent of its full professors and only 17 percent of its undergraduates. All this in a city where, according to the 1990 census, Latinos form 65 percent of the public school students and 40 percent of the total population.

A new off-campus group called Conscious Students of Color (CSC) organized a rally for May 11, 1993, to protest Young's actions and inactions. CSC included African Americans, Filipinos and Koreans; a Chilean whose father had served under President Salvador Allende; a Guatemalan; and other Latin Americans familiar with struggles in their own countries. Together they formed a very open and politically diverse group.

At the rally called by CSC, a window of the Faculty Center was broken; students entered and held a sit-in. UCLA officials summoned 200 police in full riot gear. They arrested 99 students, grabbing their heads, necks and ears, dragging them, and in some cases using pepper gas or tazers on them, according to *La Gente*, the UCLA student newspaper. "We stayed in handcuffs for over six hours," María Lara told me, before being jailed at 3 a.m. as dozens of supporters watched. Charged with a felony (vandalism), not just the usual trespassing, 83 went to jail.

The next day, 1,000 people attended a MEChA protest against the arrests, and more rallies followed with even larger numbers. In addition to the African Americans and Asian/Pacific Island Americans, who had been seeking to upgrade their own studies programs, some Palestinians and Native Americans joined the Latinos. "It was the first time the city has seen such a broad, multiracial effort," according to Professor Jorge Mancillas of the UCLA Medical School.

Several students of working-class Mexican origin, half of them women, half men, decided to go on a hunger strike demanding a Chicana and Chicano Studies department. The group eventually numbered nine, with six UCLA students, one high school student, Prof. Mancillas and a man who had participated in the 1968 student uprising in Mexico City. Housed in tents on a prominent campus quad, they took water only.

Support spread. It included several labor groups, among them Justice for Janitors (now a project of the Service Employees International Union, Local 1877), which had stood by Chicano-student demands for several years. Two hundred members left their own strike picket line and marched over to the campus rally that first day. Throughout the strike they provided bodies, material resources such as vans and bargaining experience at negotiations. Support also came from community organizations, merchants like activist-restaurant owner Vivian Bonzo, and state legislators including Art Torres and

Tom Hayden. Chicano doctors monitored the fast on a volunteer basis. Even the *Los Angeles Times* editorialized that departmental status for Chicano studies made sense in a city like Los Angeles.

Still Chancellor Charles Young refused to budge. Meanwhile, the commitment affirmed by the hunger strikers caught still more people's imagination. "They really were willing to die," said one student, 23-year-old Sergio Romero, an activist, campus writer and strike supporter from California State University, Los Angeles. This kind of idealism was one of the major forces at work, in the opinion of leading Chicano historian Rudy Acuña, who spent 12 to 16 hours daily at the hunger strikers' encampment.

"How much were you inspired by César Chávez' methods?" I asked two of the hunger strikers, María Lara and Cindy Montáñez.

"Before, I was aware of César but not as much as other people," Cindy said. "Then his death brought more awareness. I do feel his spirit was there. I think he has sparked something in all of us…. The community was very excited about our doing this hunger strike in honor of César Chávez." High school students talked about having their own hunger strikes, and small children offered to give up chewing gum in solidarity.

The hunger strike made Chicano Studies a matter of public interest—as it should be. In that spirit, the UCLA struggle went far beyond a campus issue. It became a struggle to win respect for the Latino origins and identity of El Pueblo de Nuestra Señora la Reina de Los Angeles de Porciúncula—the original, full name of Los Angeles. Even more, as Cindy said, "It was a movement for everybody. The students and faculty and community were fighting not just for something that would benefit Chicanos, but something that would affect the entire community. Students realized that, and so they were cautious about what they were doing"—which led to a policy of nonviolence and not making personal attacks on Chancellor Young in public statements.

At 7 a.m. on Saturday, June 5, with rain pouring down on them, 200 strike supporters began to march 17 miles across Los Angeles. By the time they reached the UCLA campus, 1,000 people were on hand. After two decades of opposition to a Chicano Studies department, Young met for the first time with all nine hunger strikers.

On the following Monday the weakened strikers, some now in wheelchairs after 14 days without food, signed an agreement with the chancellor. The "César Chávez Center for Interdisciplinary Instruction in Chicana and Chicano Studies" (CCC—*Si! Si! Si!*—the acronym begins) would be established, with a department's attributes if not name. Seven full-time faculty would be hired over the next three years. The charges against all but seven of the students arrested at the Faculty Center were dropped.

The fast ended, but conflict began immediately about the Implementation Committee that was to hire the new faculty—that is, about governance. The hunger strikers had demanded student and community representation equal to that of faculty on this committee—one-third for each sector. Young rejected this, and the faculty was split on the extent of student-community governance. Monday-night meetings of students, faculty and community to press their demands continued through July, with up to 100 participants at each. By late summer, academic careerism and old grudges seemed to render progress on the issue of governance impossible; some faculty had a lot at stake personally. Division and lack of maturity also plagued discussions. "The administration will use all this to block the center," one sympathetic faculty member observed.

Four years later, many faculty and students were expressing deep frustration with the center's situation. As one said, "The center people are still not listening to student needs, are very conciliatory [to] the administration, not that politically active, and in general have become like yet another traditional department.... Good courses are being offered, but where is the critical thinking, and how is it being applied?" Some said, "What can we really expect, when the person in charge of the center is a Chicano who had been opposed to the hunger strike?" In this age of ongoing backlash against the gains of the 1960s, it would take more than one hunger strike to make progress.

<<< >>>

The UCLA victory was subverted at the elite, corporate level, but the whole struggle has much to teach us about mobilizing, and organizing and about where Latino ideology is going today.

The hunger strike succeeded in large part because it won broad support. It did not let certain devils of division prevail, including that most common divisive force confronting Raza: narrow nationalism, which dictates who is brown enough, who is a real Chicano, why "Latino" is a good (or bad) word and so on. Such hassles swirled around the UCLA hunger strike, but they failed to cripple it. Strike leaders María and Cindy assured me that, although their goal was defined as a "Chicana and Chicano Studies department," this meant the broader category of Latino Studies—as has been understood in situations on other campuses. "The strikers remained committed to recognizing differences among Raza without dwelling on the differences," in the words of Jorge Mancillas.

One reason for the spirit of unity may well have been that, by its very nature, a hunger strike is a spiritual affirmation of moral authority through willingness to sacrifice. Spirituality provided a major source of strength to the hunger strikers, María and Cindy told me. At a time of discomfort and grave uncertainty, with death a plausible option, spirituality said: you are not alone. "Spirituality made them untouchable," a retired sociology professor told me, "It gave them a power, a magic. I had never experienced this before."

The concept of indigenismo, or indigenousness, provided what might be called the framework for this spirituality. It is both a worldview and a way of life, based on the belief that all living creatures on the planet are connected, no one superior to another, in a relationship of profound humility rather than domination. In the UCLA hunger strike, the indigenous worldview was articulated by one of the strikers, Paztel Mireles. A 51-year-old veteran of Mexican student struggles, he had become spiritual leader of the Grupo Danzante Cuauhtemoc, an Aztec dance group of political-cultural character, based in Los Angeles. Grupo Danzante and Conscious Students of Color provided the main leadership at the core of the UCLA struggle, with MEChA members taking an active role, according to Mancillas.

Not all Raza observers were completely enthusiastic about the role played by indigenismo in the strike. Conversations with eight radical activists in Los Angeles, all supporters of the UCLA struggle and almost all Chicana/o, revealed a range of opinions. They spoke to strengths they had seen during the hunger strike, and also to pitfalls. The most common concern expressed was that indigenismo could be manipulated to encourage patriarchy. During the hunger strike the mass media focused on male figures, some of whom confirmed their hegemony. Here was a contradiction, since women were playing leading roles as fasters, speakers and negotiators, and in spiritual work. Professors Gina Valdez and Laura Medina served on the medical team, and also conducted prayers, blessings and spiritual healings. Their quiet, crucial support lent a feminist strength to the strike.

Postscript

By spring 1998, the UCLA Chicano Studies struggle had come to seem like a classic case of those who win a victory being shoved aside by the administrators of that victory, who then betray its purpose. At every step, students were being neutralized and their promised advisory role blocked. "We are not involved in the process at all," a MEChista told me in Los Angeles. They were particularly angry because a highly respected counselor, who had served as a major link between the administration and students, had recently been removed. And so the struggle to establish the César Chávez Center as it had been conceived five years earlier continued.

But it was good to find students in 1998 still committed to a struggle that went back many years. They had not forgotten those who were willing to die in 1993. It is wrong, I thought, to assume that campus-based struggles always fade away because of the turnover in a student body. Collective memory can be nurtured, and realism does not have to mean cynicism.

UCLA students who wanted a Chicano Studies department were still fighting the same external enemies, but they had made progress in their internal organizing. "We have grown a lot in dealing with sexism and homophobia," said my MEChista friend. "We learned from the hunger strike. Now we have a new constitution to address certain issues, and new committees on gender and sexuality, high-school student outreach and other issues. We are educating the membership that our community won't be liberated unless everyone is, including our queer sisters and brothers. The last national MEChA conference was terribly sexist, even the workshop on women was led by a man. The next MEChA national conference will be on this campus, and I think UCLA MEChA is showing a new way. Let's hope so!"

chapter twenty-seven

RAZA PROTEST A DAY OF LIES AND HATE

"¡Aquí estamos y no nos vamos!"—roughly translated, "We're here to stay!"—chanted some 300 mostly Latino youths as they marched through the streets of Sonoma on June 14, 1996. It was the 150th anniversary of California's so-called Bear Flag Republic, and the young Raza were demanding to take back their history.

Sonoma is the town where 34 probably drunken Yankees took over Mexico's military outpost on June 14, 1846, declared California a "republic" and raised a flag showing a bear—now the official state flag. Anglo historians called it a bold stroke against Mexican domination inspired by a great hero, Col. John Fremont. Half of the 200,000 Native Americans in California had already died under Spanish and Mexican rule, so no problems from them were anticipated. During the Bear Flaggers' 25-day occupation of Sonoma, they terrorized the remaining native peoples and wounded and murdered Mexicans. Some 800 Fremont followers succeeded the Bear Flaggers, and eventually Mexican resistance in California was overcome. Meanwhile, the United States had invaded and defeated the rest of Mexico.

Now the town of Sonoma was going to celebrate the 150th anniversary of Manifest Destiny's triumph in California. But this year Raza, together with African-American, Anglo and Native American youth, decided to protest the Bear Flag as a symbol of division and anti-Mexican feeling in today's climate of hatred for immigrants. The demonstration was organized by the Chicano Moratorium Coalition and the Student Empowerment Project (StEP), which brought people from all over California.

Officials including Gov. Pete Wilson, champion of the immigrant-bashers, commemorated the anniversary with costumed historical characters, speeches and songs on the town plaza, and other events lasting three weeks. During the opening parade on June 14, the young protesters could not possibly be ignored. They waved their own bright turquoise, gold and red flags symbolizing the "Four Sacred Elements" of indigenous culture: land, water, fire and air. They blew whistles loudly and persistently. They shouted "Shame on you!" at the parade. How, they were asking, could anyone be proud of a day that made it national policy to beat, kill and put people to work as semi-slaves?

You could barely hear Governor Wilson drone on as he spoke to celebrants gathered in the plaza. Cries of "Deport Wilson!" were very audible, however. Anglo onlookers looked puzzled when they heard the demonstrators chant, "We didn't cross the border, the border crossed us!" "What does it mean?" Such a question speaks to a great divide. On the one hand Sonoma has an overwhelmingly Anglo population. A Sonoma Valley school trustee, Dorne Musilli, had recently proposed establishing a school for Spanish-speaking children and abolishing bilingual education elsewhere. She also proposed making it illegal to speak Spanish at any school, including outdoors on the playground. During the June 14 ceremony, those who cheered the Bear Flaggers were almost exclusively older Anglos who appeared middle-class, while the protesters were almost all young people of color, mostly working-class.

But exceptions turned up everywhere. About 10 to 15 Anglo residents organized their own demonstration. At three shops near the plaza, the Anglo owners said they would have nothing to do with the celebration. One blond, blue-eyed young man made it clear he thought the only good Wilson would be a dead Wilson. A white woman standing on her porch near the plaza offered her bathroom, telephone or cold water to passing protesters. On the other side of the color line, one Chicano yelled at the marching protesters, "Go home!" and a Chicano Republican Party official wrote in the local paper that he stood "in support of the history of California as it has unfolded" (lynching of Mexicans and all, I guess).

There was nothing new about the contradictions. Gen. Mariano Vallejo, the Mexican commander in Sonoma on June 14, 1846, eagerly collaborated in the U.S. takeover. Like other wealthy Mexican ranch owners, he believed his self-interest lay with the invaders. Thanks to Vallejo's support for annexation, he became California's first U.S. senator from Sonoma County. Sometimes Raza forget this kind of painful truth about our history. The June 14 parade included men dressed as Mexican soldiers and officials; when they marched by the first time, most of the Chicano protesters remained silent, but a few clapped or cheered. The second time, protesters booed loudly out of a delayed understanding that the Mexican upper-class and its defenders were no friend of Mexicano people. "Shame on you!" applied to them, too. Rather than commemorating Vallejo, we would do well to remember the resistance of native peoples to both the Mexicans and the Yankees.

Raza youth are learning that the roots of our struggle include the division of rich from poor. At the June 14 celebration, Gov. Pete Wilson pontificated about our "golden" state and saluted the Sons of the "Golden" West. Those moneyed references take us back to July 7, 1846, when Commodore Sloat raised the U.S. flag at Monterey, California, completing the takeover, and proclaimed that "a great increase in the value of real estate may also be anticipated." Now, 150 years later, a winery near Sonoma was cashing in on history with a big sign that announced on June 14: "IT'S A REVOLUTION! BEAR FLAG BLUSH IS HERE!" As for the workers who produce that blush wine, they are just Mexicans who came with the territory and now labor in the fields or inside the winery, going home at night to the half-hidden barrios on the city's outskirts.

But Bear Flag Day 1996 also said: the Mexicans won't always be hidden. We won't accept the denial of our complex yet sturdy reality for another 150 years. June 14, 1996, belonged to La Raza, and on the streets of Sonoma you could imagine a time when all the days would belong to all the disempowered, despised *razas* of our planet.

chapter twenty-eight

"BACK IN THE EARLY 1990S..."

As I was talking one day in July 1996 with a 27-year-old African-American organizer, we came to speak of militant youth activism against the Gulf War in San Francisco's Bay Area. "Well, yeah," he said, "but that was back in the early 1990s." Like ancient history, y'know.

Understanding those words is vital if we are to work toward a revolutionary future: youth-led groups, which are key to that future, usually have their eyes fixed on the present. Why would they look back very much in this ahistorical society that denies the linkages between past and present struggles for social justice? A society so politically bankrupt that young activists emphasize above all the need for new ideas, new programs, new language? A society that devalues the opinions of youth and is secretly afraid of empowering them, even to solve their own problems?

So it's risky for an older person like this *veterana* to analyze the struggles of activist youth, and absolutely fatal to speak *for* them. We usually end up being irrelevant, arrogant, paternalistic, nostalgic or all of the above. But it might be worthwhile to take that risk and look at various examples of politically active youth of color in the Bay Area—especially, though not only, Latinas and Latinos—for what they can teach us. Such a venture might even help meet today's acute need for mutually respectful, intergenerational communication about politics.

One of the most striking facts about the 1990s is the high level of female leadership and participation. For anyone who remembers the sexism of the 1960s and 1970s movements, today's young women in action are a joy to see. Raquel Laviña, for example, is a Chicana-Filipina who has been active since age 15 and now belongs to Standing Together to Organize a Revolutionary Movement (STORM) in San Francisco. As she told me, "Women have always been the backbone of any organization, but this wasn't recognized. Times have changed a lot just in the last six to seven years." Cindy Wiesner, a young Latina also in STORM, affirmed that "women being in leadership is key to any successful organizing." Since the mid-1990s, young Asian/Pacific Island women have been increasingly visible in Bay Area activism on a range of issues from environmental justice to immigration policy. In their work and sometimes their words too, they fit the title of the 1997 South End Press book *Dragon Ladies: Asian American Feminists Breathe Fire,* edited by Sonia Shah.

A second striking reality is youth's basic grasp of "the system." I have heard teenage Latinos break down ruling-class deceptions and double-talk almost instinctively; even junior high or elementary school students can take your breath away. Like other activist youth, they express a profound cynicism about the government, electoral politics and official institutions, especially with regard to racism. Possible reasons for this are having movimiento veterans as parents or older siblings, and the presence of universities with a tradition of activist struggle like San Francisco State University or the University of California, Berkeley. Other historic events that must have contributed to the politicization of youth: the 1991 Gulf War, the beating of Rodney King and the Quincentennial of 1992 as an occasion for year-long protest. Together those events stripped away many lies about U.S. foreign policy and domestic racism. The Zapatista uprising in Chiapas beginning January 1, 1994, and ongoing support for Cuba as demonstrated by the Venceremos Brigade have also educated and inspired.

What do we find when we look for the key issues that concern activist youth, in particular Latinos and Latinas? Five questions come to mind.

Where Is the Moral High Ground?

With youth's righteous distrust of the dominant society often comes a deep hunger for the moral high ground so absent from that society. Where to find affirmation that this country should be guided above all by a concern for human welfare rather than by hatred, greed and hypocrisy? Right-wing double-talk about "family values," all the attempted co-optation of goals like "civil rights," has not confounded students' moral hunger.

Some activist Latino/a youth seek to meet that need by adopting an indigenous worldview. Others look to Western religion for that moral high ground. They may find faith in God a key to ending the violent death enveloping their daily lives. One example: the Shotgun Theater Group, which performed a play about gang warfare that brought down the house at a big Latino/a high school student conference I attended in 1996. The play depicted a dreadful cycle of killing that finally ends with a turn to religious faith.

The moral hunger of young Latino activists includes the desire for a political culture that honors mutual respect, a culture that is not riddled with contradictions between ideals and actual conduct, a culture that does not mirror society's individualism and egoism. In a meeting of San Francisco's multiracial Youth Uprising Coalition (YUC), one young woman described with dismay a recent rally with members of an ultra-left group grabbing the mike, blowing cigarette smoke despite her protests, glaring at her angrily and acting disrespectfully in general. Stories of physical efforts to block speakers and dominate a public event, of divisiveness and sectarianism, are not uncommon—and not limited to left forces.

Moving Beyond Defensiveness

Among activists with one to three years of experience, we also find a second hunger: for less purely defensive work and a more long-range, "pro-active" strategy. Staving off attacks on immigrant rights and affirmative action, the criminalization of youth, and other forms of the right-wing blitz have consumed the greater part of young energy in the past few years. Obviously Californians of all ages face this problem. But for youth, who may put their time and energy into such efforts around the clock, then encounter an ugly political culture in their own midst, then find their efforts repeatedly defeated, a sense of hopeless disempowerment can set in that leads to burnout at age 20 or even younger. Somewhere along the line, a sense of efficacy must be found.

In moving beyond defensiveness, young people have been recognizing that their linkage to the larger community is a crucial lifeline. In San Francisco's November 1995 elections, a coalition of groups that culminated in YUC defeated the mayor's move to intensify the curfew and turn the city's only youth recreation center into a holding facility. That victory made San Francisco one of the very few U.S. cities where a curfew has been defeated by a grassroots campaign.

Although it began as yet another defensive action, the campaign taught several valuable lessons. A crucial one was the value of youth working closely with parents and teachers in their communities, projecting not only opposition to the curfew but also the need for resources such as a youth café or center. Older people came to recognize that the people most affected by a problem—in this case, youth—can lead the fight to solve it. The victory also resulted from youth learning how to work in coalition. They learned, for example, how to incorporate the valuable experience of a local group like PODER, which works on environmental justice issues. As YUC mentor Robin Templeton observed, "The positive lesson for YUC is that we can come together and win."

A major example of youth moving beyond defensiveness is the Student Empowerment Project (StEP), now Voices of Struggle (VOS), which engaged in the 1993–94 student blowouts. Unlike many student protests, their activism didn't end with that summer's vacation. Gabriel Hernández, organizer and mentor, commented: "We have put 20,000 people in the street, but that's not the important thing. What counts is that students are going into communities where they never went before, like different ethnic groups, churches, organizations doing grassroots work. Issues come and go—the important thing is to build for the long run." Voices of Struggle has maintained a flexible balance between organizational identity and the autonomy of its components; this seems a good basis for serious, long-range building.

These youths have worked intensively on immigrant rights and affirmative action (often with the statewide organization Californians for Justice), collecting thousands of names on petitions and, in the process, building a base in various communities. With these bases, they have continued pressing for long-range changes in educational policy, and have won some victories through persistent outreach. One example is getting school boards to agree to have Raza Studies taught in four high schools outside San Francisco (Daly City, Concord, Oakland and Pittsburg) for the first time. "We phone-banked parents, lobbied community people to support us, met with different groups of officials—lots of different things," said Luís Sánchez, a student who coordinated preparation of a full syllabus and a reader for Raza Studies. Here is an impressive step toward breaking through the Eurocentric educational system that has almost always failed to tell Chicanos they have a long history of achievements and struggles for social justice together with a rich culture rooted in ancient experience. Such a breakthrough is key to what we call decolonization and the whole agenda of aggressive, rather than strictly defensive, goals.

Another area of proactive work that requires Latino youth to develop good ties with the larger community is combating barrio violence, particularly gang warfare. This work goes back 20 years. Today we have the National Coalition of Barrios Unidos, with headquarters in Santa Cruz, and Daniel ("Nane") Alejandrez as chair. In April 1996 it held a "National Peace Summit" in Washington, D.C., with 500 youth attending, its fourth major gathering in two years. The conference's César Chávez Peace Plan includes gang truces, community economic development and violence-prevention initiatives with government support.

It seems likely that groups fighting gang-related violence—and there are many across this country—might sometimes be pressured to limit street activism by their dependence on foundation or public funding. It could also be that student organizers feel they don't have the resources to take on such a massive social problem. One way or the other, more communication and perhaps collaboration should develop between Latino/a student activists and those working with the most disenfranchised of all youth.

Resolving Internal Contradictions

As they stabilized, groups like VOS have worked hard to develop leaders in ways consistent with the goal of decolonization. This means training young, often inexperienced people in strategic thinking; in how to make decisions and then implement them; in planning actions and coordinating simultaneous protests in different towns; and in speaking at rallies. It often requires finding ways to get quiet people to run meetings or creating space for women to speak up.

Raquel Jiménez, then a respected student leader at the University of California, Berkeley, seemed proud when she said of VOS in 1997: "The high school students are running things now. They needed college students as mentors in the beginning, but now they can run their own meetings." This is cause for celebration when we remember VOS is mostly working-class youth. The goal has always been to develop group leadership, not individual hotshots.

Raquel also spoke of the ongoing struggle against sexism and homophobia. The commitment to fighting those forces, which was established by StEP a few years ago with specific norms like 50-50 male/female leadership, continues. Twice it held major internal discussions about sexism. But the battle is far from won. "What's improved is that women feel comfortable bringing things up at meetings. People apologize, 'I guess I need to work on my attitude.' Sometimes things change in the guys who have decided they want to change because they see rejecting sexism as part of rejecting colonization. But it's hard for them to change other men—they don't speak up when they see something wrong unless it happens at a meeting."

When it comes to homophobia, the struggle has been even more difficult. "It's not easy to do among high school Latinos," Raquel said in 1997, "especially those who may just be coming out of a gang. I brought up homophobia at the 'advance' [as VOS calls its retreats]. It's not that people make nasty jokes, it's the silence. We don't talk about the problem enough." In general, the men are more reactionary and the women are more progressive on this issue, a straight Chicano activist at the University of California, Los Angeles, told me. "Chicana lesbians are more progressive than Chicano gays."

Much has changed and some things haven't changed. Beware the unholy trinity of the 1960s, still with us: reactionary nationalism, sexism and homophobia. Too often they travel together.

Dealing with Divisions

Nationalism is, of course, one of the divisive issues among activist Latino youth—sometimes passionately divisive (see next chapter). The reasons for this vary and can be very material. For example, where you find a broad range of Latino populations, as in northern California, you usually find less Chicano or Mexican nationalism than where you find primarily people of Chicano or Mexican background, as in southern California. (However, this is changing with the growth of the Central American population in Los Angeles, for example.) Such variety of nationalities and cultures both complicates and enriches Latino youth work.

Edgar Cruz of the Committees of Correspondence in San Francisco, who is of two different Central American nationalities, points out: "There is a lot of difference in politics as a result of those different backgrounds. For example, most youth who grew up in the United States come into politics through culture and affirming their identity. Latinos from South America focus less on racism and more on class." We can add: those who come from areas of Central America that have been torn by civil war tend to think Chicanos don't know much about real struggle. But the *centroamericanos* and recently arriving Mexicans usually don't know Chicano history. We can also find class divisions and elitism. Sometimes these are encouraged, directly or indirectly, by nonprofit agencies that have forgotten their mission. Too many so-called Latino/a community leaders fail to respect youth organizing; "Young people have no money and they don't vote," the attitude goes.

Amid the divisions, most Latino youth seek to maintain unity whenever possible. Again and again they plead at public gatherings for an end to Red against Blue (gang conflict). The basis for unity should be: who is actually doing the work?—with the understanding that everyone is needed.

One of the best tools for building unity among youth of color is cultural activity. Education for Liberation showed the potential of poetry, dance, plays, drumming, crafts like beadwork, building carnival floats—a whole range of activities—for educating and uniting. Young taggers and muralists put across powerful radical messages, and so does hip-hop culture with progressive content, despite the commercial preference for gun-glorifying, "ho"-baiting raps. The growing number of mixed-race student activists, who usually oppose the demand that they choose one national or racial background over another, also resist nationalism. Mixed-race UC Berkeley students who worked in the *diatribe* magazine collective, for example, feel they avoided divisive forces as well as sexism and homophobia to a large degree. They attribute this to their being non-hierarchical, unlike other campus organizations, and to being multiracial.

What Kind of Society Do Latina/o Youth Want?

We have spoken of the moral hunger, the desire to move beyond defensive activism, and various internal problems among young Latino/a activists. What, then, is their vision of society as it should be and the kind of organization needed to win it?

Voices of Struggle recognizes the need for a vision but leaves the answers to emerge organically from practice. "We are people pushers, not paper pushers," commented Gabriel Hernández, as a metaphor for this stance. "A lot of the Left had the words but what's the action? Today the attitude is more like 'let's try x, y, z—a variety of tactics.' Young people tend to think, 'That may have worked then, but this is our reality.'"

"At the same time," said Gabriel, "young people don't see the light at the end of the tunnel. We have to have a vision beyond today's immediate action. Somebody has to throw the rock through the bank window [that is, reject capitalism]. But most of the Left skips too many hoops, and jumps to the end—the vision."

As these comments suggest, only a small number of young Latino/a activists have looked to the Left for answers to the vision question. Most will tell you that the very word "left" seems alien, not useful, even negative. Edgar Cruz says: "For some, especially if they're from El Salvador, the word 'socialism' has come to mean war, death squads. It can even mean being kidnapped by guerrilla forces, which leads them to equate socialism with fascism. That isn't right, but the idea persists." Today, a few Chicanos/as can be found in traditional Marxist and other vanguard formations, along with some Latinos who came to the United States from countries where a strong left tradition exists. In general, it is hard to find a predominantly Latino, leftist youth group in northern California.

But recently we've seen a growing interest in political study, including Marxism, among Latino/a college students or recent graduates who have a few years of activist experience and who want to study long-range, strategic ideas. Youth conferences with a left analysis, and study groups, have become common in the Bay Area. Usually they emphasize practical application; for example, discussing problems like the criminalization of youth in terms of its capitalist roots. One six-session study group was put together in 1996 by several people of color. It was impressive to see two dozen activists attend, the great majority between the ages of 18 and 25. Another group followed, even larger, that met without fail every Sunday for months. In 1998, the new Center for Political Education was launched in San Francisco with many courses and seminars, to fill an ongoing demand.

Postscript

By 1998, certain problems had intensified and new solutions were being sought. Several Latino activists who had been involved since the 1993–94 blowouts mentioned the use of alcohol and drugs as an increasingly serious obstacle to organizing. They saw this as a reflection of a youth culture focused on material consumption and self-centeredness. "It's the music, the videos, the name brands, wanting Nikes and gold stuff. During the walkouts, the music was about struggle, but now even some of the rappers from that time are doing the commercial stuff. Before, we wore huaraches as an expression of our culture, but now people want Nikes," said one young *veterana*.

"We have had long meetings to talk about this, but there is lots of denial—people don't bring it up," another Chicano said. "It's all about 'Get money, just care about yourself.' That makes the gang thing worse now, too. But there are some Raza who are different." In seeking solutions, some youth have been doing coalition work—meeting with other youth of color to discuss the problem. Latinos in the Bay Area have met with Filipino students, Young Comrades (an African-American organization) and a new anti-racist Anglo youth organization that came out of a notoriously racist city. More and more young people have been working together across color lines, and this can be seen at public events. Not that relations are good at every high school but at least some of the most experienced organizers see the importance of this. The April 22, 1998 walkout in northern California by more than 2,000 middle and high school youth of all colors marked a historic leap toward multi-racial solidarity. The students themselves were amazed at what they could do that day.

Raquel Jiménez saw new advances over the past year and a half in the struggle against sexism. "The guys have taken a lot of new responsibilities. They take notes at the meetings, make the food for events, including those who are 14 and 15 years old." The men in VOS had a men's "advance" last fall and brought in the names of five women they had disrespected, then discussed what they had done. They bring the struggle up themselves. According to Raquel,

> All the women agree that self-esteem is an issue and that they feel marginalized. They have tried to see why they don't have a lot of women as friends, and are closer to the men—they don't respect themselves as women and they see the other girls at school as Barbie dolls. But we have talked about how to reach other women. We have become closer and now we talk about the organizing outside of meetings, among ourselves. Also, we have better relations with the new women in the group.

Involving parents in the youth activism also continued in 1998.

Looking back on the years 1993–98, we see that Raza students in northern California have been working on some of the same issues today as before, such as getting Raza Studies into the high schools and combating the right-wing move to end bilingual education. A political vacuum existed, with some of the key college-age people gone and a new generation not yet in motion as before. But Sergio Arroyo, one of the most experienced youth organizers, said, "Things slowed down for a while after some of us graduated, but they are picking up again." The year 1998 would bring the 150th anniversary of the Treaty of Guadalupe Hidalgo as well as the 100th anniversary of the Spanish-American War, both landmarks of imperialist expansion, which were to be commemorated with various educational events and protests. Speaking of the new high school generation, many organizers will tell you, "They are so sharp. They see what's wrong with the system so clearly."

From this quick overview of youth activism in one area, we see a transition period unfolding, with many contradictions. A transition between the deadly Reagan-Bush climate of massive disempowerment, and a new movement backed by an angry, energetic generation with several years of activist experience seeking a long-range strategy. It ain't the revolution, but sometimes you can imagine one.

chapter twenty-nine

¡RAZA SÍ! NATIONALISM...?

It can be frustrating to realize how many internal controversies that movimiento Chicanos and Chicanas struggled with 30 years ago are still on the agenda today. Among these is the Great Nationalism Debate, which loudly demands resolution in this age of escalating divide-and-control tactics.

Can we really afford the conflicts within our own communities, and with other communities of color, that feed on nationalism? Can we really afford to have Chicano/as looking down on Central Americans and Puerto Ricans (or even Mexicans) as "other"? Can we really have Chicano student organizations in southern California refusing to admit Mexicans as members ("They're not Chicanos")? Or attacking Chicano activists for coming from Washington, D.C., instead of the Southwest, being half-white and similar "crimes"? Or holding a meeting, as has happened more than once, where everybody who walks into a meeting room is given the "brown-bag test" (the browner, the better)?

And does nationalism really make sense in an era of globalization, when it is clearer than ever that the oppressed on this planet are inextricably linked by a dominant system that knows no borders? Doesn't that tell us that we must make a priority of learning about and building alliances with others?

To all such divisions it is time to say: *¡Ya basta!* ("Enough already!") But we need to understand why they persist. The bitter truth is that in a racist society where a brown skin (along with other colors) can cost lives, people will embrace any ideology that seems to offer hope of change. Even when that ideology proves counter-productive, the hope persists. Raza nationalism, then, has to be seen as a complicated, two-edged sword. It can't be fully understood if we just dismiss it as "identity politics."

<<< >>>

In the 1960s, the cry of *"¡Viva La Raza!"* rang out from joyously defiant youth as a key slogan of the Chicana/o student movement. That *grito* expressed the ideology called Chicanismo, a form of cultural nationalism. Chicanismo (today written as "Xicanismo" or "Xicanisma") aimed to forge a new self-definition that rejected WASP culture, drawing instead on Raza history and tradition. It sought to answer the question of many youths: I'm not Mexican, I'm not gringo, but I'm some of both, so what am I? Chicanismo centered on group identification.

In this period, Raza nationalism mostly meant affirming peoplehood rather than establishing a nation-state. The concept of Aztlan, today's Southwest, symbolized that intent. Raza activists spoke of Aztlan as an ancestral homeland, not unlike a traditional nation, but more as a cultural or spiritual base than a geographic area demanding political independence. One way or the other, it implied strength, power.

Nationalists also embraced the idea of Chicanas/os as an internal colony needing to be liberated. We identified with anti-colonial struggles in the "Third World," and wanted our movement to be seen as such. Since then the internal-colony thesis has been rejected by some Chicano scholars. Yet few would deny the historic fact that the United States colonized Mexicans, laying the basis for the oppression and exploitation of Chicanos today. That reality, which has deep roots in 150 years of pain, nurtures nationalism.

In practice, Chicanismo or Chicano nationalism showed that pride in one's history, culture and language—Chicanismo—can be a powerful catalyst to joining the fight against oppression. It can mobilize youthful energy in particular, first by liberating individual minds from the chains of internalized racism, and then by inspiring participation in collective struggle. We also saw how the self-respect that flows from a new identity can change Chicana/o lives, symbolized by wearing a beret. The Brown Berets and Black Berets, groups of Chicana/o street youth who adopted a paramilitary style to express their commitment to defend Raza, made their berets, like those of the Black Panthers, carry a proud message of group identity. Still worn today, the beret speaks to the ongoing hunger of Raza youth for respect and a sense of collectivity—the same needs that drive others into gangs.

But our nationalism then, as today, could be ambiguous, if not negative. I remember during the movimiento years shouting, *"¡Viva La Raza!"* with the noisiest *carnales,* but being bothered by another popular slogan, *"Mi raza primero"* ("My people first"), because it implied an exclusion of others. We had to affirm our culture and history, I thought, but we also needed to create a whole new, non-capitalist, anti-racist social structure free of domination by a corporate ruling class. Decolonization required more than eating tortillas instead of white bread and learning to speak some Nahuatl.

In that spirit, another ideology emerged in the 1960s that distinguished between what we called narrow (or cultural) nationalism and revolutionary nationalism. It insisted on the need for the political and economic transformation of society, not just recognition of Chicano history, values and culture. The idea was adopted by Chicana/o activists who had, for example, traveled to Cuba with the Venceremos Brigade, begun to study Marxism and become aware of class—not just racial—contradictions. A few, like this writer, joined one of the Marxist-Leninist or other socialist parties that existed then. At times our Chicano leftism meant little more than picking-up-the-gun; minimal thought was given to any deeper politics than having a Che Guevara poster on the wall (forgetting that Che himself would have demanded more). But such romanticism was often accompanied by genuine commitment; we cannot forget the Chicanos who sought to be revolutionary as they understood the word, and sometimes gave their lives. Everyone was searching for the way, the unmarked road.

A sense of group identity defined Chicanismo and still stands today at the heart of Raza activism. It is also true today, like 30 years ago, that such identity alone cannot provide the long-range, overarching vision needed for a strategy of liberation. There can be no Chicano/a liberation without *structural* social change. Most controversial of all, liberation requires alliances—based on common interests—with other peoples, including whites. So we say: *To fight effectively for Raza liberation, a sense of group identity and self-respect are necessary but not sufficient.*

The Perils of Nationalism

If nationalism opens our minds in some ways, it obscures crucial realities in others. Among those realities are gender and class.

For a few people in the 1960s movimiento, Chicano liberation also had to mean an end to sexism. Unfortunately, on this issue the revolutionary brand of nationalism may have been better than others in rhetoric but not in practice. Too often questions raised by Chicanas were dismissed by our supposedly revolutionary *carnales* as "divisive" or as "a white woman's trip." We can hear those same accusa-

tions today. In fact, nationalism has been tightly linked with patriarchy—which includes sexism and homophobia—throughout Chicano
movement history.

A major reason for this is the view of Raza liberation as an expression of manhood, a concept dear to the male-dominated
movimiento. We can see how the symbols of Chicano liberation are
drawn from periods of armed struggle to assert Mexican independence from foreign rule. They range from the Aztec warrior-chief-
tain with head held high and feathered crest to Mexican revolutionary
heroes like Zapata and Villa: a host of patriarchal figures. Although
women revolutionaries are not ignored, they tend to remain nameless
or mythically named, like Adelita.

Nationalism also obscures class issues. Chicanos with some degree of privilege seek to maintain it by claiming commonality with
the vast, impoverished majority, based solely on race. Nationalism
has been used to convince the marginalized that Latino faces in high
places will empower *them*, when in fact the goal is middle-class access for their self-styled patrons. Devoid of class consciousness, nationalism can also blind us to perceiving our common interests with
peoples of other colors. Racial consciousness becomes racial determi-
nism, and directs all choices, sustaining oppression forever. Instead, it
must be combined with a broader, deeper politics that includes gender, class, sexual preference and other arenas of oppression.

Our history is full of lessons about a nationalism that negates
class. Every Cinco de Mayo, for example, we hear another round of
cheers for Benito Juárez as one of Mexico's great nationalist heroes
who led his people to victory over France's imperial invasion in
1861. Cheers are appropriate for that victory but not for Juárez' nationalist policies when they subordinated indigenous land claims to
the rule of Mexican state power and property-rights law. As Latin
Americanist Ed McCaughan has pointed out, even though Juárez
himself was a Zapotec Indian, his sense of national identity did not
include Mexico's poor, mostly indigenous majority.

In thinking about the perils of nationalism, we would do well to
remember its historical origins in European nation-state formation.
We notice only that many Third World people fighting colonialism or
neo-colonialism have advocated revolutionary nationalism. Of
course, there is a difference between nationalism as a tool of liberation and as a tool of domination. But such divisions can blur, leaving
us with nationalist horrors from contemporary Bosnia to Idi Amin's

Uganda. We need to consider what an exclusionary nationalism can unleash if we don't clarify our goal.

Nationalism in an Era of Fragmentation

Today we find a raging Right, manifested in cutbacks in social services, persistent attacks on the poor and untrammeled racism. Many people feel extremely vulnerable. Thus, just when solidarity with others is most needed, obstacles to building it mount. People of color hunker down instead of reaching out. We look at the rest of society through narrowed, fearful eyes: slits of vision when great openness is needed. "Watch your back and don't worry about anybody else" becomes the motto. As the concept of one's community takes on ever-shrinking dimensions ("homeboyism," a friend calls it), we see the predictable rise in nationalistic conflicts.

Tensions develop between Latinos, sparked by the scapegoating of migrants. Many second- or third-generation Chicanos/as seek to distance themselves from "all those" recently arrived Mexicans, Salvadorans, Nicaraguans and others. They believe the new Latinos' presence encourages racist stereotypes about all Latinos and thus hurts those who are more established. Class plays a key role here, especially if we are talking about Aspiring Middle-Class Chicanos versus Aspiring-to-Survive Mexicanos.

In his book *Walls and Mirrors,* David Gutiérrez describes various factors that explain the divisions between established and recently arrived Latinos. The most obvious, he says, is the sense among Mexican Americans that the growing number of recent arrivals represents an economic threat, that they are "depressing wages, competing ... for scarce jobs and housing, and undercutting efforts [by Mexican Americans] to achieve better working conditions." Division also rests on minor but genuine differences between the language usage, folkways and social mores of Mexican Americans and those found in Mexico (which also vary within that country). Another factor is the recently arriving Mexican's belief that the Chicano/a is a person without a country or culture, who can't even speak Spanish.

The problem intensifies when we look at relations between communities of different colors. Cultural differences are turned into divisions; turf wars or leadership competitions are masked with nationalist rhetoric; Raza politicians utilize nationalism to win votes in "our community" against politicians from other, equally oppressed populations. Too often their program is little more than brown capitalism. Hard times also increase nationalistic opportunism in government agencies, where employees from different communities of color jockey for advantage, and among academics and student groups competing for funds on a campus.

So we can say: *Narrow nationalism flourishes in communities of color at times of increased racist and economic oppression, and when left forces are too weak to counter it.*

Building Alliances

Many people in communities of color agree on the need to build alliances, but they say, in effect, "We can't work with others until we get our own community together." It would be wrong to arbitrarily dismiss such reservations. It would be equally wrong to let matters rest there. Why should we have to choose between "getting our own act together" and working with others? There is much we can and should do simultaneously.

Building alliances calls for us to break down the walls of mutual prejudice that exist. To do so, we need to hammer out strong tools. One is simply education: learning about each other's history, current experience and culture, beginning very young. In this ahistorical nation, that is no small task. Students in particular need to fight for such knowledge, demanding courses in all the hidden histories—and demanding them together, not just one color at a time. We also have to fight against the ignorance that encourages competitiveness rather than unity (for example, the way that Chicanos sometimes assert, "The Blacks have made it").

Most important, we must work together at all levels for common causes, in a spirit of mutual respect. There are more than enough areas for cooperation. They include demands for a decent wage and opposing the attack on survival programs such as welfare for the ever-growing poor. They include fighting racist hate crimes, the denial of civil rights, attacks on affirmative action and bilingual education, and the rest of the right-wing backlash agenda. We need to perceive commonalities that may not be obvious; for example, Border Patrol abuse and urban police abuse are very similar, but this is rarely understood. Within urban areas, police abuse falls constantly on people of color, and different communities should support each other when victimized, if only with a statement of sympathy. A young Chinese engineer was shot dead by northern California police in 1997 for no reason except racism; every Latino and African-American community organization in the area should have protested, not just the Chinese-American community. Such small but eloquent acts can help to break down the isolation that says, "We have to get our own act together first."

The affirmation of cultural strength, language and beauty is a very promising area of cooperation. An evening that brings together Black rappers, Chicano performance artists, Korean drummers and Native American poets, for example, can do more for cross-racial solidarity than a host of speeches. Expressions of mutual respect for cultural work may seem no more than a gesture, but gestures can be important if sincere. When an African-American music critic writes that Latinos (specifically, Puerto Ricans) developed the roots of hip-hop, it can open some eyes in both communities.

Building cross-racial solidarity must include some honest self-criticism and analysis. We all live in a society whose economic system rewards ruthless competition and aggressive profiteering above all else. It's a merciless system that prioritizes individual advancement above collective well-being, and has no room for so-called losers. How can we all grow up in such a society, breathing that air, and not be infected by it? How can we not manifest its poison in our own conduct, including relations with others with whom we should be allies? The more we keep a watchful eye on this treacherous terrain, the more likely we are to avoid the land mines that can blow away successful alliances.

All peoples of color need to be self-critical about how we sometimes let power corrupt. Within nonprofit agencies intended to serve the public, for example, we find competition for control between those of different colors. The color that's on top, in numbers and influential positions, will dominate, while the others resent and scheme to change the existing balance. Let's face it, Raza, when we get some degree of power in a racially mixed situation, we can act just as competitive as everyone else. A little humility about our weaknesses can go a long way in building solidarity. A little sensitivity can prevent unintentional sabotage of good relations.

On the positive side, Raza youth today often seem to have less investment than older activists and organizers in competing with, or hating, "the other." They know firsthand about the increasing numbers of mixed-heritage births. They see the dangers of affirming cultural identity through an ethos of violent self-aggrandizement that exalts one group above all others. They know the deadly divisiveness of gang warfare, and cry for an end to it. Again and again I have heard high school youth speak of unity as their dearest dream.

To move toward unity, we don't have to like each other personally. But we do need to work together, take risks together, march and picket and go to jail together, and perhaps even die together—or die for each other—before lasting trust can be born. In the meantime we must recognize our interdependence, and the need to build on it, as a fundamental, life-saving strategy. In short, we can work on those two big tasks at once: getting our own communities together and building solidarity with others. They facilitate each other.

If that goal sounds too difficult, think about the organizations formed in recent years by grassroots women of different colors and ages. Women have led the way in building alliances, and their growth is one of today's most promising motions. Think also about the multiracial environmental-justice movement. Think about the coalitions for decent schools, welfare rights, safe housing; again women often lead the way. Small rainbows of our own making are everywhere, to brighten the long road through today's hellish times. They point the way toward bigger rainbows in future.

If we have not yet done more, perhaps it is because the divide-and-conquer tactics of White Supremacy have blinded us to our own possibilities. To cure that blindness, we need a revolutionary vision rooted in a mass base that has been built by working among people at the grassroots. We need a vision that understands that nationalism without consciousness of the need to build cross-racial alliances will weaken, not strengthen, the struggle for social transformation. We need a vision that won't tolerate the abuse of any working-class people of any color.

The other reason we have not affirmed our strength is probably despair at the possibility of changing a very sick, very powerful society. No answer to such despair comes easily. But Latinos and others in all corners of the land are not giving up hope; they continue to work because they need to—because they must. And for one other reason, whether they articulate it or not: because no other effort is more worthwhile. What else makes us more human, in the finest sense? What else gives us the right to this beautiful planet except the possibility of being beautiful within and among ourselves?

<<< >>>

Nationalism will not end in this country until racism ends. But we must constantly struggle to revolutionize its meaning and find a more liberatory call to oneness. Failure to do so means we insist on living in the past, confused by the demands of a new multi-colored century and doomed to stumble backward blindly when we could run forward toward the light.

chapter thirty

REMEMBER SOMETHING ANCIENT, IMAGINE SOMETHING NEW

Many young Raza activists today are adopting a vision that embraces the strengths of nationalism while shunning its divisiveness. They call it "native spirituality," or "the natural way," or "indigenismo," and see it as that revolutionary worldview we urgently need.

Native spirituality rests on a profound belief in the inter-dependence of all forms of life on the planet. Instead of domination and destruction, it speaks for balance: balance between humans and other forms of life, balance among humans including male-female relations. With balance it is possible to imagine a different kind of human society, one that begins with a person's immediate community but reaches out to embrace all living creatures.

For youth in particular, indigenismo offers a passionate sense of belonging, of identity, but without competition and hierarchy. It says, You do not have to squabble over how to define yourself, over a label; there are other ways to have a sense of peoplehood. The roots of peoplehood are not simply racial or national but equally cultural and spiritual. Like the practice of circling and other non-hierarchical forms of spirituality, indigenismo rejects borders between humanity. Thus it rejects the limitations of nationalism.

At the same time, indigenismo can subvert the colonized mentality found among mestizo peoples that elevates the European and denigrates the Indian. For Chicano/a youth, discovering they have roots in indigenous, often advanced, pre-Columbian cultures can help develop a sense of potential empowerment. "My ancestors invented rubber? Wow!" exclaimed one incredulous Los Angeles gang member to a youth counselor telling him about ancient Mexico and the Olmecas (who didn't exactly invent rubber, since Nature was the inventor, but who surely did develop it). Such discoveries can be a first step toward understanding and respecting the worldview of indigenous peoples.

A degree of indigenismo could be found in New Mexico during the 1960s, when Chicano activists often spoke of the land as our mother and had contact with Native Americans, but this spirit did not become widespread in the movimiento. In 1992, it grew with the anti-Quincentennial actions in this country and all over the hemisphere. Since then, from the San Francisco Bay Area to Albuquerque and Tucson, rallies and conferences organized by Latinos have opened with participants forming a circle of indigenous inspiration. Such ceremonies can and do create an environment of openness, of coming closer, for the discussions and work ahead. Not everyone may feel personally comfortable with them, but few deny the positive, collective effect.

In recent years indigenismo has taken a new form with growing popularity among Chicano/a youth. It centers on using a Nahuatl language sound of pre-Columbian Mexico, for which the Spaniards had no equivalent letter in their language and therefore wrote "X." Today's "X" philosophy defines Chicanos/as not as mestizo but as indigenous (or sometimes as indigenous/mestizo) people. Thus Chicano/a is written "Xicano/a," and writers such as Ana Castillo speak of "Xicanisma" instead of Chicanismo/a. The possibility that the word "Chicano" comes from "Mexica," pronounced "Mechica," strengthens the "X" philosophy.

Chicano columnist Roberto Rodríguez, whose recent book *The X in La Raza II* takes on this theme, comments that "X could have the same value for Raza as it does [for] African Americans—representing the indigenous names, the language, and our history." As with Africans in the diaspora, symbolized unforgettably by Malcolm X, the Chicano "X" reminds us of original, indigenous names that have been forgotten, and thus it reaffirms a long lost identity. The "X" also symbolizes an unknown quantity, which implies flexibility. This could help us find a way out of the usual, exclusionary ways of defining our identity. Some Chicanos dislike the "X" concept because it can lead to new terminology debates. Will its appeal become fad-like, a matter of fashion? This could happen, but even if it does, the power of indigenous thought and values will not die.

Past experience with Western romanticizing of "the noble savage" suggests that there are other questions we should ask about indigenismo as applied by Chicano/as today. Does it take into sufficient account that Native Americans are not always ready to embrace Chicanos who insist on being considered "indigenous"? Many see us primarily as descendants of those Spanish and Mexican invaders who stole their land, imposed their religion, colonized them. To their ears, Chicano claims on "Aztlan" can sound downright imperialist.

Another question that has come up—for example, during the University of California, Los Angeles, hunger strike to win a Chicano Studies department: why do some who practice native spirituality treat women as lesser, as inferior? Why do they sometimes put "their" women in the traditional blouses called *huipiles* and expect them to "stand by" the men? They do this even though, in many pre-Columbian cultures, women played major leadership roles in community affairs—running the economy, transmitting the culture, serving as important spiritual leaders (sometimes as goddesses)—and in matters of war. For those cultures, male-female relations were seen as a matter of balance between living creatures rather than domination, which would include patriarchy.

A related question: why does indigenismo sometimes seem to be a new form of cultural nationalism? Why do its supporters sometimes sound as dogmatic as the most narrow nationalists when they insist they are indigenous and not, never, in no way, mestizo? Or when they reduce indigenismo to a cult politics that says: only those who go to sweat lodges are authentic?

Sometimes we also find a tendency to view everything that's indigenous as good and anything "European"—such as Spain—as evil. That view overlooks such historical realities as the Aztec empire's oppressive domination of other indigenous societies and its class system, which privileged priests and the military. That view also forgets Spain was not a typically European nation after 600 years of rule by the Moors, an Arab/Berber people from Africa.

Another, fundamental question: can a renewed spirituality by itself bring about a world without oppression and exploitation? Don't we still need to struggle in material ways for structural change? A friend put his criticism sharply: "I think indigenismo romanticizes the past at the expense of a critical history, and it simplifies the present at the expense of a criticial understanding of the everyday issues confronting our people and the working class in general." Others would simply say it's escapist.

But our analysis of indigenismo has to be thoughtful and weighed. First, it's vital to avoid a longtime error of leftist politics, starting with Marxism: failure to understand the powerful role in human society of subjective forces such as spirituality. That failure has opened the door wide to right-wing manipulation of spiritual hunger. That failure undermines the possibility of mobilizing masses of Latinos/as for whom faith has been an affirmation of heart in a heartless world. The bottom line in any organizing for social justice needs to be respect for others' needs, including spiritual needs.

To all the questions about how indigenismo has been misused, we should say: any vision, any worldview, can be interpreted differently by different people, misunderstood and abused. That does not diminish its power. Indigenismo is too new an alternative to nationalism for its long-term effects to be adequately evaluated yet.

Meanwhile, Chicano movement *veteranos* had better realize that the indigenist vision has been flourishing among youth in large part because they want something different from the old formulas for social change. Something that sounds more alive to them than both "leftism" and "liberalism," yet with the capacity to transform society. Something that gives clearer meaning to ideas like "democracy" and "socialism." Something new, with new language and symbols. Indigenismo offers this. It is also profoundly dialectical, thanks to its affirmation of interdependence, and able to embrace a host of different views. Thus it offers a way to avoid the trap of dualism. In the past, as one friend joked, "We used to debate studying Mao versus burning sage. What about trying to do both?"

To embrace indigenismo does not and should not require a rejection of *mestizaje*, although some Chicanos insist on such dogmatism. Raza are mixed, and to find shame in that truth simply echoes a racism of our own. Instead, let us see how the variety of heritages called *mestizaje* could nourish Raza's capacity to serve as a bridge between ideas and peoples. In societies where "half-breed" is a dirty word, our wild mixtures could be a precious model for learning how to treasure difference instead of hating it. What could be finer than to provide humanity with such a model in today's age of anguished fragmentation? Couldn't this be the best, the most inclusive reason, to shout, *"¡Viva La Raza!"*

<<< >>>

Indigenismo can be the soil in which to grow a revolutionary project that will meet basic human needs like health care, full employment, decent housing and education. It can draw the outline of a new kind of society, based on communal goals, cooperation and respect for the value of all life. The need for such a vision haunts Raza and all other activists today.

We can look to Mexico, where a vision for social change has been powerfully affirmed by the Maya people of Chiapas. They named their vision "Zapatismo," in memory of Mexican revolutionary Emiliano Zapata, and startled the world with an armed uprising on January 1, 1994. That day, and ever since, the Zapatistas have posed the basic problem: how to establish both identity and democracy? How to achieve a new life of dignity for indigenous people while also creating a Mexico of justice for everyone? Always the Zapatistas have said they do not want one without the other.

At a 1996 meeting of Chicanas/os with some of the Zapatista leadership, Comandante Tacho began his presentation by saying: "We don't want power. What we want is decent homes, enough to eat, health care for our children, schools." At first I thought to myself: how can you gain those things without power? Then I realized that by power he meant domination. The Zapatista vision does not find the answer to injustice in the replacement of one domination by another, but in a vast change of the political culture from the bottom up that will create a revolutionary democracy.

Who knows how, where or when such a vision can be realized. The point is to move toward it and never stop. What an agenda for a crazy bunch of dreamers! But what can match it?

AFTERWORD

The people in this book, and thousands of others, have taught many lessons about where we go from this moment on. Looking back at the stories told here, I found irresistible the temptation to say a few last words. Here is a list of thoughts, personal (though hardly just mine) and very short.

Making what we may call a revolution for the century-after-tomorrow demands that we build a unified and therefore powerful force for change. That cannot be done without overcoming racist divisions at the grassroots level.

To overcome those divisions requires white attitudes changing, and more than that. Our exclusively Black-white model of racialism must be abandoned in favor of one that includes all peoples of color. We then have a foundation for potential alliances among people of color, which are more critical than ever given today's new divide-and-conquer tactics.

For those alliances to grow, Latinas and Latinos must understand the dangers of nationalism (or its younger brother, identity politics). Nationalism obscures issues of class, often benefits only our access-hungry careerists, and can prevent Raza along with other marginalized folk from uniting around class.

For those alliances to grow, Latinos need to practice a constant, profound honesty about ourselves and our weaknesses, especially racist attitudes within our own community toward other people of color. We also need to be self-critical about how we sometimes let power corrupt.

All this points to the great need for a radical force within each community of color to pursue liberating politics and combat conservative or reactionary tendencies within each community. The good news of 1998 was that the first national Black Radical Congress (with 2,000 people attending), the first Asian American Left Forum, and various meetings to build a New Raza Left all took place within the same six months. There's hope!

To build unity requires recognizing the central role of young activists. They are vigorously fighting the attack on this century's Reconstruction. Their anger at today's ugly society often translates into a passionate drive for unity across color lines.

And the best lesson of all: women are the world's most consistent alliance-builders. When women of color lead the way in a movement, it will almost always be stronger. When any women lead the way in uniting people, let tyrants beware.

All very nice, you say, but get practical. Where and when can alliances be built?

A common agenda for people of color should include, for starters, standing together against hate crimes. Against police abuse, which intensifies as poverty deepens today. Against the denial of adequate health care (walk into the emergency room of any big-city public hospital and who's waiting there along with poor whites?).

Surely we should all be able to unite for our children's well-being. Against the drug traffic, gang warfare, and the demonization of youth. Against neglected, under-funded, inequitable education, beginning with the inner-city schools. We need one million parents and teachers of all colors to march on that too-White House calling for the nation to stop wasting millions of minds. We also need to see how dance, music, theater, art, poetry, are major arenas for alliance-building, especially among youth. Culture can usher in new visions.

Education without language rights is impossible. Sometimes bilingual programs have been made a divisive issue between Black and brown. But recognition of "Black English" as a lingua franca, with its own structure and norms, can provide a bridge for appreciating why children should not be forced to forget their home language in order to learn English. Let them know both! The June 1997 vote to end bilingual education in California showed that division is not inevitable; a majority of African Americans opposed that measure along with the great majority of Latinos.

Of the many arenas for alliance-building, none is more fundamental than the workplace. In recent years, community organizing has unleashed new forces everywhere. Imagine if that were combined with creative, democratic union organizing that genuinely involves the rank and file. Imagine a new labor movement that incorporates millions of the unorganized—for example, day laborers and domestic workers.

The dream of social transformation from the bottom up then becomes less elusive. Can't you see the Rainbow Warriors smiling, when they win a victory here and there, knowing they fought the good fight? Yes, and they also know more good fights lie ahead.

Index

About South End Press

South End Press is a nonprofit, collectively run book publisher with more than 200 titles in print. Since our founding in 1977, we have tried to meet the needs of readers who are exploring, or are already committed to, the politics of radical social change. Our goal is to publish books that encourage critical thinking and constructive action on the key political, cultural, social, economic, and ecological issues shaping life in the United States and in the world. In this way, we hope to give expression to a wide diversity of democratic social movements and to provide an alternative to the products of corporate publishing.

Through the Institute for Social and Cultural Change, South End Press works with other political media projects—Z *Magazine*; Speakout, a speakers' bureau; Alternative Radio; and the Publishers Support Project—to expand access to information and critical analysis. If you would like a free catalog of South End Press books, please write to us at: South End Press, 7 Brookline Street, #1, Cambridge, MA 02139. Visit our website at http://www.lbbs.org/sep/sep.htm.

Related Titles

Zapata's Disciple: Essays
by Martín Espada
$14.00 paper; $40.00 cloth

The Last Generation: Poetry and Prose
by Cherríe Moraga
$14.00 paper; $30.00 cloth

Colonial Dilemma:
Critical Perspectives on Contemporary Puerto Rico
edited by Edwin Meléndez and Edgardo Meléndez
$16.00 paper; $40.00 cloth

When ordering, please include $3.50 postage and handling
for the first book and 50 cents for each additional book.
To order by credit card, call 1-800-533-8478.

ABOUT THE AUTHOR

An activist, author, and teacher, Elizabeth ("Betita") Martínez's political work began as a United Nations' researcher on colonialism. In the 1960s, she served full-time in the Black Civil Rights Movement with the Student Nonviolent Coordinating Committee (SNCC) in Mississippi and as coordinator of its New York office. She also participated in the women's movement (becoming an honorary member of the legendary Women's International Terrorist Conspiracy from Hell—WITCH).

In 1968, she moved to New Mexico and co-founded and edited the Chicano movement newspaper *El Grito del Norte* for five years; she then went on to co-found and coordinate the Chicano Communications Center, a barrio-based project. Since 1976, she has lived in the San Francisco Bay Area, working with youth groups, teaching part-time at various universities, and speaking about Latino issues on dozens of campuses nationwide. She initiated and is co-chair of the Institute for MultiRacial Justice.

Out of her activist experience came many articles and books, including *Letters from Mississippi* and *The Youngest Revolution: A Personal Report on Cuba* (both under the name Sutherland); *Viva la Raza: The Struggle of the Mexican-American People* (with Enriqueta Vásquez); and *Guatemala: Tyranny on Trial* and *The Art of Rini Templeton*, as co-editor. Her best-known work is the popular, bilingual volume, *500 Years of Chicano History*, in print since 1976 and the basis for the video she co-directed, *Viva la Causa: 500 Years of Chicano History*. She has received many awards for community service and leadership, and has one daughter, Tessa, an actress, who also lives in San Francisco.